THE
ENEMIES
OF ROME

PHILIP MATYSZAK

THE
ENEMIES
OF ROME

*From Hannibal to
Attila the Hun*

with 72 illustrations

Thames & Hudson

*To the Ancient Briton Reg Barrance,
and his daughters Diana and Barbara*

FRONTISPIECE *Kirk Douglas as Spartacus. But how close is
the Hollywood legend to reality? The real Spartacus was a great
leader and general, but he was no freedom fighter.*

First published in 2004 in hardcover in the United States
of America by Thames & Hudson Inc., 500 Fifth Avenue,
New York, New York 10110

thamesandhudsonusa.com

Library of Congress Catalog Card Number 2004101031
ISBN 0-500-25124-X

Printed and bound in Slovenia by Mladinska Knjiga Tiskarna

CONTENTS

N

CHAPTER 11
BOUDICCA
AD 25–61
BRITANNIA

CHAPTER 10
ARMINIUS
18 BC – AD 19
GERMANIA

CHAPTER 7
VERCINGETORIX
80–46 BC
GAUL

CHAPTER 16
ALARIC THE GOTH
AD 368–410

ATLANTIC
OCEAN

CHAPTER 3
VIRIATHUS
180–139 BC
LUSITANIA

CHAPTER 6
SPARTACUS
105–71 BC
ROME

CHAPTER 1
HANNIBAL
247–182 BC
CARTHAGE

CHAPTER 4
JUGURTHA
160–104 BC
NUMIDIA

Almost all dates of birth are approximate, as are some
dates of death, eg. Zenobia, Josephus.

300 miles

500 km

Boundary of the Roman Empire at its greatest extent
under the emperor Trajan (AD 98–117).

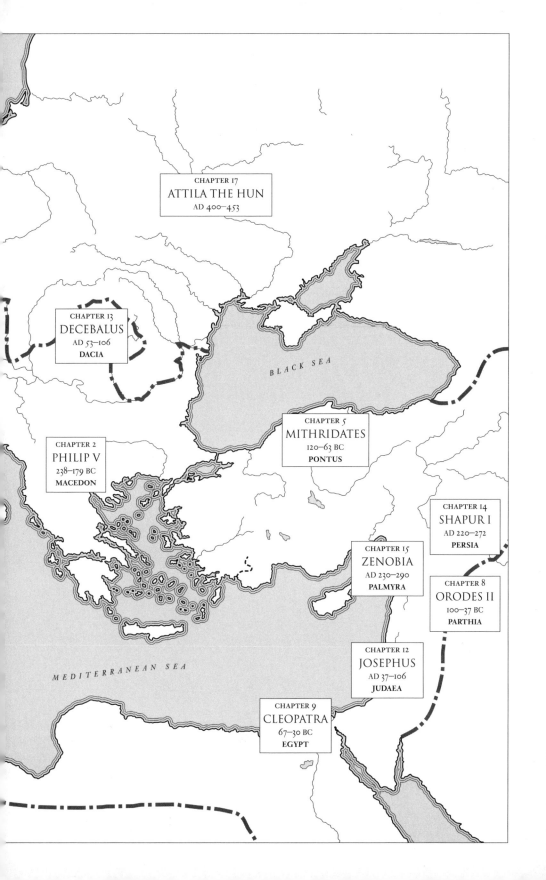

CHAPTER 17
ATTILA THE HUN
AD 400–453

CHAPTER 13
DECEBALUS
AD 53–106
DACIA

BLACK SEA

CHAPTER 5
MITHRIDATES
120–63 BC
PONTUS

CHAPTER 2
PHILIP V
238–179 BC
MACEDON

CHAPTER 14
SHAPUR I
AD 220–272
PERSIA

CHAPTER 15
ZENOBIA
AD 230–290
PALMYRA

CHAPTER 8
ORODES II
100–37 BC
PARTHIA

CHAPTER 12
JOSEPHUS
AD 37–106
JUDAEA

MEDITERRANEAN SEA

CHAPTER 9
CLEOPATRA
67–30 BC
EGYPT

ACKNOWLEDGMENTS

Thanks are due to Adrian Goldsworthy with whom I first discussed the idea, the Classics Library in Cambridge University for the use of their facilities while I put it together, to Barbara Levick for putting it together again, but correctly this time, and to the staff at Thames & Hudson who supported the project from beginning to end.

PREFACE

Until recently it was automatically assumed that Roman civilization was a Good Thing. Rome carried the torch of civilization into the barbarian darkness, and after the unpleasantness of conquest, Rome brought law, architecture, literature and similar benefits to the conquered peoples. When the Dark Ages descended on western Europe, the idea of Rome, and memories of her lost grandeur, provided the inspiration for reconstruction, even as the Roman language of Latin united the church and scholars across Europe.

There is now an alternative view, which suggests that Rome became the only civilization in the Mediterranean area by destroying half a dozen others. Some of these civilizations were as advanced as Rome's, or even more so. Others were developing, and the form they might have finally taken is now lost forever.

In the third century before Christ, when our story begins, there were a number of different, lively and competing cultures scattered about the Mediterranean. In the East, the Macedonian conquest of Asia Minor had created the Seleucid Empire, an exotic mix of western Greek ideas, Zoroastrian spiritualism, and ancient Persian culture. In Egypt, the Ptolemaic dynasty had identified with its Egyptian subjects, and Egypt's mainly Greek capital of Alexandria was the intellectual centre of the world.

The Hebrews and the Phoenicians had cities which were thousands of years old when Rome was founded. In fact the Phoenician alphabet was the precursor of the Greek, which in turn was the basis of the alphabets still in use in most of modern Europe. Both Greeks and the Phoenicians had expanded westward to found cities such as Marseilles in modern France and Naples in modern Italy. Sicily was divided between the Greeks in the east and Phoenicians in the west, these Phoenicians coming from the city of Carthage which dominated the southwestern Mediterranean.

The Celtic peoples of northern Europe were expanding rapidly. Like the Romans, they learned much from the ancient Etruscan civilization even as they helped to extinguish it. While the Celts were not a developed civilization, they were far from barbarians. Their metalworking was as good as, or better than, the Romans', and they were competent builders and traders. It is one of the tragedies of history that, just as the Celts of Gaul were pulling these threads together to develop more representative government, a monetized economy and written tradition, they were Romanized by a savage conquest. The subsequent massacres and famine cost millions of lives, and effectively obliterated the nascent Celtic civilization.

Therefore at the time of Hannibal's invasion, Rome was far from being the only civilization on offer in Europe. The social pattern of the continent was changing rapidly, and everywhere urbanization, writing and long-distance trade were transforming the way that people lived their lives. This trend would have continued and developed even had Rome never existed. In fact, until after the Punic wars, Rome's overall contribution to Mediterranean culture was minimal. Early Rome produced no great paintings or sculpture, no historians, poets or philosophers. Even the Romans who lived there admitted that the architecture of Rome was sub-standard, its greatest edifice being a sewer – the *cloaca maxima* – built during a period of Etruscan dominance.

What Rome did have to offer was a society optimized for war – a warrior culture where every peasant was a soldier, and the aristocracy competed for military success. When this book starts, Rome had already conquered most of mainland Italy. Hannibal could not have known it, but his failure meant that Rome would develop an unstoppable momentum that would take it from the Thames to the Euphrates, turning each conquered nation into a model of itself. Hannibal unwittingly represented the last chance for a Europe of diverse cultures and civilizations which could grow and develop together.

Naturally, Rome absorbed much from the peoples she conquered. Indeed, so much was absorbed from Greece and the Greek peoples of Asia Minor that the culture of Roman civilization is quite correctly described as Graeco-Roman. The problem was not that Rome's was an exclusionist culture, but that it became a monoculture. For the peoples of the Mediterranean the choice became Roman civilization or no civilization.

Over the centuries, that civilization became sterile, sick and ossified. Those peoples who still opposed Rome changed their perspective, and regarded Rome less as a potential threat than as a profitable target. Rome fell back on the defensive, scourged by barbarian incursions from outside even as civil wars devastated her from within. By the death of Attila the Hun, Rome had returned to the position it had held before the birth of Hannibal. It was no longer the driving force of culture and civilization in western Europe. But when Rome failed, there was no civilization to take Rome's place, as there would have been had Hannibal destroyed Rome in 215 BC. The Goths, Franks and Vandals had only ruins to build upon. Had Rome not triumphed so thoroughly, both militarily and culturally, the Dark Ages need never have happened.

In this book we see many of the alternative European and Mediterranean cultures in their last years before they were overwhelmed. We meet the leaders who, out of pride, greed, idealism or self-preservation stood against the Roman juggernaut. Few withstood conquest, and fewer still died in their beds. And as each one fell, the civilization of the Mediterranean became that much poorer.

PRELUDE TO EMPIRE

It is quite unremarkable that the Romans believed that their founders, Romulus and Remus, had been fathered by Mars, the god of war. From its very first years of life the infant state was almost constantly at war – with the neighbouring Sabines, with savage hill tribes, and with the city-states of Etruria to the north.

In central Italy in the sixth century BC war was a way of life. To survive, a state had not only to practise warfare, it had to become extremely good at it. The Romans, led by their warrior kings, had a number of advantages. Firstly, in its haste to increase its population, Rome had not been fussy where it found its citizens. Deserters, escaped slaves and former brigands all adapted readily to military life – all the more so because military service was from the start the key to social success in Rome.

Secondly, at a very early point in its existence the Roman electorate was organized along military lines. Legend says this occurred under Servius Tullius, the fifth king of Rome, but the story of early Rome is as much myth as history. In Rome's democracy, the equestrians, who rode their horses into battle, were allowed the most votes. Those who could afford enough armour to fight as heavy infantry formed the block with the second greatest voting weight. At the bottom of the scale were the *capite censi* (or 'head count') – those so poor that they were excused military duty, but who also had minimal voting rights.

Thirdly, because the Roman army consisted of its citizenry in arms, Rome was extraordinarily resistant to tyranny. Rome's last king, Tarquin the Proud, discovered this when the Roman people overthrew the monarchy in 509 BC. Tarquin could not use the army to put down the people, because the people were the army. Feeling that they had a stake in their society made the Romans fight ferociously to defend it. The Etruscans who backed Tarquin decided that Rome was not worth the pain of conquering, and the new Republic flourished.

Over the following decades Rome overcame the Sabines, the marauding Volsci, and the rival city of Veii, though it gives some indication of how small the affairs of Rome were, even to the rest of Italy, that the remains of Veii now lie within the northern suburbs of modern Rome. Had the rich and sophisticated states of the eastern Mediterranean considered Rome at all, they would merely have seen yet another semi-barbarous tribe squatting in their hilltop fort.

Yet there was one dangerous difference. Those conquered by Rome became not subjects, but citizens. Within a few generations the defeated peoples considered themselves Romans, and willingly lent their money and manpower to the state in return for the benefits brought by further conquests.

Rome was now governed by consuls, elected magistrates with many of the executive powers of kings. The consuls led the Roman armies in war, and presided over the deliberations of the senate in Rome. However, the senate was not the parliament of Rome – it had no powers either to make or pass laws. Although the considered opinion of the foremost men of Rome carried huge weight, laws were actually proposed by the magistrates and voted on by the people.

Roman democracy constrained the power of the aristocrats, and led to bitter class warfare which pitched the common people (the plebs) against the aristocrats (the patricians). This conflict led the plebs to secede twice from the Roman state, each time to be drawn back by concessions from the patricians. Among these patricians were the noble houses which would dominate Rome throughout the Republic and early Empire. The Horatians, Claudians, Valerians and Domitii Ahenobarbi are among the names which occur again and again in the history of the early Republic.

In 396 BC Rome destroyed the rival city of Veii but, soon afterwards,

Rome was itself captured and plundered by the Gauls, who were now at the high point of their territorial expansion. With astonishing resilience, the Romans rallied, re-took their city, and forced the Gauls back to northern Italy. Within a generation, Rome was as formidable as ever, and starting to expand southward through Italy.

In the years when Alexander the Great was conquering the Persians and pushing Europe's frontiers to the Indus, the Romans were engaged in a series of wars with hardy mountain peoples of central Italy called the Samnites. Sometimes allied with the Greek cities of southern Italy, the Samnites stubbornly opposed the domination of Rome and their resistance was not to be fully crushed for centuries. The Greek cities called for aid to their homeland and this, in 281 BC, brought Rome against its most dangerous opponent yet: Pyrrhus, one of the successors to Alexander the Great, and the greatest general of his day.

Rome's introduction to the wider world of the Mediterranean powers was a bloody one. The city was defeated in a series of battles in southern Italy, yet it fought on with the tenacity for which it was becoming renowned. Finally, bruised by the loss of much of his army, Pyrrhus decided, like the Etruscans before him, that conquering Rome was too expensive. He withdrew, leaving the Romans masters of the Italian peninsula.

Yet, as so often with the Roman Republic, victory brought not peace but new and greater challenges.

·PART I·

HANNIBAL

PHILIP V

VIRIATHUS

JUGURTHA

From the Ebro to the Nile –
the Birth of the Roman Superpower

As Rome prospered and grew strong, across the Mediterranean sea Carthage watched with a jealous eye. Carthage was long used to dominating the western Mediterranean and her leaders quite rightly saw the growing power of Rome as a threat to that dominance. It was inevitable that the two greatest powers in the western Mediterranean should clash, and they did so in 264 BC. The war began because of Roman support for a Sicilian city hostile to Carthage, and the battles of this war were fought in Sicily and the seas about that island.

Rome, which had so far confined itself to the Italian peninsula, was forced to become a maritime power. It has been said that the Romans took to sailing like a brick to water: their inability to keep their ships afloat in anything but the calmest waters lost them entire armies through shipwreck. On those occasions that they stayed above the surface (for example at Mylae in 260 BC), the Romans did well in their naval battles, often defeating the more experienced Carthaginians. By the time the Carthaginians were forced to terms in 241 BC both Rome and Carthage were drained of money and manpower.

Then, in 218 BC, the Romans discovered that they had to do it all again. The Barcids, one of the leading families of Carthage, had always regarded peace with Rome as a truce during which they could muster fresh forces. Rome was becoming increasingly assertive and was interfering in areas such as Spain, which the Carthaginians saw as within their sphere of influence. Furthermore Carthage had recovered quickly from the earlier war, and could reasonably hope that Rome's recovery had been slower. Friction in Spain caused war to break out again, but Carthage's leaders had decided to take the war to their enemy. Led by **Hannibal** (Chapter 1), the Carthaginians invaded Italy itself. The following years were among the darkest in Roman history. Hannibal was a superb tactician who defeated the Romans in battle after battle. The low point came in 216 when the Romans were trounced at Cannae. Several of Rome's subject cities rebelled, and for a moment it seemed as though Rome itself might fall.

Hannibal's success encouraged the Macedonian king **Philip V** (Chapter 2) to ally himself with Carthage against Rome. The Mediterranean powers were now taking note of Rome, and their attention was not friendly. Philip had observed the rise of Rome and the narrowness of the seas that separated his realms from this new and expansionist power. He realized that if Rome became involved with the feuding city-states of Greece, his own rule would be threatened. Philip made an alliance with Hannibal. His military involvement in the war against Rome was minimal, but his hostile intent was noted. Immediately after Carthage had once again been forced to surrender, Rome launched a serious attack on Philip. Their victory left them with interests to defend in Greece, and conquests to consolidate in Spain. The Romans, hereto uninterested in affairs outside Italy, suddenly found themselves embroiled in diplomatic and military adventures from Andalusia to Athens.

Even before the end of the Carthaginian wars, a more cosmopolitan outlook was taking hold among the Roman elite. Scipio Africanus, the general who eventually defeated Hannibal, was among those who admired Greek life and culture, much to the disgust of curmudgeonly diehards such as Cato the Censor who saw these new foreign ways as subverting old Roman values.

The wars with Carthage had changed Rome forever, and not for the better. The huge loss of Roman manpower led to the extensive use of slave labour in the countryside. This process was worsened by the fact that Rome's citizen army now campaigned ever further afield. The small peasant farmers who made up the backbone of the army were unable to farm their lands, which began to fall into the hands of the Roman elite.

Even as Rome's peasantry were excluded from the fruits of victory,

Rome abandoned its old inclusionist policy and began to divide its peoples into 'conquerors' and 'conquered'. While Roman citizens enjoyed the benefits of Empire, Rome's new subjects in Spain were mercilessly exploited by a string of venal and corrupt governors. The Iberian peoples did not take this lying down and, for decades after Hannibal's war, the mood of the Celtiberians and Lusitanians varied between restlessness and outright revolt, a situation made worse by Roman inexperience. Most of Rome's conquests to date had been against people close to their own level of civilization; governing wilder tribes far from Rome was a new experience. Furthermore, the Romans did not have as their primary interest the welfare of the Iberians, but rather the exploitation of the peninsula's natural resources, especially silver. In the cycles of brutal oppression and bloody revolt which resulted, Rome was eventually victorious, but the price in blood and economic devastation was high. The great Lusitanian leader **Viriathus** (Chapter 3) showed the Iberians that the Roman legions were not invincible, and that the rugged Spanish countryside was well suited to small wars and the sudden ambushes at which the peninsula's warrior peoples excelled.

Carthage and Macedon had been world-class powers, and defeating them gave Rome confidence which sometimes crossed into arrogance. With Philip V of Macedon forced to cede to Rome his hegemony over Greece, the Seleucid kings took Philip's discomfiture as an opportunity to extend their western borders. Several bruising clashes with the Roman war machine eventually made it plain to the Seleucids that the eastern Mediterranean did indeed have a new master – but it was not themselves.

The Romans brutally exploited their superiority. When Carthage began to recover strongly from her crushing defeat of two generations earlier, Rome provoked a war and then razed Carthage to its foundations (though it later rose again as a Roman city). At home, two reformers from one of Rome's greatest families, the Gracchus brothers, tried to correct some of the imbalances in social justice that were threatening the Roman state. They ran into venomous resistance from vested interests which selfishly and corruptly killed not only the reform programme but also the brothers themselves. The death of Tiberius Gracchus in 133 BC marked the beginning of the slow death of the Roman Republic.

After the Punic wars, Roman culture blossomed under foreign influences. The playwrights Terence and Plautus produced plays that entertain audiences even today, and Polybius (a Greek exile) introduced the Romans to historiography. Among Rome's first home-grown historians was Sallust, a former politician who was deeply disillusioned with the situation in Rome. His history of the war with the Numidian king **Jugurtha** (Chapter 4) pitilessly exposes the arrogance and corruption of Rome's ruling class. This greed and selfishness was unscrupulously exploited by Jugurtha to his own advantage, and public disgust with the venality of their own ruling class helped to bring a new generation of demagogues to power.

Despite internal stresses, this period sees the Roman Republic at its height. Rome was supreme from the shores of the Atlantic to the beaches of the Lebanon. Rome was trying new styles of poetry, theatre and architecture. Even the traditional Roman pantheon was having to accommodate new gods in its midst. Though the aristocracy kept a tight grip on political office, internal conflicts among the great families meant that the votes of the common man counted, and the people had an important part in Roman political life. But beneath the surface, all was not well.

CHAPTER 1

VENDETTA: HANNIBAL'S LONG FEUD WITH ROME

Everything that happened to both peoples, Romans and
Carthaginians, was, at base, caused by one thing –
by one mind, one man. By this I mean Hannibal.
Polybius 9.12

More than five hundred years before Hannibal was born, while the site of Rome was still a barren marsh, a storm blew a shipload of refugees onto the African shore near the newly founded city of Kart Hadasht, known today as Carthage.

The queen of that city was Dido, daughter of a Phoenician king. Fleeing from her native land, she had been offered by an African ruler both sanctuary and all the land she could cover with the hide of a bull. With the spirit that was to typify Carthaginian merchant venturers of future generations, Dido had the bull's skin cut into tiny strips, and used these strips to enclose an area of land large enough to form the basis of her future city.

Now, with this city thriving, Dido welcomed the newcomers from the sea in the hope that they would swell the ranks of Carthage's citizenry. The new arrivals were led by Aeneas, a favourite of the goddess Venus, and a nobleman from the fallen city of Troy. Dido fell passionately in love with him. While out hunting, the pair sheltered from a storm in a cave, and there consummated their love.

Dido had no sooner found pure happiness than it was snatched from her. While he slept, Aeneas was visited in his dreams by Mercury, the messenger of the gods. Mercury reminded Aeneas that his destiny lay in

Italy, and that he should forthwith abandon his present dalliance.

Dido noted the change in her lover, and became hysterical at the thought that he might abandon her. Torn between love and duty, Aeneas could not bring himself to bid Dido a proper farewell. Instead, one morning, Dido awoke to find that Aeneas had boarded his galley, and was even then setting sail. Distraught, she ordered her sister Anna to make a pyre of all those possessions which the Trojan had left behind in his guilty flight. Before anyone could suspect her intentions, she threw herself into the flames and perished. Her last words were a malediction to Aeneas and his descendants:

'These are my prayers, and this my dying will;
And you, my Carthaginians, must every curse fulfil.
Perpetual hate and mortal wars proclaim,
Against that prince, his people, and their name....
Our arms, our seas, our shores, opposed to theirs;
And the same hate descend on all our heirs!'

Virgil *Aeneid* 4

So, according to legend, began the enmity between Carthage and Rome. The reality was hardly better. Their first-known diplomatic contact marked the warmest point in their relationship, and even that was no more than wary tolerance. At the time, Rome was a fledgling power in Latium, while Carthage was the dominant power in the western Mediterranean. The first known treaty between the two states was in 508 BC, by which the Romans agreed not to interfere with Carthaginian trade in the region, and Carthage agreed to stay out of Rome's affairs in Italy.

In 280 BC, the Carthaginians shared with Rome a common interest in repelling the invasion of one of the successors to Alexander the Great, King Pyrrhus. In fact the Carthaginian fleet fought on the Roman side. But the growth of Roman power after the war caused deep unease in Carthage, and hastened the inevitable clash.

This clash came when the Romans involved themselves with affairs in Sicily. Messana in north Sicily was seized by a band of mercenaries called the Mamertines. At this time Carthage controlled the west of the island, and the Greeks the east. Wars between the two were frequent and both sides now hastened to seize Messana for themselves. The Mamertines sought protection from the remaining regional power – Rome. War was not inevitable, but neither goodwill nor diplomacy was forthcoming. In 264 BC Rome and Carthage became locked in a grim struggle that lasted for the next twenty-three years.

The war cost hundreds of thousands of lives and was fought in Africa, Sicily and the adjacent seas. The Romans invaded Africa, but their general, Atilius Regulus, was defeated and his army destroyed. In the war at sea the Romans raised fleet after fleet, only to see each destroyed in turn. Some were sunk by the Carthaginians but more by the weather, since the Romans were remarkably poor sailors.

In Sicily the Romans had more success. As formidable by land as they were vulnerable at sea, the forces of Rome rapidly drove the Carthaginians from the hinterland and penned them under siege in their port cities. That they did not drive Carthage from the island altogether was due to the efforts of a remarkable Carthaginian commander, Hamilcar Barca.

Hamilcar was a Barcid, one of the leading Carthaginian families of that time. He had begun his war by raiding along the Italian coast, and when he arrived in Sicily, he established himself near the modern city of Palermo. From there he conducted a daring guerrilla campaign. In 244 BC he captured the city of Eryx, and made this his base of operations. By 241 Carthage, though almost completely drained of money and manpower, made a last desperate effort to supply Hamilcar with men and munitions. At the Aegates Islands, the Romans under the admiral C. Lutatius Catulus intercepted the Carthaginian supply ships and destroyed them. For Carthage, this was the last straw. They made peace with Rome, agreeing to abandon their possessions in Sicily and to pay a huge indemnity of 3,200 talents of silver (a talent was a weight of just over 25 kilograms).

This treaty indirectly precipitated another conflict. The size of the indemnity meant that Carthage could not afford to pay the mercenaries who had fought for her, and who now rose in mutiny. Hamilcar returned from Sicily and played a leading part in the subsequent campaign, the viciousness of which can be judged from its name – the 'truceless war'. To Carthage's impotent fury, Rome took blatant advantage of her rival's weakness and annexed the Carthaginian province of Sardinia.

With the mercenaries defeated, Hamilcar set off north again, this time to Spain, where Carthage intended to build a new empire and gain from it the silver and manpower to stand against Rome. Polybius takes up the story at the point where Hamilcar had sacrificed to the gods for the success of his mission.

Then he [Hamilcar] called his son Hannibal to him, and asked him with fatherly tenderness if the boy wanted to go with him [to Spain]. As a boy would, the overjoyed Hannibal begged his father to allow him…. Hamilcar took Hannibal by the hand and led him to the altar. There he commanded Hannibal to lay his hand on the body of the sacrificial victim, and to swear that he would never be a friend to the Romans.

Polybius 3.11

Hannibal was about nine years old at this time. He must have had an exciting boyhood in Spain as Hamilcar expanded Carthaginian influence from his base at Gades (modern Cádiz). Spain was not a united country but a patchwork of different and often warring peoples whom Hamilcar subdued with a mixture of force and diplomacy. In 231 the Romans sent an embassy to find out what Hamilcar was up to, and he satisfied them by saying that he was seeking in Spain the money to pay the Roman indemnity. When, two years later, he drowned while crossing a river, command went to his son-in-law Hasdrubal, who continued his policies. Roman concerns were alleviated by the 'Ebro Treaty' of 226 by which Hasdrubal promised to confine his activities to the south of the Ebro river.

Hannibal saw negotiations at first hand and witnessed dozens of minor sieges and skirmishes. The modern concept of teenagers as somewhere between child and adult did not exist in the ancient world, and Hannibal was given charge of troops at an early age. He also became a married man, taking a wife from the city of Castulo. By his mid-twenties, Hannibal was an experienced commander.

Hasdrubal was assassinated in 221. By this time, the troops in Spain were determined that they wanted as Hasdrubal's successor none other than Hannibal. This was not least because Hannibal resembled his distinguished sire in looks, mannerisms and most importantly, in military acumen. The popular assembly in Carthage confirmed this choice, and at the age of twenty-five, Hannibal was given supreme command in Spain.

According to the historian Livy, Hannibal then acted as though carrying out a pre-formulated plan to make war on the Romans. This is not entirely impossible. From what we know of Hannibal's character, he was both quick-witted and firm of purpose when resolved. But there is much we do not know about this man, though he was one of the greatest generals in antiquity. No surviving ancient biography makes him the subject, and Hannibal slips in and out of focus according to the emphasis that other authors give his deeds and character.

Of his mother and of his wife we know almost nothing. Much of our knowledge of the rest of his family comes from their having commanded armies against the Romans. No coin or ancient author gives us any clue as to Hannibal's appearance. A bust found in Capua may be that of Hannibal; it dates to about the time of the Punic wars, so if it is he, it may be a realistic likeness. The bust shows a man with Semitic features, a short, curly beard and a reflective and rather cruel expression.

Indeed, says Polybius, for the Romans, Hannibal's overriding trait was his cruelty. Livy agrees.

Inhuman cruelty; perfidious, even for a Carthaginian, caring absolutely nothing for truth, honour, religion, the sanctity of oaths or for anything else that men hold sacred.

Livy 21.4

But Livy also says that Hannibal was the first into action, and the last to leave the field. He was 'reckless in courting danger, and showed superb tactical ability when the danger materialized'. He was indifferent to hunger, fatigue and stress, and often slept on the ground wrapped in his cloak. He was ready to gamble his life and the lives of his men if the cause seemed justified, but he never did it needlessly.

He inspired devoted loyalty from those under his command, as can be seen from the admiring words of Polybius:

For sixteen years he fought a war against the Romans in Italy without a pause, and in all that time he never released his army from service in the field, and yet kept those great numbers under his control, and free from disaffection either toward himself or to each other. And this, despite the fact that he employed troops who belonged not only to different countries, but to different races. He had with him Africans, Spaniards, Celts, Ligurians, Italians, and Greeks, men who had nothing naturally in common in their laws, their customs, their language, or in any other way. Still, the skill of their commander was such that he could impose the authority of a single voice and a single will even upon men of such totally diverse origins. And he achieved this under conditions which were not consistent, but perpetually changing with the winds of fortune; often in his favour, but also at times in the opposite direction.

Polybius 9.22–26

One other thing is known of Hannibal: he could hold a grudge. From his earliest boyhood until his death, he continued unwaveringly in his quest to harm Rome with all the means at his disposal. And in 221 BC, fate had handed him as powerful an instrument as he could ask for – a battle-hardened army equipped and paid for with the resources of half the Iberian peninsula.

In 220 Hannibal advanced against two tribes which inhabited an area beyond the river Tagus – the Vaccaei and the Carpetani. As he brought these over to his side, the coastal city of Saguntum became involved in a dispute with some allies of the Carthaginians. Hannibal had a decision to make. He could abandon his allies, and lose all credibility with the Spanish tribes, or he could support them against the Saguntans. But Saguntum was an ally of Rome, and Rome was already deeply concerned about Carthaginian activities in Spain.

Characteristically, Hannibal hardly hesitated. Although Saguntum was well situated and strongly defended, he began a siege without even consulting the authorities in Carthage. Eight months later, he stormed the city. Rome reacted furiously, sending an embassy to Carthage with the demand that Hannibal and his senior commanders be handed over to Roman justice.

The Carthaginians retorted that they had never ratified Hasdrubal's settlement with the Romans and, in any case, Saguntum was south of the Ebro; moreover, Rome had shown none of this delicacy about her treaty arrangements when she had blatantly annexed Sardinia from them. There are different accounts of what happened next, but the most common version says that the leader of the Roman delegation, Fabius Maximus, gave the Carthaginian senate an ultimatum: surrender Hannibal, or face the consequences. The Carthaginians replied that they would not give up Hannibal, and the Romans could do what they liked about it. The Romans declared war. Later they were to discover that Hannibal had already unilaterally done so, and was by then moving to invade Italy.

It was a testament to the Spanish policy of the Barcid clan of Hannibal that Carthage had recovered enough to be able to defy Rome as she did. The silver from Spain not only directly stimulated the Carthaginian economy, but it funded merchant ventures in a city that earned more from trade than any other in antiquity. That trade went mostly by sea, but unlike Rome in later years, Carthage was never dependent on the import of food supplies from abroad. The city was supplied by its hinterland in Africa – a region that was to become one of the breadbaskets of Rome in late antiquity.

While the area that Carthage controlled directly was relatively small, the city exerted powerful cultural dominance over much of the region, and many nominally independent cities and peoples were in fact well within its sway. Despite this, Carthage never produced a distinctive style of its own in architecture or the fine arts. And while we know that there were Carthaginian poets and historians, none of their work has come down to us.

Politically, Carthage was controlled by an oligarchy of powerful families, of which – at the time of the Second Punic War – the Barcids were the strongest. Membership of the Carthaginian senate was for life, but two leaders, rendered in Latin as the *suffetes*, were elected annually. The actions of Carthaginian commanders in the field were checked by a board of some hundred supervisors, a device which had allowed the city to remain free from military takeovers throughout its five-hundred-year history. Carthaginian justice was hard on failed commanders. For example, Hanno, the admiral whose defeat brought about the end of the First Punic War, was crucified for his mishandling of the battle.

The gods of the Carthaginians included the goddess Tanit, who, in the years before the war, had come to be as much worshipped as her consort, Baal Hammon, the patron god of the city. The patronage of Baal, incidentally, is why so many Carthaginian names end with '-bal'; Hannibal, for example, means 'grace of Baal'. The Roman claim that the Carthaginians sacrificed children to their gods has recently been strongly substantiated by child and animal remains found in places of sacrifice. Credence must therefore be given to writers like Diodorus, who claimed that it was not uncommon for the children of leading families to be sacrificed in times of national crisis.

Apart from this repugnant habit, there were features of Carthage – such as oligarchic family factions dominating a senate with two annually elected leaders, a mix of patriarchal and matriarchal gods, susceptibility to Hellenization, and recent imperial success in Spain – which made the city very similar to another situated only three days' sailing north across the Mediterranean: Rome. No matter what the rights and wrongs of the matter, Hannibal's war was going to determine which power, Roman or Punic, would dominate the western Mediterranean in the coming century.

Hannibal's plan was daring in the extreme. He proposed to march on Italy from the north, taking his army over the Alps. The gamble was as much political as it was military. Hannibal was counting on his army remaining intact and cohesive despite a passage through mountains filled with treacherous passes and equally treacherous tribes. There were immense difficulties with transporting his elephants – prized for the

1 *Hannibal's odyssey. Between crossing the Alps and returning to Africa, Hannibal spent more than a decade and a half on Italian soil, during which time the Romans never once defeated him in battle.*

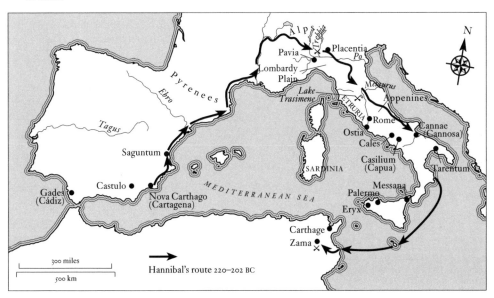

effect they had on untried Roman cavalry – but any thoughts of taking a siege-train had to be abandoned at the outset. This meant that the Carthaginians would have to rely on desertions and betrayal to capture any of the major cities of Italy, and it signalled Hannibal's belief that the subject peoples of Italy needed only a credible protector before they cast off the shackles of their Roman oppressor.

This idea was not unrealistic. The Samnite tribes who inhabited the mountains of central Italy had only recently succumbed to Rome after a struggle lasting centuries, and the Greek cities of the southern coasts had a proud history of independence. Of course, this had been even more the case a generation before, a fact that has prompted some historians to suggest that Hannibal was executing a plan laid out by his father. And it is true that, while Hannibal was superb at winning battles, his strategic vision was to prove limited and faulty.

Hannibal's first step, in the spring of 218, was to set out from Nova Carthago (modern Cartagena), the capital which his predecessor Hasdrubal had founded. He left Spain in the care of a younger brother, also called Hasdrubal, and was accompanied by another brother, Mago. Hannibal's army contained 90,000 infantry and 12,000 cavalry. Over the following months this army subdued Spain from the Ebro to the Pyrenees, comprehensively shredding whatever remained of Hasdrubal's agreement with Rome. Then Hannibal waited, intending to destroy whatever army the Romans sent against him before following the remnants back into Italy.

But Scipio, the Roman commander, was delayed by a Gallic uprising in north Italy. This boded well for Hannibal's plans to detach Rome from her subjects, but it did mean that Hannibal set off for Italy without his preliminary battle. The Romans did eventually dispatch one consular army to Spain and another to Sicily, never imagining that the Italian peninsula itself was in peril. The army bound for Spain missed Hannibal's army coming the other way. When the situation became apparent, there was no little consternation in Rome, and both consuls were hastily recalled.

Hannibal's route across the Alps is unknown, though subsequently much discussed. It certainly included the lands of the Allobroges, a Gallic tribe who took a dim view of the new arrivals. The Allobroges harried the Carthaginians, who were inexperienced both in mountain warfare and at coping with the mountain snows. Hannibal's losses were heavy.

As they reached the end of their arduous climb, Hannibal gave his men a rousing speech. He showed them the Lombardy plain waiting below them, and promised that it was ripe for the picking.

All the wealth that Rome has piled up in her years of conquest; all those rich possessions, yes; and also they who possess them, are there, yours for the taking. Draw your swords and let us go forward to claim this prize! … You have travelled far, across rivers, through mountains and hostile tribes. Now you have a chance to win a rich reward of money and the good things in life.

Livy 21.43

In all, the crossing took just over two weeks. Since leaving Nova Carthago, Hannibal had been burning his resources at a terrific rate. Of his huge army, about 6,000 horses and about 30,000 infantry remained, their ranks thinned by battle, privation and desertions. No wonder then that Hannibal now rested his troops in preparation for the coming clash with the Romans. To the Carthaginian's astonishment, Scipio had managed to pull his troops back to Italy after missing Hannibal on his way from Spain. No less surprising was the feat of Tiberius Sempronius, the other consul, who brought his troops up the length of Italy in about forty days.

Now the Roman generals had good cause to be confident. They knew how gruelling the crossing of the Alps must have been, and rated Hannibal as no more than a headstrong youth who could be quashed by Rome's fresher and better-disciplined troops.

The two sides met at the river Ticinus near Pavia in October 218, and whether the clash can be dignified with the name of 'battle' is open to question. Scipio, advancing up the north bank of the river Po, encountered the Carthaginians advancing in the other direction. Sempronius had not yet come up in support, and Scipio found his cavalry outmatched by the faster and lighter Numidian horses of Hannibal. The disconcerted Romans found themselves being pushed back and close to rout.

Scipio tried with great personal bravery to rally his men. Plunging

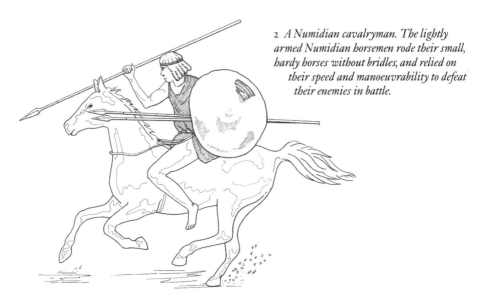

2 *A Numidian cavalryman. The lightly armed Numidian horsemen rode their small, hardy horses without bridles, and relied on their speed and manoeuvrability to defeat their enemies in battle.*

into the fray, he was wounded and almost captured. Some reports say that he was rescued by the bravery of his young son, others more prosaically attribute the deed to a Ligurian servant. Chastised, Scipio pulled his troops back across the river, destroying the bridge behind him. He took refuge in the fortress town of Placentia, there to nurse his wounds until Sempronius caught up with him.

Delayed by the broken bridge, Hannibal was forced to retrace his steps to a point further upstream. On crossing, he immediately marched on the Roman position and offered battle. Scipio declined, a show of timidity that caused some of his Gallic allies to desert to Hannibal. With his position deteriorating by the day, Scipio was forced to retreat across the river Trebbia, with Hannibal's Numidian cavalry snapping at his heels.

Scipio had retreated to a strong position, which Hannibal was reluctant to try to storm. Hannibal was already making useful political gains among the Gauls, and his fortunes received another boost when the commander of the Italian garrison at Clastidium surrendered the fortress to him. This was not only useful propaganda – the defection of some of Rome's Italian allies was bound to encourage the rest – but the Romans had stored their grain supplies for the campaign in this fortress. Hannibal could now relieve his own supply shortage at the expense of the Romans.

In December 218 Sempronius arrived. The sources (which tend to favour the Scipionic view of events) relate that Sempronius was impatient with what he saw as the pusillanimity of Scipio. He immediately initiated an action against the Carthaginian troops, who were scattered across the countryside in search of plunder. The Carthaginians hastily put out troops in battle order to protect their men, and with both sides feeding soldiers into the skirmish, it seemed as though a spontaneous battle was about to break out.

Hannibal did not want to fight in a time and position not of his choosing, so he pulled his men back behind his fighting line, and escorted the stragglers back into the camp. He noted the aggressiveness of Sempronius, and laid his plans accordingly.

Therefore, soon afterwards, the Roman camp was attacked at dawn by Numidian light cavalry. Despite Scipio's misgivings, Sempronius had the Roman army drawn up into battle order, in the expectation that the main Carthaginian army was not far behind. In fact, Hannibal had not yet moved from his camp. He was aware that the combined consular army outnumbered his, and that his men were still weak from their long journey. His intention was to push the Romans off-balance.

The Numidian cavalry retreated across the Trebbia, and the Romans followed, adding the misery of wading across a river in December to their breakfastless start. Scipio's troops were relatively green recruits (Polybius says that Scipio had hoped to spend the winter training and hardening them). Now they went into what, for many, was their first battle with their morale much lower than that of Hannibal's veterans, who had woken at a decent hour and had the benefit of a leisurely breakfast whilst their enemies toiled across the river.

Occasional showers of sleet started to fall as the two armies formed up. Hannibal was facing four legions of the finest close-order infantry in the world – about 16,000 Roman legionaries accompanied by some 20,000 allied troops, including the last of the loyal Gallic tribes. Even with the Gauls who had deserted to him, Hannibal was outnumbered in infantry, but he now had a substantial advantage in the cavalry.

The two sides engaged. The Carthaginian skirmishers easily bested their Roman counterparts, and the cavalry battle went the same way. It helped that at this time Hannibal still had some elephants, which terrified the Roman horses, most of which were as inexperienced as their riders. But the Roman infantry shrugged off the setback on their flanks, and crashed into the main body of Hannibal's army. Tired, weak, and partly demoralized as they were, these were still Roman legions. They believed themselves unbeatable, and Hannibal knew that many on his own side concurred.

At this critical point, Hannibal's brother Mago, accompanied by 1,000 cavalry and infantrymen, burst from where they had been waiting in ambush and flung themselves at the rear of the Roman line. Mago's men had spent a cheerless night hidden in scrub where the Trebbia plain dipped into a watercourse. They had waited for the advancing Roman army to pass them by, and attacked when the two battle lines were fully engaged. The shock of this unexpected attack caused confusion out of all proportion to the number of troops involved, and it was yet another blow to Roman morale.

Shedding allied troops right and left, the legions threw themselves at Hannibal's centre. With his troops fully engaged in routing the Romans on the left and right wings, Hannibal could do little but watch as some 10,000 legionaries crashed through the middle of his army. The commanders of the Roman legionaries realized that the day was lost and did not attempt to re-engage Hannibal, instead withdrawing in good order towards Placentia, and making camp near that city. About this nucleus the scattered remnants of the Roman army reattached themselves, while survivors of the rout straggled back in dribs and drabs.

At first the Romans tried to pretend that the engagement had ended with honours even on both sides. But as the casualty figures became clearer, so did the result of the battle. Hannibal had handed his enemies a beating.

Emboldened by his success, and hoping to save the local Gauls the strain of supporting his army through the winter, Hannibal struck out for Etruria. He was pushed back at the Apennines, not by the Romans but by the terrain and winter storms. Unaccustomed to the bitter cold, all of his elephants perished except a hardy animal nicknamed 'the Syrian'. Partly to relieve the pressure on his supplies, and partly for propaganda reasons, Hannibal released all the Italian prisoners he had captured at the Trebbia without demanding the customary ransom.

He then spent a nervous winter among his Gallic hosts. Polybius reports:

He was well aware of the fickleness of the Celts … and was constantly on guard against assassination. Therefore he had a set of wigs made, each of which made him look like a man of a different age. He changed these constantly, each time changing his apparel to match his appearance. Thus he was hard to recognize, not just by those who saw him briefly, but even by those who knew him well.

Polybius 3.78

The Gauls too were becoming restless and eager for plunder so, early in the spring of 217, Hannibal launched his offensive. Once again, his approach was original and daring. In a three-day march, he pushed through the marshes near the river Arno, arriving in Etruria with his army intact and unchallenged. However, Hannibal himself did not come through unscathed. He was attacked by a severe infection which was later to take the sight from one eye, and he had to be carried for a part of the way on his last surviving elephant.

Facing Hannibal was Gaius Flaminius, a Roman consul accompanied by a full-strength Roman army. Flaminius was a demagogue who had a long history of friction with the senate. He was also a competent general, as the Gauls in Hannibal's army could testify – he had campaigned very successfully against them. Flaminius was as eager to defend Etruria as the Gauls were to plunder it and, on hearing that Hannibal had arrived and was devastating the country, he hastened to meet him. It seems not to have occurred to him that he was being deliberately provoked.

In part through his superior cavalry, Hannibal was kept well informed about what the Romans were doing. Thus it happened that on the morning of 21 June the Carthaginian army was drawn up in battle array on a misty hillside overlooking lake Trasimene. So dense was the mist, and so good the Carthaginian discipline, that the Roman army strung out in line of march along the lakeside was blissfully unaware of their presence.

Flaminius was expecting to do battle that day, but probably believed that Hannibal was waiting at his camp at the end of the lake. The idea that a large army of diverse nationalities – many with only an tenuous grasp of military discipline and order – could have been moved silently during the night and perfectly positioned on broken terrain must have seemed absurd. That Hannibal achieved it is a testament to his genius as a commander.

When the Carthaginians struck, they struck hard, and the battle was over almost as soon as it began. The Romans were disorganized and confused, with their backs to the lake and nowhere to form line of battle. They rapidly disintegrated into struggling groups, each overwhelmed by a tide of attackers. The Gauls were especially eager to avenge themselves on Flaminius, who by one account was wearing glorious armour, the helmet topped off by a Celtic scalp. Some reports say that Flaminius panicked, others that he died fighting bravely, but certainly he did not survive the battle.

By the end of the day, Flaminius' shade had been joined by those of some 12,000 Roman soldiers, with about the same number captured. His army had been obliterated as a fighting force, and Hannibal re-equipped each of his Libyan soldiers with a fresh shield and a second-hand set of armour, courtesy of his defeated foes.

Hannibal's army hardly had time to rally when word reached them that the surviving Roman consul, Servilius Geminus, had dispatched some 4,000 cavalry to Etruria. A strong force of cavalry would impel Hannibal to keep his army together, without the chance to plunder and forage, and the Carthaginian needed to do both. Accordingly he dispatched his own cavalry, under the rash but brilliant Maharbal, to meet this new threat. Maharbal almost exactly emulated his commander's success, killing half the enemy and capturing most of the rest.

Hannibal had now crippled the Roman army as a fighting force, and he was eager to finish with the rest of it. But this remainder of the Roman army proved strangely elusive; it was always close enough to threaten battle, but Hannibal could never actually bring about a decisive clash. He rapidly discovered that the general behind these new tactics was Fabius Verrucosus, a general from a leading Roman military family. Fabius had been elected sole commander – dictator – in Rome after Hannibal's victory at Trasimene, and was determined to preserve Rome's surviving army in Italy.

Fabius intended to wear Hannibal down and to keep him on the move while Rome recovered her strength, for which tactic the Romans called their leader *Cunctator* or 'The Delayer'. Hannibal himself referred to his opponent as 'The Schoolteacher' from the speed and severity with which he punished any mistakes that the Carthaginian made.

One such mistake was almost Hannibal's undoing. As he pillaged

Campania, Hannibal allowed Fabius to slip a garrison into Casilinum, near Capua. From here, the river Volturnus blocked Hannibal's retreat while Fabius waited in the mountains between Casilinum and the colony of Cales. This put Hannibal in a trap. He could not remain in a plain which he had stripped of supplies, nor could he launch his army in a suicidal assault against a Roman army entrenched in a superior position. Yet these appeared to be his choices.

Eventually, it seemed that Hannibal chose to try a night break-out. The Romans saw the torches of the army streaming towards a well-guarded pass. Confident that the garrison there could intercept the attempted break-out, Fabius refused to move from his camp, despite the pleas and imprecations of his subordinates, who saw a chance of breaking the Carthaginians once and for all.

But when Fabius' garrison carried out their interception, they found thousands of cattle with torches tied to their horns, but no Carthaginian soldiers. Hannibal's army was streaming through the position which they had abandoned, taking their booty and heading for winter quarters in Apulia. Hannibal had written another chapter into the annals of military deceptions, and made Fabius look a fool into the bargain.

With Fabius' credibility weakened and their allies wavering, the Romans decided to revert to the warfare they knew best – to engage and crush the enemy in open battle. Accordingly they gathered together no fewer than eight legions, each of about 5,000 men. Together with their allies and cavalry, they had at least 85,000 men to Hannibal's 50,000.

It may well be that Hannibal was late in realizing the change in Roman strategy. In the summer of 216 he swooped on the fortress of Cannae (modern Cannosa), and seized the corn

3 *A Roman triarius. The triarii were the third and final rank in the Roman battle line, and the most experienced warriors. Note the leg armour (greave) which was worn only on the left leg, and that legionaries in this period wore chain mail rather than the 'lobster-plate' armour of the imperial era.*

35

supplies designated to feed Rome's massive army. The same move placed Hannibal between the Romans and the cornfields of Apulia. The Romans had either to retreat to a secure source of supply or offer battle. That is, they had either to fight or go away, which is what Hannibal had been trying to make Fabius do for most of the preceding year.

Hannibal was of a like mind with the two consuls who opposed him – eager for battle. The Romans, Terentius Varro and Aemilius Paullus, were charged with the immediate destruction of Hannibal, and Hannibal must have felt that just one more crushing victory would break even Roman willpower, and bring Rome's wavering allies over to him *en masse*. The stakes could hardly have been higher.

The clash came on the morning of 2 August 216 BC. Hannibal had anchored the left flank of his army on the banks of the river Ofanto. This flank consisted of his Spanish and Gallic cavalry. In the centre of his army Hannibal had positioned his Spanish and Gallic infantry, with Libyan heavy infantry on each side. On the other flank was massed the remainder of his 10,000 cavalry, probably Numidian light horse under the dashing Maharbal, who had mauled the Roman cavalry after the victory at Trasimene.

Hannibal commanded the centre, for there he intended his troops to stage one of the most difficult manoeuvres to pull off on a battlefield – to fall back under pressure without breaking. In ancient warfare, the majority of casualties in a battle were inflicted on enemy soldiers as they fled in rout. But those who fled first had the best chance of survival. Thus for an army to fight effectively, each soldier had to trust that his comrades-in-arms would not leave him in the lurch. And this trust was strained to its uttermost when the battle line started to move backward.

Nothing shows Hannibal's ability as a leader of men better than that the Gauls and Spaniards, fighters more noted for their ferocity and mercurial temperament than their discipline, fell back exactly as Hannibal had intended. Meanwhile, on his left flank, his cavalry had routed the Roman horse in a ferocious charge. The Roman commander, Aemilius Paullus, left his cavalry to their flight and joined his heavy infantry in the centre, where the fighting was now intense. Meanwhile, on the right flank, Maharbal's light horse were holding back the Italian cavalry under Varro.

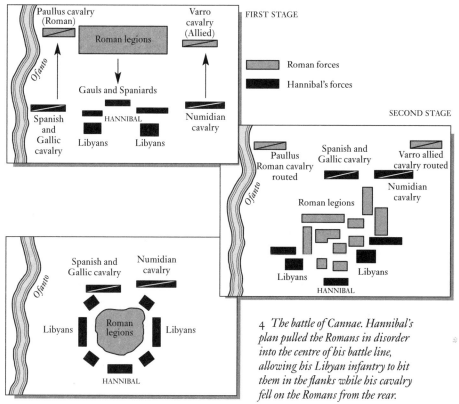

FIRST STAGE

Roman forces

Hannibal's forces

SECOND STAGE

THIRD STAGE

4 *The battle of Cannae. Hannibal's plan pulled the Romans in disorder into the centre of his battle line, allowing his Libyan infantry to hit them in the flanks while his cavalry fell on the Romans from the rear.*

Now the Spanish and Celtic infantry began to buckle and, scenting victory, the Romans surged into the gap in the Carthaginian centre. No matter that the Gallic horsemen had returned from the left flank and joined Maharbal in breaking the Italian cavalry. The Romans won their battles with the infantry, and the legions seemed on the brink of victory. Until then, Hannibal's Libyan infantry had played little part in the fighting. Now they turned on the disordered Romans, pushing past their flanks, and closed in from left and right like the jaws of a vice. At the same time, the Gauls and Spanish ceased to fall back, and threw themselves at the front of the Roman line, even as the Carthaginian cavalry hit the Romans in the rear. The encirclement was complete.

At this point the battle ended, and the massacre began. But though their cause was hopeless, the Romans neither surrendered nor died quietly. As many as 45,000 Romans and their allies fell that day – a figure unrivalled for a single day of battle in Europe until the efforts of Allied commanders at the Somme in 1916. Another 4,000 Romans were captured, so of the massive army raised to rid Italy of the Carthaginians, some 17,000 men remained, many wounded, and all beaten and demoralized. The consul Aemilius Paullus lay among the Roman dead, and with him, somewhere between a quarter and a third of the entire Roman senate. It was Hannibal's greatest victory.

Having mopped up the dregs of Roman resistance and secured his prisoners, Hannibal gave his troops a well-earned rest, despite the urging of the fiery Maharbal:

'Follow up! If you understand what this victory means, in five days you can be feasting on the Capitol (in Rome). I will go first with the cavalry, and we can be there before they know we are coming.' This was too much for Hannibal to grasp immediately. He commended Marhabal on his attitude, but said that he needed time to consider his advice. At this Marhabal said 'Indeed, the gods do not give one man everything. You have the ability to win battles, Hannibal, but you do not know how to use victory.'
> Livy 22.54

According to Livy, Hannibal's delay saved Rome and her Empire.

Hannibal had good reasons for not following up, though with hindsight this mistake cost him his one good chance of final victory. But Hannibal's army was exhausted, as he was himself. The Romans had taken some 5,000 to 8,000 of Hannibal's men to the grave with them, and many more had suffered wounds. They needed time to regroup.

Anyway, Hannibal probably considered the war already won. Any other Mediterranean state would have sought terms even before the crisis at Cannae. Surely the scale of this defeat would break even the legendary Roman stubbornness? And if it did not, which of Rome's allies would now stand with her, given that Hannibal appeared able to defeat Rome at will? Certainly not most of southern Italy. The Greek cities and Samnite tribes, recently and reluctantly absorbed into the Roman hegemony, declared for Hannibal almost as soon as word of his victory reached them. This included Capua, a significant gain, for its citizens were Roman, albeit of a junior class which did not have the vote.

Welcome as these new allies were, they came at a cost. In the months that followed the victory at Cannae, it became disappointingly clear that Rome intended to fight on, and the first to feel her wrath were those who had defected to Hannibal. Mago was dispatched to Carthage to ask for reinforcements. The elite equestrian class of Rome were distinguished by the rings they wore. To show that he was not exaggerating the scale of Hannibal's victories, Mago poured a sackful of these rings onto the floor of the Carthaginian senate house. Every one had been taken from captured or killed equestrians, and to the sackful on the floor, Mago added another, and another, until the heap numbered thousands of rings.

But the absence of the Barcids from Carthage had allowed their enemies to grow stronger. Hannibal's opponents in the senate asked contemptuously that if Hannibal was asking for help while he was winning, what would he demand when things went against him? In fact, throughout the long war which followed, Hannibal was only once to receive significant help from his native city.

In the field, Hannibal remained unmatched. In 212 and 210 he took on the Romans and defeated them. But he now understood that the wound Rome had received at Cannae had not been mortal. The flow of defections to the Carthaginian side slowed and then stopped; though not before the strategic port of Tarentum fell into his hands in 212. Rome put four armies in the field against Hannibal, then increased this to six. In 208 two more Roman consuls died in separate engagements, but in Spain the war was turning against Carthage.

Hannibal's brother, Hasdrubal had been hard pressed by Scipio the Younger, son of the Scipio whom Hannibal had defeated at the Ticinus in 218. Now Hasdrubal decided to abandon Spain and bring his army to Italy. The Romans reacted promptly and bravely to this new incursion. Leaving only a light force to screen their departure from Hannibal, they rushed northward, intending to destroy the younger Barcid before he could join Hannibal in the south.

They were brilliantly successful. In 207 they met the invading Carthaginians on the banks of the river Metaurus in northern Italy, destroyed their army and killed Hasdrubal himself. Hannibal knew nothing of this, for the messengers sent by his brother had been intercepted by the Romans. The Romans returned to their lines in the south without Hannibal even being aware that they had gone. The news was broken to him by Roman cavalry who threw the head of Hasdrubal over the ramparts of Hannibal's camp, and then sent two Libyan prisoners to give the full, morale-sapping story.

Legend has it that Hannibal stared into the face of his dead brother and remarked, 'Now indeed, I can clearly see the fate of Carthage'.

Hannibal was losing ground. The Romans had retaken Tarentum. In a desperate effort to keep possession of Capua, Hannibal had marched his army to within four miles of Rome; the closest he was ever to get to the city of his enemies. To no avail. Roman nerves held, and the assault on Capua continued. Without siege weapons, Hannibal could achieve nothing outside Rome, and he eventually withdrew. But for centuries after, mothers would terrify restless infants into silence at night with the words '*Hannibal ad portas!*' ('Hannibal is at the gates!').

In 203 the Romans broke the stalemate. The initiative was taken by Scipio the Younger, a general of Hannibal's own calibre. After master-minding the defeat of the Carthaginians in Spain, he had persuaded the reluctant Roman senate to bypass Hannibal in Italy, and invade Africa directly. Ironically, many of the troops Scipio took with him were disgraced survivors of the battle of Cannae, sent in quasi-exile to Sicily.

Scipio's intelligent and energetic campaigning rapidly forced the Carthaginians to agree a truce until a peace treaty could be worked out. One condition of that truce was that Hannibal leave Italy forthwith. Hannibal was now forty-five years old. He had been twenty-nine when he led his troops into Italy, and still he remained unbeaten in the field.

'Few exiles have left their motherland with as much sorrow and bitterness as Hannibal left the land of his enemies. Again and again he looked back at the shores of Italy, accusing gods and men and calling down curses on himself for his failure.'

Livy 30.20

Yet Hannibal was to have another chance at the Romans. The Carthaginians were heartened to have their champion back on his native soil, and began spoiling to resume the fight. Indeed, the Romans believed that the entire ceasefire had been a perfidious plot to allow Hannibal to return to Africa unmolested by the Roman fleet.

In 202 BC near a place called Zama (the exact site in Africa is now lost) the Romans under Scipio squared up against the Carthaginians under Hannibal. It was truly to be a clash of the titans. With the preliminary manoeuvrings, both political and military, out of the way, Hannibal called for a meeting with Scipio; ostensibly to negotiate peace, but probably because Hannibal was curious about the young man who had done so much harm to his cause. The two met between their battle lines, accompanied by a sole interpreter. Hannibal offered to give up all but Carthage's native lands in Africa – but Scipio would settle for nothing less than complete surrender.

Hannibal opened the battle with an elephant charge, hoping to disorganize the Romans who would have seen nothing like it before. Scipio's well-drilled troops opened their ranks to let the elephants through, and tormented them with javelin-throwing light infantry. The elephants were driven back in rout sowing confusion in the troops following up behind them. This confusion was augmented by a successful charge by the Roman cavalry. These now outnumbered the Carthaginian horsemen, for the Numidian king, Masinissa, had deserted and taken his cavalry over to Scipio.

Hannibal had organized his infantry into three lines, with his Italian veterans as the last. To prevent each line from becoming disorganized as the Romans broke the line ahead, fleeing Carthaginian troops were not allowed through the ranks. Instead they had either to stand and die, or to make their way around the flanks. Hannibal's idea was that the Romans should have exhausted themselves by the time they reached his veteran troops, and this is what happened. The battle at the third line was grim and prolonged, and ended only when the Roman cavalry returned from routing the Carthaginian horse and hit the Carthaginians in the rear.

Some 20,000 Carthaginian soldiers died, and about the same number were taken prisoner. This defeat brought the war to an end and proved that, after all, Hannibal could be beaten. In fact, given Rome's superiority in both infantry and cavalry, it was only Hannibal's genius that might have affected the outcome of the battle, as Hannibal implicitly pointed out later to Scipio, who received the title of Africanus after his victory.

Scipio asked Hannibal who was the greatest general. In response Hannibal proclaimed Alexander, the Macedonian king, the greatest as his crossing of unexplored territory with a small force 'transcended human hopes'. When asked who the second greatest was Hannibal proclaimed Pyrrhus for his teaching of making camps and the art of winning men over. When asked who was the third greatest, Hannibal pronounced himself. With a laugh, Scipio asked how Hannibal would rank if he had defeated Scipio in battle. 'Then, beyond doubt', Hannibal replied, 'I should place myself before all other generals.'

Livy Book 10

The empathy between Scipio and Hannibal proved good for Carthage. Hannibal the statesman now led the country as effectively as had Hannibal the war leader. With Scipio keeping the vindictiveness of the Roman senate at bay, Hannibal worked ceaselessly for the next seven years, from 202 to 195 BC, to rebuild his shattered nation.

Hannibal's overhaul of the city's administration and finances made him many enemies, and these people eventually complained to the Romans that Hannibal was once more plotting against them. Scipio's enemies in Rome seized upon the denunciation, and sent for Hannibal to be arraigned in Rome. Rather than face the mercy of a Roman court, Hannibal fled to Tyre, and from there to the kingdoms of Asia Minor. At the court of the Seleucid king Antiochus III, he found an ally who was also struggling against Rome.

Hannibal acted as an advisor to Antiochus. Because the king did not fully trust him, Hannibal was not given command of any troops. Instead he had the opportunity to try his hand as an admiral against the citizens of the island state of Rhodes, which was allied to Rome. The Rhodians were the finest sailors in the Mediterranean at that time, and it is a credit to Hannibal's skill that, despite inexperience on the part of himself and his sailors, he outmanoeuvred his enemy and came close to capturing their admiral. However, Hannibal's fleet took a mauling from the close-combat skills of the Rhodian ships, and he was eventually forced to concede defeat and break off the battle.

Antiochus himself went down in defeat to the Romans at the battle of Magnesia in 189. Hannibal correctly divined that his surrender would be one of the clauses of the subsequent peace treaty, and he abandoned his command and fled once more, with the agents of Rome hot on his heels.

They ran him to ground at the court of King Prusias of Bithynia in 183. Faced with the overwhelming might of Rome, Prusias saw no choice but to give Hannibal up. It may well be that Hannibal too was tired of running. He was sixty-five and had been at war with Rome for most of the preceding forty years, but he had no plans to surrender.

'Let us put an end to this life, which has caused so much dread to the Romans.' With these words Hannibal took poison, and died by his own hand. The epitaph which he pronounced for himself was entirely fitting. For those they fought against, the Romans of the Republic felt anything from respect to deepest contempt. Amongst all these enemies, Hannibal was unique; for in a nation which affected not to understand the meaning of the word, he had inspired fear.

CHAPTER 2

PHILIP V OF MACEDON: ALEXANDER'S HEIR AGAINST THE ROMANS

I know Philip to be a man with a proud heart and a warlike temperament. There is a fierce anger in his heart, like that of an animal penned into a cage, or kept on a chain.

Character assessment of Philip by his contemporary
Alexander of Arcarnia – Livy 35.18

Philip V was born in 237 BC, five years after the end of the First Punic War. But the affairs of Rome, a semi-barbarous state across the Adriatic, were not a major concern to Philip's father Demetrius II, king of Macedon.

The Macedonian king had other preoccupations, for the Mediterranean world of the late third century BC abounded in perils and opportunities. Macedon lay between the barbarian tribes of Illyria and Thrace, and above Greece, over whose rival and fractious city states Macedon held an uneasy hegemony. Macedon was equal to the other great powers of Egypt and Syria which dominated the eastern seaboard.

In both Asia and Greece, petty kings and cities maintained a shifting mosaic of leagues and alliances, and periodically their small wars drew in their neighbours. The small states often clubbed together to exploit any signs of weakness in one of the great powers, and the barbarian tribes waited to launch plundering raids across the northern frontiers if they could catch the Macedonian army off-guard.

Macedon was a prosperous country. It lay between Greece and the Balkan tribes, with the Danube serving as a further trade link. The climate – a mix between the Mediterranean and more temperate Euro-

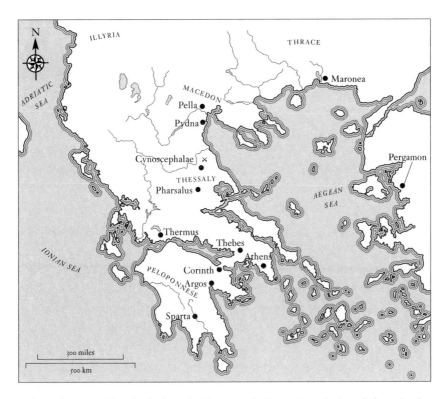

5 *Greece in 200 BC. Macedon had exercised hegemony in Greece since the time of Alexander the Great, but the land was constantly troubled by wars between feuding city-states.*

pean – produced fertile crops and abundant forests. Beneath the soil were reserves of iron and silver, which Macedon exported for a profit.

The Greeks of the south felt the Macedonians to be at best uncouth cousins (there was some debate about whether they could compete as a Greek state in the Olympic games); but the Macedonian kings themselves claimed descent from the sons of Heracles who were exiled from Greece after their father's death. In the years 360–330 BC one of Macedon's greatest kings, Philip II, extended Macedonian rule into Thessaly, and made Macedon the dominant power in Greece. His son, Alexander the Great, went on to conquer the Persian Empire and Egypt.

But Alexander's kingdom soon split into different and warring factions, of which Macedon itself was one. Though the Persian threat was now ended, the kings of Macedon faced dynastic competition from the related royal houses of the Seleucids and Ptolemies.

Consequently, when King Demetrius died in 229 BC, he made careful arrangements for the succession of his eight-year-old son. The new king, Philip V, inherited the crown, but not royal power. In his will, Demetrius had appointed a regent, Antigonus Doson, to shepherd the kingdom through Philip's childhood. Antigonus ruled as a king in all but name, regarding Philip more as his heir than as rightful monarch.

The young king must have felt some relief when Antigonus died in 220 and the royal power passed smoothly to himself rather than to the sons of the regent.

The seventeen-year-old Philip firmly took up the reins of power, to the chagrin of one Apelles, his new guardian, who had hoped to rule the state through its teenage king.

As Demetrius had foreseen, it was not long before neighbouring states tried the new king's mettle. The Aetolians, a people who lived to the southwest of Thessaly, attacked the Achaeans, who lived in the Peloponnesian peninsula south of the Aetolians, and who were allied to Macedon. Philip was slow to respond, concentrating on building a coalition of allies. Many of these alliances were purely for diplomatic purposes as Macedon and the Achaeans did most of the actual fighting (it is from the Latin for allies – *socii* – that this war gets its name of the Social War).

The war was to last for three years, in part because Philip was compelled to hasten to Macedon's northern borders to drive back a barbarian invasion. As it was late in the campaigning season, no one expected the Macedonians to return before the spring. But Philip appeared suddenly with a hand-picked strike force at Corinth. He launched a series of lightning raids on his opponents before wintering at Argos. Such sudden manoeuvres became a part of Philip's campaigning style; that summer he made a surprise dash for the Aetolian capital of Thermus, where he looted the treasury and set fire to the city before turning to maul the Spartan allies of the Aetolians in 218.

Philip seemed a king in the mould of Alexander the Great, who had occupied the throne of Macedon almost exactly one hundred years before. He was active and audacious, yet moderate in his conduct and merciful toward his enemies. He was also intelligent and a lively talker, though with a vicious streak. Once, when an advisor, who happened to be sightless, made a telling point against him, Philip turned to his council and said sarcastically, 'Take note – even a blind man can see that.' Over the years, Philip's character was to become darker and more savage – not altogether surprising in a man who spent his life among faithless allies, perfidious enemies and disloyal subjects.

Among the first of the latter was Philip's guardian, Apelles. Disappointed in his hopes for monarchy at second hand, Apelles and his faction plotted treason. Apelles was discovered and executed, and Philip now looked for his advisors outside Macedon. One of these was Demetrius of Pharos, an Illyrian ruler and former ally of Antigonus Doson. In his chequered career in Illyria, Demetrius had been both an ally and an enemy of the Romans. He had fled to Philip for protection, and he now drew his patron's attention to Rome's problems with Hannibal in Italy.

Demetrius found it easy to awaken the ambition of Philip. The king was young, yet had been successful in everything he had tried, he had a reputation for audacity, and above all, was descended from that family, which, like no other, had ambitions to rule the world.

Polybius 5.102

Another of Philip's advisors was Aratus, a pro-Roman Achaean nobleman. Philip was very attentive toward Aratus, and the king's moderation owed much to the Achaean's counsel. But Philip had noted that the affairs of Greece and Rome were now intertwined, and eventually he was going to have to deal with the power across the Adriatic. After Hannibal's victory at Cannae in 216, Philip decided to throw in his lot with the Carthaginian. Matters were not helped by the death of Aratus, quite possibly from tuberculosis, though Aratus himself suspected slow poison. A friend who found him coughing blood was bitterly told: 'this is evidence of the king's love'.

Philip obtained a treaty of alliance from Hannibal; but his ambassador was captured by the Romans, who shifted a fleet to the Adriatic coast to prevent Philip from crossing to Italy. Before committing himself to an invasion, Philip literally tested the water by launching a small fleet against Roman positions in Illyria. A brief action against a Roman flotilla forced him to destroy his ships and retreat by land, a chastening experience that he did not venture to repeat even after Hannibal seized the very accessible port of Tarentum.

At this time, according to our sources, Philip's character began to change.

> He had enjoyed a good run of success. Prosperity had puffed up his ambitions, and extravagant desires began to take root in his mind. His natural inclination to evil broke through the barriers he had built against it, and he began to show his true and proper character.
>
> Plutarch *Life of Aratus* 52

Preoccupied with Hannibal, the Romans could not open a second front against Philip. But even their moral support caused the Aetolians and Illyrians to declare against Macedon, and Pergamon – a Roman ally in Asia Minor – promptly joined this coalition.

At such times, the historian Livy says that 'Philip showed the spirit worthy of a king'. He attacked his Greek enemies so ferociously that they quickly agreed to a peace brokered by Ptolemy of Egypt. Predictably, the Aetolians reneged after hearing of Pergamese reinforcements for their cause and of a barbarian invasion of Macedon.

Unfortunately for the Aetolians, the Pergamenes were distracted by a war nearer home, and the barbarians withdrew from Macedon on Philip's return. This left the Aetolians unsupported, and the wrathful Philip plundered their lands with a vengeance. Consequently, when the Roman expeditionary force finally arrived, it found few allies in any condition to fight. The Romans retreated to a secure port, and remained there until peace was negotiated in 205. This 'Peace of Phoenice' was intended to keep Philip at arm's length until Hannibal was disposed of. Thereafter Rome had very clear plans for Macedon:

> It is not a question, Romans, of whether there will be peace or war. Philip has already made that choice, and he is actively mustering his forces for war on land and sea. All we have to decide is whether to take our legions to Macedon, or wait to fight him here in Italy…. Let Macedon be the theatre of war. Let it be their cities and countryside that are devastated by fire and the sword.
>
> The consul Sulpicius to the Roman assembly – Livy 31.8

Philip meanwhile turned his attention to the Pergamenes, and swiftly defeated them in battle. He had also allied himself with the Seleucid king Antiochus III, with an eye to stripping Ptolemy V of Egypt of his overseas possessions. Philip's fleet had defeated another set of Roman allies, the Rhodians, in a sea battle at Lade. In the light of all this activity, no one was surprised when the Romans declared war in 200, though the senate had difficulty selling the idea to its own war-weary citizens.

The Romans entered the field as allies of Athens, which Philip had under siege. Predictably, the Aetolians resumed their war with Macedon, and the Dardanian barbarians swarmed across the frontiers. Philip responded with his usual vigour, sending half his forces north to see off the barbarians, and with the remainder destroying an Aetolian force which was ravaging Thessaly. Business as usual was terminated by the arrival of Quinctius Flamininus and a Roman field army. The long, phoney war with Rome had suddenly become serious.

With Hannibal's fate in mind, Philip refused battle and attempted to negotiate. Flamininus opened talks with the demand that Philip quit Greece, including Thessaly, which Macedon had held for decades. It was an impossible demand, and Flamininus, who was eager for military glory, had deliberately made it so.

Flamininus forced the mountain pass which Philip was holding, and pushed him into Thessaly. Though Flamininus claimed to be freeing Greece from Philip, the first Thessalian town he came to resisted him fiercely. It was reduced to ashes as a warning to others who withstood their liberators. Far from being cowed by this savagery, the Thessalians were outraged, and every city now opposed the Romans, sometimes with desperate heroism. In frustration, Flamininus ravaged those parts of the countryside not already ruined by the scorched earth policy of Philip's retreating army.

Observing Philip's difficulties, Macedon's old allies, the Achaeans, now went over to the Roman side. With this desertion, Philip redoubled his attempts to make peace. The Roman commander appeared to entertain the prospect, while at the same time sending urgently to Rome to find whether his command was to be renewed for another year. He instructed his friends in the senate to make peace with Philip if he was to be replaced in Greece, but otherwise to vote for the war to continue.

With his command renewed, Flamininus returned to his original demand that Philip withdraw from Greece. Philip resolved to fight on, though his army was in worse shape than that of the Romans. He had made an alliance with King Nabis of Sparta, but after using this treacherously to seize control of Argos, the Spartan switched sides, leaving Philip abandoned by all his allies except the Arcananians.

Philip spent the winter of 198 strengthening his army until it was the same size as his enemy's. He then marched south, determined to bring the issue to a head as soon as possible. Flamininus was just as eager for battle, and on a spring day in 197 the fate of Macedon was decided near Pharsalus, at Cynoscephalae, where some hills shaped like dogs' heads give the battle its name.

It was not ideal ground for Philip's Macedonians. His army fought in a close formation called the phalanx. Each member of the phalanx carried a fifteen-foot pike, allowing the first three ranks to present as a hedge of spears to the enemy. Going forward, the phalanx was almost unstoppable. Contemporary military experts had long debated whether the phalanx was superior to the Roman cohort (Polybius gives a whole chapter to the

6 *A Macedonian phalanx. The enormously long pikes of the phalangites allowed them to present a hedge of spearpoints to the enemy, but the phalanx was difficult to manoeuvre and vulnerable when disordered.*

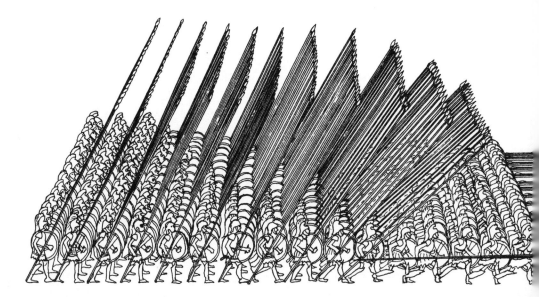

subject, and Livy spends a good part of his Book 9 explaining how the Romans would have dealt with the Macedonians had Alexander the Great turned his attention to the west). Now the question was to be resolved.

The greater flexibility of the cohort proved decisive. The Romans hit Philip's left wing as it was deploying, broke it, and fell upon the flank and rear of the rest of Philip's army. Their long pikes and close formation made it almost impossible for Philip's men to manoeuvre, and once the Romans were in among them with their short stabbing swords, the Macedonians stood no chance.

Philip lost some 8,000 to 10,000 men that day, and another 5,000 were made Roman prisoners. He again asked Flamininus for terms, and this time agreed to give up control of Greece. Flamininus' Aetolian allies were incensed that the Romans intended to leave Philip in his kingdom, and that kingdom intact. However, Flamininus and Philip had established a personal rapport during their negotiations, so Flamininus curtly told the Aetolian leader to 'stop ranting'. There were practical reasons for his decision as well. Without Macedon as a bulwark, Greece was vulnerable to raids from barbarian tribes to the north.

In the formal treaty which was ratified by the senate, Philip had also to pay an indemnity of 1,000 talents, limit his army to 5,000 men and give over his son as a hostage. Seeing that the Romans had him at their mercy, Philip seems to have been agreeably surprised by the treatment he received. He was not at all surprised when the Aetolians and Spartans fell out with Rome, and he cheerfully assisted his conquerors in defeating King Nabis of Sparta in 195.

Rome now turned its attention to Antiochus III of Seleucia, an erstwhile ally of Philip who had been conspicuously inactive during his recent tribulations. Flamininus had withdrawn the Roman army from Greece, and Antiochus saw this as an invitation to step in. When Antiochus allied with the Aetolians, Philip, already unsympathetic to Seleucid ambitions, joined the Roman side. In 191 he campaigned in Thessaly with Baebius, a Roman praetor.

Philip fought a canny war, re-absorbing many of his old possessions into his kingdom, and watching the Roman and Aetolian armies tear at each other. His good humour was such that an Aetolian commander who fell into Macedonian hands received no worse than Philip's company at dinner and an escort back to his lines. Inevitably, the Aetolians were broken, and forced into abject surrender. All that saved them from extinction was Flamininus' perception that Aetolia was a valuable counterweight to Macedon.

When Antiochus was finally driven from Greece, Philip speeded the Romans on their way, assisting over the Hellespont an army which included Scipio Africanus, the conqueror of Hannibal, and his brother Lucius. Also, the messenger sent to tell Philip of their coming was a young man with a distinguished future – Tiberius Sempronius Gracchus. Philip sent congratulations to Rome on their victories, and received in return the remission of his remaining indemnity and the return of his son Demetrius.

Like his father, Demetrius got on well with the Romans at a personal level; and he had used his stay in Rome to cultivate a number of personal acquaintances for future use. These were soon required. Philip was unable to shake off completely the predatory habits of a Hellenistic monarch. He began to expand aggressively into Thessaly until, in 181, a sharp warning came from Rome to pull back. Philip did so, and in a fit of frustrated savagery, massacred the leading citizens of Maronea, one of the towns he had been told to leave.

Demetrius hastened to Rome and contained the diplomatic damage, but suspicion between Rome and Macedon was growing. Philip grimly began to prepare his kingdom for war. He deported a part of the civilian population and executed those political prisoners whom he most distrusted. Nor did Philip trust Demetrius, his Romanophile son. This suspicion was encouraged by Philip's older son, Perseus, who was jealous of Demetrius' popularity, and the fact that Demetrius was the son of Philip's wife, while he was born of a concubine.

Perseus produced a letter from Flamininus which showed that Demetrius was plotting against Philip. Hearing that he was to be arrested, Demetrius attempted to flee, but this was taken as proof of his guilt. He was captured and executed.

Philip was feeling the strain. He was girding his reluctant country for a difficult war and was highly unpopular, even loathed, by many of his people. As a further blow, the letter which had caused the execution of

Demetrius proved to be a forgery. In a fury, Philip disinherited Perseus. The prince might well have suffered further, but while still on campaign against the barbarians in 179, the old king died of sickness and (allegedly) a broken heart.

Perseus seized the throne, swiftly executing Philip's proposed heir, and launched his new kingdom into a confrontation with Rome. We will never know what might have happened if canny old King Philip had led Macedon's army at Pydna, but his son was no match for Rome. Perseus suffered the fate that Philip had managed to avoid – being led through Rome as a prisoner in a Roman triumph.

CHAPTER 3

VIRIATHUS: FROM SHEPHERD TO GUERRILLA LEADER

He had the greatest qualities of a commander (for a barbarian);
and he was foremost among his men in facing danger.
Appian *Hispania* 12 (75)

Viriathus, ancient Iberia's greatest leader, came from Lusitania, an area roughly bounded by the modern Guadiana and Douro rivers and taking in much of modern Portugal. Though rich in minerals, the land was mountainous and the soil poor. The peoples of Lusitania made their living in part by preying on tribes from more fertile lands. This was in keeping with the tribal values of the Celticized peoples of the region, the main tribe of which was the Lusitani, after whom the region was named, and this tribe alternately allied itself with or feuded against the other principal tribal groups, the Vettones and Celtici.

When their neighbours came under Roman sway during the early second century BC, the fierceness of the tribesmen and their lack of anything worth possessing kept Rome from Lusitania. However, the Lusitanians did not see any reason to abstain from raiding their neighbours, and this inevitably led to a clash with the neighbours' Roman suzerains. After a period of frequent clashes when the Lusitanians repeatedly agreed to and then violated peace accords, Rome lost patience in 151 and launched a full-scale attack under Servius Sulpicius Galba (an ancestor of the Roman emperor of AD 69).

Again the Lusitanians sued for peace. Galba replied that the poverty of the Lusitanians' native soil made it impossible for them to desist from raiding for long, so he proposed a whole-scale resettlement on three

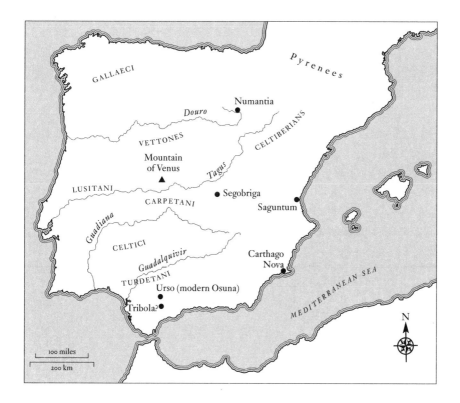

7 *Hispania in 150 BC. The mountains and rivers of the Iberian peninsula made it an excellent environment for guerrilla warfare, and Spain was not properly subdued for at least another hundred years.*

fertile plains. On an agreed date in 150 the Lusitanians gathered in three separate groups to await resettlement. Galba insisted on disarming them, weapons being superfluous for an agrarian way of life. Then, with the nation in three separate, unarmed groups, Galba ordered the Roman army to surround each group in turn and massacre everyone there – men, women and children. It was an atrocity that sickened even the brutal Romans. 'He avenged treachery with treachery – an unworthy Roman imitating barbarians.' (Appian *Hispania* 10 [60].)

Not all, and probably not even the greater part of the Lusitanians were caught by this trick. Among those who escaped was a shepherd called Viriathus. Like the rest of his countrymen he took up the vendetta against Rome, and was soon commanding several of the guerrilla bands which struck at the Romans from mountain strongholds.

These attacks became bolder and more frequent, until by 147 BC the Lusitanians launched a wholesale invasion of neighbouring Turdetania. They came against the army of the Roman propraetor Vettius. The Lusitanians went into battle lightly armoured, and mainly protected by a shield which was either the distinctively spined Celtiberian shield, or smaller, rounder shields called 'targes'. The main offensive weapon was a spear (the *saunion*) and a formidable sword of the *falcata* type, the curving blade of which resembles a large Gurkha kukri. Combined with their natural ferocity, this made the Lusitanians a formidable fighting force, but they were no match for the disciplined legions of the finest army in antiquity. The Romans quickly pushed the bulk of the Lusitanian forces into a fortified town and besieged them there.

Being desperately short of supplies, the Lusitanians were tempted to accept the terms offered by Vettius, although they bore a suspicious resemblance to the terms previously offered by Galba. Viriathus vigorously argued against surrender, and when he offered to show his countrymen a way out he was elected as their leader. The next day, he led out the Lusitanians as if for battle, then, as the Romans formed up against them, the tribesmen scattered, with each seeking safety for himself. Hastily Vettius called up his cavalry, but these were unable to follow up the fleeing tribesmen because Viriathus had retained 1,000 of his best horses and horsemen to cover his countrymen's retreat. The Roman cavalry had to break these first, but the Lusitanians remained just out of reach and skirmished with the Romans until their foot soldiers had reached broken ground and safety. With his faster horses and lighter riders,

8 *Some Lusitanian warriors used straight swords in place of the falcata shown here, and often carried light javelins for use in preliminary skirmishes. Some warriors wore shirts of chain mail and others may have used cuirasses of stiffened linen, but armour was probably the exception rather than the rule.*

Viriathus then outran the Roman cavalry to rejoin his army safely, making his rendezvous at the town of Tribola.

Vettius followed, and Viriathus pretended to retreat while leading the Romans to a suitable ambush position. The ambush was a complete success. Caught between the Lusitanians and a cliff edge, some 4,000 of Vettius' army of 10,000 were killed, including Vettius himself. A Roman junior officer took command of the survivors. With his men too demoralized to fight, the Roman resorted to bribing the Celtiberians, and thus managed to send 5,000 of them into battle against Viriathus. Flushed with their earlier success, the Lusitanians made short work of the Celtiberians; according to Appian, after a short battle every one of them was killed. Viriathus went on to stock his nation's larders by comprehensively plundering Carpetania (around modern Toledo).

The year 146 BC saw another Roman army enter the fray, this one commanded by C. Plautius. Once more Viriathus withdrew to his home ground. There, on a hill called the Mountain of Venus, the Romans were setting up their camp among the olive trees when Viriathus attacked and overwhelmed them. Plautius was so shocked that he took his army to the security of their winter quarters and refused to move even when Viriathus went rampaging through the lands of Rome's allies, confiscating and destroying crops and pillaging the major Celtiberian centre of Segobriga. The destruction of the Segobrigan army was recorded by a Roman military historian:

Viriathus sent men to carry off the flocks of the Segobrigans. When the soldiers saw this they rushed out in great numbers. The marauders pretended to flee and drew the Segobrigans into an ambush where they were cut to pieces.

Frontinus *Stratagems* 3.10.6

But it was in the nature of the Romans to try, try again. The next year brought Quintus Fabius Aemilianus, the son of the conqueror of Perseus in Macedon, and with him an army of some 15,000 foot soldiers and 2,000 cavalry. While these troops were mustering at Urso (modern Osuna), word reached them that Viriathus had attacked Plautius' successor, Claudius Unimanus, and almost wiped out his army. Claudius' symbols of office were taken as trophies to the Lusitanian stronghold.

After meeting and defeating another of Fabius' subordinates, Viriathus was prepared to take on the general himself. Fabius, however, knowing his troops to be raw and untrained, refused a decisive engagement. Spain was treated to the sight of Iberian soldiers repeatedly offering battle to a Roman consular army which, just as steadfastly, refused to face them. In 144 BC Fabius finally risked an engagement and drove the Lusitanians back, but the damage to Roman prestige had been done. The Celtiberians rose in revolt against Rome, and so began the long and bitter Numantine War (named after the Celtiberian capital, Numantia).

Next in the sequence of commanders to try their mettle against Viriathus was Q. Pompeius. Viriathus followed his usual pattern when under attack and fell back towards the mountains. At the same Mountain of Venus that had been the downfall of Plautius, Viriathus chose to fall on the Romans. Pompeius lost about 1,000 men and pulled the survivors back into camp, while Viriathus decided that his army's summer excursion would be to ravage the area about the Guadalquivir river.

The year 142 BC arrived, bringing with it yet another Roman army, this time under the command of a step-brother of Fabius Aemilianus – a man called Fabius Servilianus. As a reflection of the seriousness with which Rome was beginning to regard the activities of Viriathus, Servilianus brought with him two full legions (about 16,000 men), 1,600 cavalry, and elephants donated by King Micipsa of Numidia (see Chapter 4).

The Romans enjoyed some initial successes and pushed Viriathus back into Lusitania. Servilianus also isolated and killed some guerrilla bands which were operating away from Viriathus' main force. With Viriathus in full retreat, Servilianus took over several cities which had been under Lusitanian control, and in 141 BC he made the fateful decision to besiege a city called Erisone (present location unknown).

The siege was not tightly maintained, and Viriathus smuggled himself and a large contingent within the walls by night. In the morning these reinforcements and the garrison sallied out against the Romans and took them by storm. The Romans retreated in complete disorder, hounded by Viriathus' cavalry, and with the infantry hot on their heels.

The running battle came to an end in a valley, and Viriathus had taken the precaution of plugging the pass out of the valley with a strong fortification. The Romans were trapped exactly as Fabius Maximus had trapped Hannibal almost eighty years earlier. But this latter-day Fabius had already proved that he was no Hannibal. He was utterly helpless in the trap which the Iberians had laid for him, and now he and his army faced extinction.

This was not a war waged with gentility and chivalry. For example, when Servilianus captured some tribesmen he made sure they would never bear arms against him by lopping the hands off all nine hundred prisoners. And Frontinus mentions a Lusitanian massacre of the innocent:

When Viriathus proposed to return their wives and children to them, the inhabitants of Segovia preferred to witness the execution of their loved ones rather than fail the Roman side.

Frontinus *Stratagems* 4.5.22

Given these circumstances, it must have been with considerable trepidation that Servilianus did the only thing possible to him – unconditional surrender to the Lusitanians. To his surprise and delight, Viriathus imposed only the mildest of conditions on his defeated enemy. The Romans were to withdraw from Lusitania and recognize the independence of their lands. Viriathus himself was to be considered as a friend and ally of the Roman people.

It has sometimes been asked why, with his hated enemy at his mercy, Viriathus let them off the hook so easily. There are several possibilities. One is simply that Viriathus considered this the end of the war. He had defeated everything Rome had sent against him, and had now brought a consular army of two legions to its knees. Rome had sued for peace. It was over, and he had won. Also, Viriathius and his men may have been tiring of constant battle. Had they put the Roman army to the sword (and it takes an army with a strong stomach to massacre that many men) Rome would never forget and never forgive. However long it took, it would be war to the death. Only by imposing the mildest of terms did Viriathus feel he could get a peace treaty from the famously arrogant Roman senate, and so it proved. His settlement was ratified, albeit grudgingly.

The extent of this grudge became apparent when the next governor arrived in the province. Servilius Caepio was the brother of the recently defeated general, and he definitely considered Viriathus and the Lusitanians as unfinished business. Caepio is generally regarded as having wanted war for glory and profit and to avenge the family honour. But he might also have realized that the root cause of the war had not yet been addressed. There were too many Lusitanians than could be supported by their land; if they and their families were to survive, it would be by plundering the neighbouring provinces. Despite the amity of the recent peace, this inconvenient fact had not gone away and at some point the Lusitanians were bound to return to their bad old ways, especially as they now felt they could defeat the Romans at will.

Caepio began a series of calculated provocations, testing the tolerance of the senate on the one side, and the patience of Viriathus on the other. Though secretly encouraging Caepio, the senate would not permit an open breach of faith. Knowing this, Viriathus refused to be provoked; but it seems that eventually some of his more hot-headed tribesmen took matters into their own hands and finally gave the Romans the excuse they needed to break the peace. In 140 BC the war was resumed.

As a leader of men, Caepio was less inspirational than Viriathus. At first it seemed that the bad blood between the Roman general and his men would do the Lusitanian's work for him:

Caepio…was a source of harm to his own men, and they in their turn came close to killing him. He was harsh and cruel to all of them, and especially the cavalry. Consequently, they told all sorts of coarse jokes about him at nights, and the more that he was angered by this, the more they made jokes to infuriate him. Though he knew what was going on, there was no one that Caepio could accuse directly. He suspected the cavalry, and not being able to blame an individual, he punished them collectively. All six hundred were ordered to cross the river and, with no more escort than their grooms, to get wood from the mountain on which Viriathus had his camp. This was so obviously dangerous that Caepio's lieutenants begged him not to destroy the cavalry. These waited for a little while, thinking he might listen to reason. Caepio would not be moved, and the cavalry would not beg him themselves, knowing that was what he wanted. Choosing to die rather than say a single respectful word to their commander, they crossed the river, with allied horsemen and other volunteers accompanying them. They cut the wood, returned across the river, and piled it in all around their general's quarters, intending to burn him

to death. And he would have died in the flames had he not run away in time.
Cassius Dio *History* 22.78

Though lacking in morale, the Roman army was large and dangerous, so Viriathus resorted to his usual tactic of falling back before an aggressive enemy. He had returned reluctantly to arms, and still felt that a deal was possible. Accordingly, he dispatched his most trusted advisors – a trio called Audax, Ditalco and Minurus – to see what terms the Romans would accept.

Given the temper of his men, Caepio knew the risks of battle with Viriathus, both for the Roman cause and himself personally. Therefore he tried another tactic. Viriathus' envoys were treated royally, and overwhelmed by the sumptuousness of Caepio's camp in the field. Caepio assured them that this standard of living, and much more, could be theirs. All they needed to do was kill Viriathus and obtain a massive reward. Because of the frequency of night alarums, Viriathus slept in his armour. On the other hand, he also received messengers and his lieutenants at all hours, so the returning delegates were admitted to Viriathus' tent without question. Once there, they stabbed their leader through the throat – the only point where the armour did not protect him – and fled to the Roman lines before the murder was discovered.

Iberian treachery met Roman treachery. Caepio coolly assured the assassins that they had misunderstood his meaning, and that he would never encourage men to kill their own commander. The killers were turned out of the Roman camp without a penny to reward them for their deed.

The Lusitanians were grief-stricken and demoralized by the killing of their leader. They gave him a magnificent funeral and elected a man called Tantalus as his successor. But the heart had gone out of their cause, even as Roman morale surged. Caepio easily obtained the victory that had evaded his predecessors, and the Lusitanians were obliged to sue for peace. Wisely, Caepio did just as Galba had promised in 150. A decade of war had depopulated much of the country, and Caepio could now deliver the Roman promise to settle the Lusitanians on land fertile enough to support them without resort to brigandage. Western Iberia was at peace. What honourable generals had failed to do in years of open warfare, a duplicitous bully had accomplished by treachery in a single campaign.

Little is known of Viriathus the man, as opposed to Viriathus the commander. It is known that he had a son-in-law (whom he allegedly killed rather than surrender to the Romans) and therefore, by inference, a wife and daughter (Diodorus gives a fanciful account of his wedding). We know nothing of his appearance, and for his character we have to rely on reports from the Romans, who seem to have rather admired their antagonist:

Viriathus was of very obscure origin but gained great fame through his actions. He went from being a shepherd to being a robber, and from there to being a general. Starting with a natural aptitude and building on this with training, he was swift in pursuit and in flight, and he had great stamina in hand-to-hand fighting. He was happy with whatever food he could get his hands on, and was satisfied to bed down in the wild. Consequently, he was above suffering from heat or cold, and was untroubled by hunger or any other hardship; as content with whatever was on hand as he was with the very best.

Through nature and training he had a magnificent physique, yet this was far less in excellence than his mental powers. He could quickly plan and execute whatever needed to be done – and he had always a clear idea of what that was. Furthermore, he knew exactly when to do it. He could pretend ignorance of the most obvious facts and just as cleverly hide his knowledge of the most hidden secrets. In everything he did, he was not only the general but his own second-in-command as well. His obscure origins and reputation for strength were so balanced that he seemed neither inferior nor superior to anyone, and the man himself was neither humble nor arrogant. To sum up, he waged war not for personal gain, power or revenge, but for the sake of waging war; he was considered both to love it, and to be a master of it.

Cassius Dio fragment 78

CHAPTER 4

JUGURTHA: AMBITION AND TREACHERY

*…so versatile in adapting to changes in his fortunes, and possessing
a combination of great cunning and courage.*

Plutarch *Marius* 12

In the year 112 BC, a small group of envoys arrived from Africa with this desperate appeal to the Roman senate.

It is not my fault, Fathers of the Senate, that I have to turn to you yet again. No, I am forced to do this because of the violence of Jugurtha. He so desperately wants to destroy me that he pays no attention either to you or to the immortal Gods. More than anything else, he thirsts for my blood. That is why, even though I am an ally and friend of the Roman people, he has besieged me now for more than four months. Neither the services of my father Micipsa nor your decrees are any use to me; I don't know whether the sword or hunger are oppressing me more.

… But since I was created merely to be a monument to Jugurtha's crimes, I no longer pray for escape from death or unhappiness – I just want to escape from the tyranny of my enemy, and avoid physical torture. As to Numidia, you are welcome to it – do as you want, but keep me out of Jugurtha's godless hands.

Sallust *Jugurtha* 23–25

The letter was written by Adherbal, Jugurtha's cousin, to whom Jugurtha seemed as much a violent force of nature as a rival to the throne. What kind of man could attack a loyal friend of Rome, usurp his kingdom and then defy the Roman senate to do its worst? That, in a nutshell, was Jugurtha's policy, even though he knew full well the power of Rome.

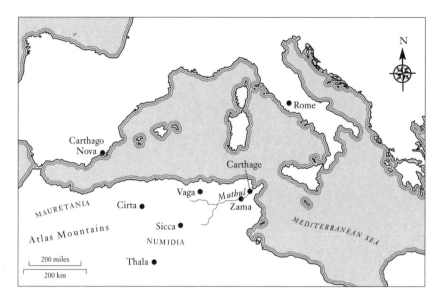

9 North Africa after Hannibal. The destruction of Carthage left a power vacuum which Jugurtha planned to fill. The Roman legions were unbeatable on the coastal plains, but they struggled to match Jugurtha in his own hinterland.

When Scipio Aemilianus had destroyed Numantia in Spain, Jugurtha was there – not as an observer, but as a fighting soldier on the Roman side.

Jugurtha was from Numidia, an African kingdom allied to Rome since Masinissa, Jugurtha's grandfather, had sided with the Romans against Hannibal. Jugurtha was the illegitimate son of Mastanabal, the youngest of Masinissa's sons. He was unlikely to succeed to the throne, but he was popular, good-looking and energetic. Masinissa's successor, Micipsa, decided that this young man could best expend his energies elsewhere, and dispatched him with a Numidian contingent to support Scipio's war in Spain. It would not have greatly distressed Micipsa if Jugurtha had not returned.

However, Jugurtha proved to be a natural soldier. 'By his unquestioning obedience and his indifference to danger he soon became a hero to the Romans and a terror to his enemies', says the historian Sallust, who is our principal source for the story of Jugurtha. Sallust quotes the glowing recommendation from Scipio Aemilianus with which the young hero returned to Micipsa.

'I am sure that you will be pleased to hear that in this war your nephew Jugurtha has distinguished himself above all others. I have a high regard for what he has done for us, and I will do everything in my power to pass that esteem on to the Roman senate and people. Speaking as your friend, I have to congratulate you personally for finding a man who is worthy of yourself and your father.'

Sallust *Jugurtha* 8

Micipsa took the hint and obediently adopted Jugurtha. He made Jugurtha joint heir with his own sons, Hiempsal and Adherbal, and on his deathbed in 118 commended his sons to Jugurtha's care. Later, Jugurtha pointed out that Micipsa had been senile, and suggested the repeal of all his recent decrees. Young Hiempsal agreed, and suggested that Jugurtha's adoption of three years previously should be repealed as well. Soon after this, soldiers burst into the house where Hiempsal was staying, discovered him hiding in the maids' quarters, and killed him. They took his head back to Jugurtha.

Adherbal quickly took to arms. He had the majority of the populace behind him, but Jugurtha had the better soldiers and greater military ability. Adherbal was defeated and forced to flee to the Roman province of Africa, which had been created from the territory of fallen Carthage.

Jugurtha had learned more than soldiering in Spain. He knew that success or failure in Rome depended on holding office, and that elections to even the lowest magistracies were phenomenally expensive. Adherbal came to Rome with right on his side and a plea for justice. Jugurtha's envoys came with gold. To the indignation of unbribed Romans, Jugurtha obtained a decree that divided the kingdom between himself and Adherbal, with Jugurtha awarded the richer part.

This settlement lasted for a few years while Jugurtha consolidated his new kingdom and put it on a war footing, and for a few months after that, as Adherbal steadfastly refused to respond to Jugurtha's ever more violent provocations. Finally, Jugurtha lost patience and blatantly invaded Adherbal's lands, rapidly driving him back to the fortress town of Cirta.

This, and Adherbal's fervent pleas to Rome (one of which starts this chapter), brought a commission from Rome to investigate. Jugurtha alleged that Adherbal had tried to kill him, and made much of his friendship with Scipio. Then as soon as he was sure that the commission had left Africa, he resumed the siege. In response to Adherbal's ever more frantic imprecations, the Romans sent yet another commission, this time composed of senior senators, including the great Marcus Aemilius Scaurus.

Jugurtha blandly refused to make any concessions. The commission retired in frustration and the defenders of Cirta, abandoned by Rome, were forced to terms. Jugurtha offered the defenders and Adherbal their lives in return for their surrender; but once in the city, Jugurtha slaughtered every adult male he had captured. Adherbal, as he had feared, was tortured to death.

When word of the fall of Cirta reached Rome in 112 BC war became inevitable, not least because many of the defenders of Cirta had been Italian traders with their own friends and patrons in the senate. When Jugurtha's son came to soothe the Romans with polite words and a lot of money, he was told to go straight home unless he intended to offer unconditional surrender.

The consul, L. Calpurnius Bestia, arrived in Africa with a large army and immediately commenced operations. Jugurtha responded with peace overtures, which the Roman accepted. A peace treaty was made by which Jugurtha had to declare his submission to Rome, pay a modest indemnity, and hand over thirty elephants. Given the extent of Jugurtha's misdeeds this was a light punishment indeed. There was a near-universal suspicion that Jugurtha had once again managed to bribe his way out of trouble, though he might simply have been extremely fortunate.

Rome was being threatened from the north by a huge migratory army of Germanic tribesmen, who had already defeated an army under the vainglorious and incompetent Papirius Carbo. In 111 the storm was holding off, but the Roman elite knew that at any time the barbarian horde could flood across the Alps. Bestia may have decided this was not a good time for Rome to be involved in an African adventure, and combined sound statesmanship with the receipt of a large cash contribution from Jugurtha.

The Roman plebs smelled foul play, and a commission was set up to investigate exactly whom Jugurtha had paid off. The Numidian king was summoned to Rome, and offered immunity in return for his testimony. Jugurtha came, but before he could say a word to the commission, a tribune stepped forward and forbade him to speak. Jugurtha must have considered the entire proceedings a farce, but he made good use of his time in Rome. Massiva, another grandchild of Masinissa, had been claiming the Numidian throne, pointing to the evident unsuitability of Jugurtha, so now Jugurtha had his rival assassinated. He made little attempt to conceal his culpability, and the Romans, respecting Jugurtha's safe conduct, could only furiously order him to quit Italy immediately.

There is a story that as Jugurtha was leaving Rome, he looked back and commented 'Now there is a city for sale; once it finds a buyer, it is doomed.'

Probably Jugurtha really did believe that Rome was rotten to the core. Whatever he did, to avoid retribution he needed only a general or politician to bribe. Despite the polemics of Sallust (who, before taking up history, was a politician from a faction hostile to the ruling Roman oligarchs), Rome's government was still principled enough to be affronted by this presumption. There were to be no further peace deals.

In 110 Jugurtha was followed to Africa by an army under Postumius Albinus, the outraged patron of the deceased Massiva. Postumius achieved little before having to return to Rome for the elections, leaving his brother Aulus to confront Jugurtha. The king immediately opened negotiations, though he probably knew that matters could no longer be repaired by a quick bribe. Nevertheless, Jugurtha dragged the talks out until almost the end of the campaigning season. With nothing to show from his time in command, Aulus tried to make amends by attacking the town of Suthul, where Jugurtha kept much of his treasury. He never reached the city.

Jugurtha's defining characteristic was his audacity. Not waiting for the Romans to come to him, he launched a surprise attack on their camp which cut much of the Roman army to pieces, forcing the rest to surrender. These captives were made to pass under the yoke – a symbolic gesture by which each defeated soldier acknowledged the superiority of the enemy. After inflicting on Albinus' men this, the greatest humiliation possible for an ancient army, Jugurtha gave the Romans eleven days to leave the country.

The Roman defeat was not due only to Jugurtha's superior generalship. He was on home ground and the legions, devastatingly effective in the low coastal plains, struggled on the upland plateau of the Numidian interior. There, a mixture of scrub and broken ground hampered movement. The summers were hot and arid, and in spring and winter cold winds blew off the Mediterranean onto the mountains, bringing rains that turned the few roads into mud, and every stream-bed into a torrent. Supplies from the coast had to be brought through mountains thickly forested with conifers and evergreens, and just as thickly populated with bandits ready to swoop on any lightly guarded convoy.

Where the ground was open, the Romans had to contend with Jugurtha's formidable cavalry. These men had been nomadic horsemen only a few generations before, and they re-adapted easily to their semi-desert environment. More lightly armed than their Roman opponents, they were more mobile, and knew the ground much better. In short, Numidia was not an easy nut for a Roman expeditionary force to crack.

Jugurtha's victory produced venomous fury from Rome. A corrupt cartel of oligarchs might have decided to cut their losses and end the war; but if this was Jugurtha's reading of Rome's government, the army that landed on his shores in 109 must have come as a severe shock to him. The Roman commander, Quintus Caecilius Metellus, was not only at least as good a soldier as Jugurtha, but also famously incorruptible. Alarmed, Jugurtha attempted peace negotiations. Metellus proved ready to talk.

When Jugurtha sent a message to Metellus in regard to peace, the latter made many demands upon him, one by one, as if each were to be the last, and in this way got from him hostages, arms, the elephants, the captives, and the deserters. All of these last he killed; but he did not conclude peace, since Jugurtha, fearing to be arrested, refused to come to him.

Cassius Dio *History* 26.89

Jugurtha was bitterly disappointed to find that Metellus had been delaying – using Jugurtha's own tactics – while he trained and acclimatized his army. Then Metellus struck westward, taking the trading city of Vaga, and engaging Jugurtha on the banks of the river Muthul. Before the battle Jugurtha gave his men a brief but accurate pep talk.

'You have fought these men before, beaten them, and passed them under the yoke. They won't be any braver under their new commander, while I have given you everything that troops can expect of their general. You are not outnumbered or outclassed. You know the land, and you know what is expected of you. The Romans don't know what they are up against.'

Sallust 49

And indeed the battle was a close one. It was not particularly bloody, for the more lightly armed Numidians could neither severely harm the heavier Roman infantry, nor be easily caught by them. But after the battle many of Jugurtha's soldiers – for the most part graziers and poor farmers – simply dispersed to their homes. They had done their duty by their king in battle, and now they had their own affairs to attend to.

Jugurtha set about raising a new army, while his opponent tried to seize as many of Jugurtha's cities as possible. Jugurtha constantly sent envoys asking for peace, and Metellus made unstinting efforts to turn these envoys against him. Even Bomilcar – the man who had effected the assassination of Massiva – was suborned, and Jugurtha was forced to execute him to forestall a plot against his own life.

There was a certain irony in the situation: the man Jugurtha could not corrupt was using his own weapons of corruption, deceit and delay against him. For the rest of his life, Jugurtha could trust no one, and every close aide was a potential assassin. The atmosphere of fear and suspicion that resulted caused many of Jugurtha's closest advisors to desert him before they too were accused of plotting against their leader.

The campaign of 109–108 BC ended inconclusively. Jugurtha had lost another major city, Sicca, but had kept the Romans from Zama, and regained the city of Vaga through treachery. With his command renewed for another year, Metellus retook Vaga and pushed Jugurtha toward a now-unknown location called Thala. Here Jugurtha made a stand, but was defeated and forced to flee, leaving many of his stores and much of his treasury behind. Thala was a bitter blow, for Jugurtha had reckoned that its isolation and aridity should have made it inaccessible to the Romans.

But if fortune favours the brave, it now seemed to offer some reward to Jugurtha for his spirited resistance. Metellus was ousted from command by the plots of his subordinate Marius, and Bocchus – king of Mauretania – began to take an interest in his neighbour's affairs. Bocchus was a long-time ally of Jugurtha, and had married his daughter. He smelled advantage for himself in the situation and felt more prepared to ally himself with his father-in-law than with the Romans, who seemed dangerous neighbours.

Marius had realized the fruitlessness of chasing Jugurtha around his kingdom. Instead he methodically reduced the number of forts and cities loyal to Jugurtha, depriving the king of a base in his own realm. In desperation, Jugurtha promised a third of his kingdom to Bocchus in return for his support.

Numidian and Mauretanian joined forces, and fell on Marius as he was retiring to winter quarters. Though outnumbered and taken by surprise, the Roman army proved magnificently disciplined and superbly generalled. The legions staged a fighting retreat to some nearby hills, rallied, and drove the Numidians back. Once again Jugurtha had misjudged, assuming Marius to be a scheming subordinate rather than a highly skilled commander in his own right. (Interestingly, it may be that Jugurtha had some personal knowledge of Marius, who had also served with Scipio Aemilianus in Spain.)

The Romans resumed their march, and two days later Jugurtha attacked again. In the thick of the battle, he attempted to use his knowledge of Latin by riding to the Roman lines and waving a bloody sword with which, he assured the astounded legionaries, he had personally slain Marius. This was a lie, but a credible one because both commanders led from the front and, with both lines engaged in combat, it was impossible for most Roman infantrymen to know how their commander was faring. On one occasion, it is said that Jugurtha,

… in order to keep his men in the field, and hoping to seize the victory which had been so close, finished up in the middle of the Roman cavalry, with his companions on either side cut down. He himself had to force his way out through a storm of missiles.

Sallust *Jugurtha* 101

A Roman cavalry charge to the flank finally broke Jugurtha's army, and demolished it as a fighting force (for as usual after a setback, the Numidians promptly dispersed). This left Jugurtha wholly dependent on Bocchus, who had deserted the field at the first sign of difficulty and thus had his forces largely intact.

But the Moorish king, having seen the Romans in action, had second thoughts about his alliance. He discreetly enquired to Rome about the possibility of making peace. The senate replied that Bocchus would have to earn his pardon, and sent Lucius Cornelius Sulla, one of Marius' deputies, to continue negotiations. Word of this soon reached Jugurtha, who had carefully planted spies in his ally's camp. On one occasion, he became suspicious of Bocchus' son Volux, and followed Bocchus to see what Volux was up to. Volux and his cavalry met Sulla, and while returning passed through the Numidian camp. Jugurtha evidently had not managed to insert a spy into Volux's retinue, for he was unaware that Sulla was now concealed among Volux's followers.

Once Sulla was in Bocchus' court, Jugurtha immediately knew about it. He promptly suggested that the Roman be handed over to him as a hostage, even as Sulla was telling Bocchus that peace with Rome depended on his handing over Jugurtha. This left the king with the interesting problem of whom to betray: his father-in-law, or a Roman envoy with the might of Rome at his back. After wavering to and fro, Bocchus finally invited both his potential victims to a conference. They came eagerly, for Bocchus had played them against each other and promised each of them that he was going to hand the other into his power.

The conference began with both sides waiting for Bocchus to give the signal that would bring his soldiers springing from ambush. The signal duly came, and the companions of Jugurtha were cut down. The Numidian king was seized and handed, with all ceremony, to the triumphant (and very relieved) Sulla.

Jugurtha's capture and Bocchus' surrender effectively ended the Numidian War. As a reward for choosing the right side, Bocchus received the portion of Numidia he had demanded of Jugurtha, and the rump of that kingdom was handed to the rule of yet another of Masinissa's numerous descendants. Jugurtha's sons were spared and exiled to the Italian town of Venusia.

In 104 BC Jugurtha returned to Rome. The Romans were no longer

interested in the political battles of five years earlier, when Jugurtha's testimony had been so keenly sought. Rome was under threat of extinction
from the Cimbric hordes of northern Europe, just as the senate had
feared, and the captive king was required for a different function – to be
paraded in chains through the streets of Rome as a morale-building
exhibit at Marius' triumph. Plutarch reports:

> While he was being led in the triumph, he went mad. At the prison, his tunic
> was torn from his body, and the scramble for his golden ear-ring was so greedy
> that his ear lobe was torn off. Then he was shoved, naked, into the pit. He
> looked around him in complete confusion, and said with a grin 'By Hercules,
> this Roman bath is cold!'
>
> Plutarch *Marius* 12

The 'pit' was Rome's most feared dungeon – the Tullianum. (This
dungeon had formerly been a water cistern, or *tullus*, and is today a
chapel, as it reputedly held St Peter over a century later.) The only entry
was through a trapdoor in the roof. Once within, there was absolutely no
way short of divine intervention for a prisoner to escape. There in that
cell, as Marius settled down to his victory feast, Jugurtha was left in the
silence and dark until his executioners arrived to kill him by strangulation. Or, according to another tradition, Jugurtha was left to a slow death
through starvation. This would at least have given him time to prepare
for his eventual meeting with the considerable number of vengeful
spirits who were waiting for him to join them.

· PART II ·

MITHRIDATES

SPARTACUS

VERCINGETORIX

ORODES II

CLEOPATRA

Plots, Treason and Civil War – The Slow Death of the Roman Republic

By 100 BC the complacency of the Roman senate was beginning to waver. Twenty years previously, the senate's power had seemed unbreakable. The domestic programme of the reforming Gracchus brothers had been seen off with a minimum of compromise, while abroad Rome had faced no serious military threat. Her armies were supreme from the Black Sea to the Atlantic. Niggling wars remained with the Spaniards and some restless alpine tribes, but Rome's warrior aristocracy looked upon these as opportunities for glory rather than as problems to be overcome.

Then came a series of setbacks. A relatively minor war in Africa turned into a drawn-out campaign. Although the energetic and capable Metellus Numidicus helped to win that war, the military incompetence and shameless corruption of their so-called betters severely damaged the common people's faith in the system.

They turned to the demagogue Caius Marius. To the Roman public, Marius' main qualification for high office was that he bitterly disliked all that the Roman governing class stood for. Marius took command in Africa, and soon brought the war to a close. To get the extra recruits he needed for this, Marius made the *capite censi* – those too poor to own military equipment – eligible for military service, using state money to pay for their weapons and armour.

While Marius was still consul, the migration of a huge Germanic tribe

74

called the Cimbri threatened Rome's northern borders. Thanks to the arrogant stupidity of their commander, the army sent to stop them was wiped out almost to a man. Rome was saved by luck, for the Cimbri decided to plunder Spain before turning to Italy. When the Cimbri came back, Marius was waiting with a carefully trained army and destroyed the invaders in northern Italy. But Rome had problems which could not be solved by military might.

Rome's aristocracy were paying for the stubbornness of the previous generation. The conservatives (the *optimates*, or 'best men', as they called themselves) had defeated social reformers by brutal violence rather than rational debate. Now reaction was setting in, and the election of Marius was only one symptom of dissatisfaction among the electorate. They elected radical demagogues to the tribunate, an office which had distinct appeal for reformers. Tribunes enjoyed special status in Rome. They could protect their fellow citizens by vetoing oppressive legislation, and even arrest the consul himself. Above all, tribunes could propose legislation and use their considerable authority to force it into law.

This was done by the disreputable Saturninus, and again in the 90s BC by the high-minded Livius Drusus. Drusus had identified a major fault-line in Roman society – the citizenship. Rome now gave the privilege of citizenship sparingly, and those who enjoyed its considerable advantages were reluctant to dilute their benefits. This enraged the subject peoples of Italy. Many of them had served alongside the legions in Rome's wars and were an integral part of the Roman fighting machine. When Drusus was murdered, the frustration of the Italian people exploded into a rebellion that threatened the very existence of Rome.

This rebellion was called the Social War from the Latin word *socii* or 'allies'. In this war, Rome's army was largely fighting against itself. Instead of barbarians or Asiatic hordes, the Romans faced a disciplined, highly motivated army that matched them manoeuvre for manoeuvre. Rome only 'won' this war by giving citizenship to any rebel who laid down his arms. This meant that the Roman army came to include soldiers who had been fighting Rome a few years previously. Many were from mountain tribes with little experience of democracy, and even less loyalty to the senate. They marched under the banner of SPQR (*Senatus Populusque Romanus* – 'the senate and the people of Rome'); but in truth their loyalty was mainly to themselves and their general; especially since the changes instituted by Marius meant that the *capite censi* looked to their general for land on which to retire after their service with the legions.

The poisonous political atmosphere in Rome did not help. The state was polarized between die-hard conservatives and radical demagogues who took it in turn to savage anyone who tried to hold the political middle ground. It was only a matter of time before one of the losers in this bitter political battle turned to the army for support.

The man who did so was Lucius Sulla. Rome fell to its own soldiers, first led by Sulla, then by his opponents and then once more by Sulla. Each fall was followed by a bloody purge of Rome's proudest families. Marcus Crassus, of the aristocratic Licinian clan, was forced to flee to Spain. Julius Caesar, related to Marius by marriage, was dragged from hiding and only spared execution at the last minute.

The war was not confined to Italy. Rome's domination of Asia Minor resulted in the largest transfer of capital in ancient history as Rome's warlords extorted every ounce of gold from the unfortunate provincials to pay for their internecine strife.

The king of Pontus, **Mithridates** (Chapter 5), was an energetic and ambitious monarch. Rome had slowly devoured the petty kingdoms which had sprung up after the fall of the Seleucid Empire, and Mithridates was determined that Pontus would not also become a victim of Rome. Almost as soon as he took the throne Mithridates set about expanding and fortifying his kingdom. It was difficult to do this without antagonizing Rome, especially with Rome's generals greedy for the glory and loot which went with conquest. Inevitably, Mithridates provoked Rome once too often and war broke out. While the Romans were distracted by the civil war between Marius and Sulla, Mithridates captured the Greek cities of Asia Minor. His command for the execution of the Romans and Italians in those cities was obeyed enthusiastically. Yet even with its leaders locked in civil war, Rome's armies remained formidable. At one point, Mithridates only escaped capture because the Roman army and fleet were on different sides of a civil conflict, and would not combine even to capture one of their greatest enemies.

The Romans repeatedly invaded Pontus, yet one of Mithridates' greatest strengths was the determination of his people not to be absorbed into the Roman Empire. Every town and castle resisted the

Romans and the countryside was hostile. When Mithridates was driven from Pontus, his subjects fought on and enthusiastically welcomed him when he returned. As in Spain on the other side of the Empire, Rome's reputation for venal misgovernment made the job of its armies much harder.

Even as the war against Mithridates went on, Italy was rocked in the 70s BC by the revolt of **Spartacus** the gladiator (Chapter 6). That an obscure Thracian bandit could so terrorize Italy reflected the malaise that gripped the state. Spartacus was a slave under sentence of death, right at the bottom layer of the Roman social hierarchy. In theory he should have been a man from whom everyone turned with scorn and contempt. Yet so thoroughly alienated were the common people of Italy that instead of resisting Spartacus, they flocked to him in their thousands. Later generations of Romans regarded the revolt of Spartacus as a deeply humiliating episode in their history. That they had to talk of a rabble of escaped slaves and gladiators as though they were worthy enemies of Rome was embarrassing enough. That they were defeated by that rabble in battle after battle was a shame that the Romans felt deeply. How Spartacus achieved his victories has baffled historians. There can be no doubt that he was a leader and general of the highest order, and it was only when the Romans reluctantly acknowledged this fact that the tide turned against Spartacus.

They gave command of the campaign against Spartacus to Marcus Crassus, a plutocrat and highly accomplished general. He was a wily political operator, and his keen business sense made him for a while the richest man in Rome.

Though he overcame Spartacus, Crassus was overshadowed in popular prestige by Pompey, who gained immense wealth from campaigning in Asia Minor. The role of money and influence in Roman politics gave Pompey such power that he sometimes overshadowed the institutions of the state in a manner resembling the later emperors of Rome. Yet Pompey had rivals for power. The senate, led by the idealistic young Cato, hounded him at every turn. And in the streets the Roman mob was led by the fiery Clodius, a Claudian from the cream of the aristocracy who championed the popular cause until he was killed in a riot.

Another young aristocrat seemed set to take Clodius' place – the ambitious and unscrupulous Julius Caesar. Caesar was believed to have been implicated in the plot of the decadent aristocrat Catiline to seize power in a coup. Catiline's conspiracy was frustrated by the orator and consul Marcus Cicero, and Caesar managed to escape punishment, partly because he was protected by the powerful Marcus Crassus.

Crassus and Caesar joined forces with Pompey. Their partnership, later called the First Triumvirate, dominated the Roman political landscape and allowed Caesar to secure himself a governorship in southern Gaul. Caesar had no mandate from the senate to expand Rome's frontiers northward – indeed most of the senate were so hostile to Caesar that they had not wanted to give him any foreign command at all. Caesar, on the other hand, wanted a war for precisely the same reason that the senate did not want him to fight one: victory would bring wealth and glory which could be converted into greater political power.

Thus Caesar's Gallic Wars – wars which would lead to the death and dispossession of millions of people – were fought neither for strategic advantage nor to defend the Roman state. They were fought so that an ambitious and ruthless aristocrat could improve his standing in the political struggles at home.

A young Gallic nobleman, **Vercingetorix** (Chapter 7), led the resistance to Caesar's legions. Vercingetorix's inspirational leadership and fear of Rome managed the unprecedented feat of uniting the rival tribes of Gaul against the invader. But this heroic rebellion was doomed. Vercingetorix was outmatched in almost every sphere of war, and even his advantage of numbers was considerably less than Caesar reports it as being. Nevertheless, Vercingetorix forced Caesar to gamble his career and his very life on the outcome of a single siege, and for a while Caesar was far from certain of winning. Eventually, however, Gaul was conquered and absorbed into Rome's growing Empire, becoming so thoroughly Romanized that even today the native tongue of the region is directly descended from Latin, and the laws based on the Roman code.

During the second century BC the empire of the Seleucids, based on the conquests of Alexander the Great, had slowly crumbled under the pressure of its enemies. These included the Romans who crushed the Seleucid ruler Antiochus III at the battle of Magnesia in 190 BC. In place of the Seleucid Empire, numerous small kingdoms had sprung up in western Asia Minor, but in the east the peoples of the Iranian plateau were united under the Arsacid kings into the Parthian Empire. Rome came into contact with the Parthians in the early first century, and the Euphrates river came to mark the respective limits of the influence of the two powers.

This agreement was shattered by a blatant piece of Roman aggression in 53 BC, when Crassus attempted to emulate Caesar's feats in Gaul by conquering the Parthians. However, Crassus had badly underestimated his enemy. His legions were ill-equipped both for the conditions in which they had to fight and the style of fighting which the Parthians adopted. Furthermore, the Romans took the fawning servility of the Parthian people to their rulers as a sign of slavish decadence, and they were unpleasantly surprised at the determination and bravery of their enemies when they faced them in battle.

Parthia's king **Orodes II** (Chapter 8) was a skilled general and diplomat. He isolated Crassus from his allies, and his soldiers crushed the Roman invasion at Carrhae where Crassus lost his life.

Rome was unable to avenge this defeat because Caesar, following in the footsteps of Sulla, had led his army against the Republic. Pompey led the Republican cause, which went down in defeat to Caesar's veteran army at Pharsalus in Greece in 48 BC.

Pompey fled to Egypt. He chose Egypt because it was the last Mediterranean power which remained outside Roman control. Egypt too was a breakaway part of Alexander the Great's old empire, and it had been ruled ever since his death by the family of Ptolemy, one of Alexander's former generals. Though they had ruled Egypt for centuries, the Ptolemies were still pure-blooded Macedonians – very pure-blooded, as they had inbred incestuously for generations.

At the time of Pompey's arrival, the marriage of Ptolemy XIII to his sister **Cleopatra** (Chapter 9) was under some strain. So much strain in fact that Cleopatra had been forced from the palace, and at one time believed that her life was threatened. The addition of Pompey into this fraught political scene was a complication that Ptolemy's courtiers felt was best removed as soon as possible. This was expedited by assassinating Pompey as he tried to land at Alexandria.

Caesar arrived soon afterwards in pursuit of Pompey, but stayed to assist Cleopatra in her struggle with her brother. In fact Cleopatra aligned herself so closely with her Roman protector that she gave birth to Caesar's son; but by then Caesar had returned to Rome as master of the city and its Empire. He was planning to extend that Empire by the conquest of Parthia when he was assassinated by his fellow senators on the Ides of March, 44 BC.

Cleopatra supported Caesar's second-in-command, Mark Antony, in the civil war which followed. Again she became romantically involved with her protector. While playwrights and novelists have made much of Cleopatra's charms, her kingdom also had valuable resources to offer Antony's cause. Antony was engaged in a power struggle with Caesar's heir Octavian, who had control of the Roman Empire in the West. Relations between the two men became increasingly strained and eventually broke into open hostility. Antony was unable to match the political skill of Octavian, or the military skill of his generals, and he and Cleopatra were defeated at the battle of Actium in 31 BC. The victorious Octavian took the name Augustus Caesar, and launched Rome into the imperial era. His immediate successors were to take Rome's Empire to its greatest extent.

CHAPTER 5

MITHRIDATES: AN ENEMY FOR ALL SEASONS

He fought against the greatest generals of his day ... he was always
in good spirits, and indomitable in misfortune. Even when beaten,
he tried every way he knew to harm the Romans.

Appian *Mithridatica* 16 (112)

While other opponents challenged Rome's growing Empire for years, or
even decades, Mithridates fought soldiers whose fathers had been children when he started his long war. For almost half a century Mithridates
kept Rome at bay through military skill, political cunning and sheer luck.

A creature of his time, Mithridates moved easily between the Greek
and Asiatic cultures of his kingdom. He was fluent in over a dozen languages, a master of political intrigue, and a connoisseur of poisons. He
was the king of Pontus, one of the largest of the clutch of kingdoms which
had sprung up in Asia Minor after the fall of the Seleucid Empire. The
sixth king to bear that name, he is sometimes called Mithridates VI
Eupator, or 'Mithridates the Great'. Mithridates means 'given by
Mithras', a sun-god who, ironically, later became a cult in the Roman
army of the second century AD.

Though Mithridates claimed descent from Darius, king of Persia, and
even Alexander the Great, his family probably came from a Persian
dynasty from the town of Cius in northern Asia Minor. Mithridates
Ctestes (or 'the founder') fled from local political troubles in Cius to
Pontus, which was then a political backwater under the loose and weakening control of the Seleucid Empire. There he rapidly established a
kingdom and a dynasty. After his death in 266 BC his son, Ariobarzanes,

brought the vital Black Sea port of Amastris into the fast-expanding kingdom.

The ancient geographer Strabo was from the Pontus, and his description shows a land of contrasts. The seafaring Greeks had established coastal cities and conducted a lively trade with the Mediterranean world, while the mountain ranges that stretched inland from the coast contained both settled, fertile valleys and mountains with wild tribesmen who were still defying the Roman Empire three hundred years later. The mountain ranges lay across lines of communication from east to west, and in consequence Pontus was made up of semi-autonomous city-states, confederations of villages, and feudal baronies. The kingdom had a strong priesthood, particularly that of the national deity and royal protector, the Iranian fire god Ahuramazda in his thinly Hellenized aspect of Zeus Stratios.

The mild, damp climate of Pontus produced an abundance of olives, timber and grain. To this was added mineral wealth in copper, silver and iron – indeed, ancient tradition believed that in this region it was first discovered how to make steel. Abundant natural resources and a mainly rural people who needed little central government made Pontus capable of withstanding major invasion with little disruption; and the kingdom's hardy mountain peoples made excellent warriors.

Pontus was a highly desirable kingdom, and competition for the crown was traditionally intense. In about 120 BC, Mithridates Euergetes, father of Mithridates the Great, was assassinated by his closest advisors. As his eldest son, though only eleven years of age, Mithridates succeeded to the throne as Mithridates VI. In reality, power devolved upon his mother, who ruled in uneasy alliance with some of the advisors who had assassinated her husband.

Mithridates was in a precarious position. That faction of the nobility which favoured his younger brother conspired to make his reign a short one, and his mother's favour was uncertain. At this time, according to legend, Mithridates started taking homeopathic doses of poison, intending to develop resistance to as many as possible. Feigning an addiction to hunting, he removed himself from the royal centre of Amaseia and spent his teenage years in some of the wildest and remotest parts of the country.

10 *Greece and Asia Minor in the time of Mithridates. The cultured Greek cities of Asia Minor resented Roman domination and extortionate taxation, many seeing Mithridates as a liberator. At the peak of his power it seemed as though Mithridates might wrest even Greece from the Romans.*

Returning to the bosom of his family as a young man, Mithridates immediately arranged the assassination of his mother and younger brother, and followed this with a purge of the nobility. He may also have contemplated revenge on Rome for annexing the Pontic dependency of Phrygia during his self-imposed exile.

Next, the young king set about extending the kingdom through conquest. Pontus had long dominated the neighbouring states of Cappadocia and Paphlagonia, but these had recently allied themselves with Rome. Therefore Mithridates drove north and west instead. Commanded by two competent generals, Diophantus and Neoptolemus, his armies conquered the Scythians and extended his kingdom almost right around the Black Sea towards the borders of Macedonia. Among those conquered were the Sarmatians, a tribe whose armoured horsemen were a valuable addition to the Pontic army.

To barbarians who valued physical prowess, Mithridates was a formidable king. He was exceptionally tall, and strong enough to control a sixteen-horse chariot. Until late in life he enjoyed good health, despite being wounded several times; once by a Roman centurion who found himself alongside the king as Mithridates pursued the fleeing Romans, and once with a wound under the eye which was treated by the Scythian Agari tribe. As the Agari used poisonous snakes to effect their cures, the treatment was probably just as dangerous as the original wound.

Mithridates then turned his attention to the south, forcing the small and vulnerable state of Lesser Armenia into becoming a virtual satrapy (client state), and gaining control of its valuable port of Trapezus. Mithridates also cultivated Armenia itself, marrying his daughter Cleopatra to Armenia's king, Tigranes. Next he claimed sovereignty of Paphlagonia, saying this had been the intention of its recently deceased king, but backed down when Rome intervened, and turned instead to the nearby kingdom of Cappadocia. He may have been there earlier, since tradition holds that he travelled the region anonymously in the last years of the second century to see the situation for himself (and executed his wife who tried to poison him on his return).

As with most kingdoms in Asia Minor, dynastic affairs in Cappadocia were lively and confused. The ruling house was named after the Ariarathes who had carved his kingdom from the Seleucid Empire, and his successors were loyal to Rome. The widow of Ariarathes V had ruled since 130 BC, killing all of her five sons to remain in power. When the nobility forced the succession of Ariarathes VI, he was assassinated by one Gordius, who rapidly came under the control of Mithridates. On the assassination of Gordius, his widow Laodice, the sister of Mithridates, ruled in the name of her infant son Ariarathes VII. This did not go down well either with the Cappadocians or with Nicomedes, the king of Cappadocia's neighbour, Bithynia. Mithridates and his army were forced to intervene several times to maintain Pontic hegemony.

Nicomedes appealed to Rome, and under Roman protection the Cappadocians removed Mithridates' puppets and instead installed a noble called Ariobarzanes as monarch. Unwilling to risk a direct clash with Rome, Mithridates tried subtlety, and invited his father-in-law, Tigranes, to invade Cappadocia. Obligingly the Armenian army conquered Cappadocia, Ariobarzanes fled, and a Pontic puppet was installed. Rome responded by sending the rising and ambitious politician Lucius Sulla as an envoy. The Roman skilfully arranged the restoration of Ariobarzanes, effectively thwarting Mithridates' plans. To both the

Romans and Mithridates, it was becoming clear that a future conflict was inevitable.

This conflict came a year later when Nicomedes of Bithynia died. With the Pontic army at his back, Mithridates established a pretender called Socrates on the Bithynian throne. Then, demonstrating his impressive persistence, Mithridates invaded Cappadocia and ejected Ariobarzanes. Not coincidentally, Italy was being wracked at that time by the dangerous and distracting revolt of the Italian allies against Rome.

Nevertheless when Rome protested, Mithridates meekly deposed his puppets in Cappadocia and Bithynia. This acquiescence greatly displeased the avaricious M. Aquillius, head of the commission sent to restore the kings. Aquillius wanted a war and booty from Pontus, so he urged the Bithynians to provoke Mithridates by a series of plundering raids. Mithridates protested bitterly to the Roman senate, but in the face of Roman inaction, he attacked the Bithynian raiders himself, thus beginning the first Mithridatic War (89–85 BC).

Aquillius and his allies seized the chance to invade Pontus, but Mithridates was ready for them. With his general Archelaus, he defeated the Romans and Bithynians in battle and drove them back in disorder to their province of Asia. Oppressed by corrupt Roman administrators and greedy tax farmers, the people of Asia rose joyfully in revolt, and delivered the province into Pontic hands. Aquillius was captured and exhibited through the region tied to a donkey. Then Mithridates granted Aquillius the gold he had so eagerly sought – in molten form, poured down his throat.

Though Greek cities hailed Mithridates as a saviour, the Pontic king knew the loyalty of his new subjects was fickle. To bind his new allies to him, he sent secret orders that every Roman and Italian in their power was to be massacred. In a single day (called the 'Asian Vespers') up to 80,000 Romans and Italians were slaughtered. Appian gives a bloodcurdling description:

At the temple of Artemis in Ephesus, the fugitives clinging for sanctuary to the statue of the goddess were pulled away and killed. In Pergamon, they used archers to shoot them while they still held to the statues. The Adramyttines followed those who ran into the sea and killed them, drowning their children afterwards … the Canuii … killed first the children under the eyes of their mothers, and then the mothers, and their husbands after them. By the way they acted it was plain that the people of the province were not driven only by fear of Mithridates, but by hatred of the Romans.

Appian *Mithridatica* 4 (23)

Mithridates had a fleet, said to number over 300 ships, which totally over-whelmed the tiny Roman naval presence in the Aegean. He soon conquered all the islands except Rhodes, which held to its allegiance with Rome through an intense siege. The main part of the Pontic forces went to Greece under Archelaus, and there seemed set to repeat the victories of Asia Minor. The Roman governor of Macedonia was distracted by a barbarian invasion, and in 88 BC Ariston, tyrant of Athens, opened his gates to the Pontic army. Euboea fell soon afterwards, and the army of Mithridates advanced into Boeotia. The people of Thespiae resisted, and while they were overcoming this setback, the Pontines learned that a Roman army of five legions had arrived, commanded by the same Sulla who had reinstated Ariobarzanes five years previously.

The Romans advanced on Athens. Archelaus led a heroic defence and, when his cause was lost, he evacuated his army by sea and joined forces in Thessaly with another Pontic army which had advanced from the north under the command of Mithridates' son Arcathias. In 86 BC the combined Pontic army met the Romans at Chaeronea. The Pontic phalanx, composed largely of freed slaves from the Greek cities, fought heroically; and the Roman cavalry were totally disconcerted by a charge of scythed chariots from the Pontic lines. But in the end Sulla's skill as a general, and the discipline of the Roman legions, caused the army of Mithridates to first lose confidence, then break. The rout became a massacre, destroying all hopes of a permanent Pontic presence in Greece.

Mithridates had already shown himself skilful in command and merciless in victory. Now he proved resolute in defeat. He promptly raised a new army to face a Roman force which had landed in Asia under Fimbria, a rogue general who had assassinated the commander appointed by Rome. Fimbria defeated the new army, led by another son of Mithridates, and laid siege to Pergamon, forcing the Pontine king to escape by ship. Lucullus, Sulla's admiral, had his fleet ideally positioned to capture him, but Fimbria belonged to a party in Rome which was opposed to Sulla; so rather than share the credit for defeating Mithridates, Lucullus stood idly by while he escaped. Already blessed with fortitude and skill, Mithridates had added the final quality needed by a long-term opponent of Rome – good fortune.

This good fortune now became yet more pronounced, as Sulla's domestic problems mounted. The competition to command the campaign against Mithridates had been so intense among Rome's glory-hungry elite that Sulla had only resolved the issue by first leading his army against Rome itself. The anger that this had created boiled over into an anti-Sullan coup, and now Sulla needed to return to Rome, where he had been declared an outlaw and a public enemy.

Mithridates too had domestic problems, both with ex-Roman subjects looking to return to their old allegiance and with his recent conquests around the Black Sea. He sent envoys in 85 BC to remind Sulla that Pontus had once been allied to Rome. Mithridates suggested renewing that alliance with Sulla to defeat his enemies at home. In reply Sulla commented: 'It is unfortunate that it took the death of 160,000 of your men to remind you of our friendship.' He then invited Mithridates to withdraw from all his conquests, disband his fleet, and pay an indemnity of 2,000 talents. Archelaus, chief negotiator for Mithridates, sent the details to his master by messenger, remaining the guest of his enemy rather than carry such terms to his king.

But Mithridates was a realist, and knew that even this treaty would outrage those who remembered his 80,000 Roman and Italian victims. In a peace which was patched together at Dardanus that August, Sulla got his terms, and Mithridates received the improbable title of Friend and Ally of the Roman people. Dardanus was a truce, pure and simple, so that each side could deal with pressing concerns before returning to unfinished business.

With Rome off his back, Mithridates restored order in his restless provinces. His son Mithridates Philopater was sent as regent to the Black Sea tribes, but an unsatisfactory performance led to his being recalled and executed. In 83 BC Mithridates was preparing to go himself with a large army when it became evident that the Romans were spoiling for a fight. Murena, the Roman commander, had taken exception to the slow withdrawal of Mithridates from Cappadocia, and repudiating the peace entirely, set about ejecting the king by force.

Mithridates and his general Gordius mounted a spirited defence, and Murena was compelled to fall back. As Mithridates prepared to follow up, a firm order from Sulla stopped the fighting and forced a resentful peace. Mithridates helped himself to a slice of Cappadocia for his trouble, and Ariobarzanes resumed his oft-interrupted kingship of the rest.

A fresh expedition was launched against the rebels in the north, and Mithridates sent another son, Machares, to take the reins there. An ill-judged drive to extend the northern border of the kingdom failed with heavy losses. While his army regained its strength, Mithridates turned to diplomacy. Another peremptory order from Sulla forced him reluctantly to withdraw from all of Cappadocia, and the senate still refused to ratify the peace of Dardanus.

A possible ally against the Roman senate was Sertorius, a Roman general who was fighting the Sullan regime from Spain. Mithridates courted the rebel as an ally, but whatever his disagreements with the senate, Sertorius was a Roman and angrily refused to betray his country. The most Mithridates could get was an offer to recognize his claims to Cappadocia, should the king assist Sertorius against the Sullans in Rome. Mithridates had more luck in finding allies in Cilicia, a mountainous region to the south whose people were skilled seafarers and pirates.

On news of Sulla's death in 78 BC, Tigranes of Armenia again invaded Cappadocia, taking away almost a quarter of a million Cappadocian citizens to add to his new capital. Then, some time in 75 BC, the king of Bithynia died, and Rome took the opportunity to annex the entire kingdom. Mithridates was not going to stand idly by and let his archenemies dominate the Black Sea, so he promptly invaded Bithynia, and while he was at it, launched a fresh attack on Cappadocia, from where Tigranes had now withdrawn.

It took Rome several months of fierce political intrigue before command against Mithridates was given to Lucullus, the same general who had let Mithridates slip through his fingers almost a decade earlier. Another stroke of luck for Mithridates was that Lucullus had inherited his soldiers from the late Fimbria – soldiers with a tradition of indiscipline who, quite justifiably, felt they had spent long enough under arms already.

The Fimbrians lived up magnificently to Mithridates' expectations, stirring themselves so reluctantly and tardily that Mithridates was free to turn on Lucullus' colleague, who was defeated after being forced to offer battle. To make matters worse, the Pontic fleet followed up this success and captured sixty Roman ships. Emboldened by his success, Mithridates hurried to take the port of Cyzicus. He was followed by Lucullus, who had finally stirred his army into action. The Roman aimed to pin Mithridates between the town and his army, while Mithridates was gambling on capturing Cyzicus and escaping through the port. He might have succeeded had not word that Lucullus was on the way inspired the townspeople of Cyzicus to a desperate defence.

Though harried by the Romans, Mithridates showed his staying power by pushing ahead grimly with the siege even as disease ravaged his army and a shortage of supplies forced the men to cannibalism. A last desperate attempt to storm the city failed, and Mithridates finally abandoned the siege under cover of a snowstorm. Lucullus caught up with him, and killed tens of thousands of Pontic troops as they tried to cross the swollen rivers. Yet more fell at the hands of the Cyzicans who swarmed out of the city after their erstwhile besiegers. Mithridates escaped with the remnants of his army by ship, though his fleet suffered losses from the severe weather. Mithridates himself had to be saved from shipwreck by friendly pirates from Cilicia.

Now, in 73 BC, with his army in tatters and allies wavering, Mithridates threw himself into the defence of his kingdom. He called for help from Tigranes, and probably also from Parthia. He dispatched an envoy to bring the Scythians over to his side, and summoned his son from the north. The cavalry had mostly survived the debacle at Cyzicus, and were now sent to harass the approaching Romans. Towns in the Roman line of advance were strongly garrisoned and ordered to hold out for as long as possible. In short, Mithridates met the challenge of invasion with ability and resolve of the type that the Romans so admired in themselves.

However, Armenia wavered, and the envoy dispatched to the Scythians promptly deserted with the gold, but by the spring of 72 BC Pontus was as ready as possible for the Roman assault. Too canny to resist the Roman advance directly, Mithridates concentrated on cutting Lucullus' supply lines. He had some success until his cavalry unwisely attacked a

Roman convoy in a valley too narrow for them to manoeuvre properly. The tattered remains from the subsequent defeat created a panic when they appeared in Mithridates' camp, especially as they brought the news that Lucullus was following up fast.

Mithridates attempted to retire, but this only hastened the collapse of his army. He himself was in danger of capture until – by chance or design – one of the donkeys carrying the royal treasure shed its load. Collecting and dividing this delayed the avaricious Fimbrians more effectively than any phalanx, but it was not enough to save the Pontic force from eventually being cut to pieces. Expecting the imminent fall of Pharnaceia, the town which housed his harem, Mithridates ordered the ladies to be killed to save them from falling into Roman hands. He himself fled to Armenia.

For the next five years, until late 68 BC, Mithridates was almost a prisoner in the hands of his son-in-law Tigranes. He played no active part in resisting the Roman advance through Armenia, though perhaps he was consoled by the determined defence which his fortress towns offered the Roman invader, some holding out for almost two years into his exile. But fortune had not abandoned Mithridates. Like Alexander's Macedonians, Lucullus' army lacked enthusiasm for conquering the East. After years of unremitting campaigns, the Fimbrians simply refused to fight any more. At a stroke, Lucullus lost his army.

Tentatively, with a handful of his own soldiers and a borrowed Armenian contingent, Mithridates set about reclaiming his kingdom. The Roman talent for misgovernment in the East led to his citizens giving him a rapturous reception, and his Thracian mercenaries, who had gone over to the Romans, now returned to their former paymaster. Mithridates made his position yet more secure by taking possession of the fortress which held the Roman winter supplies, and handily beat the Roman force which attempted to prevent him. With Ariobarzanes (yet again) on the run from Tigranes in Cappadocia, and Pontus again secure, Mithridates was back where he had started. In Cicero's words, 'He accomplished more after his defeat than he dared to hope for before it.'

The repercussions were felt in Rome. Lucullus was replaced in 66 BC by the unscrupulous but brilliant Pompey, the later antagonist of Julius Caesar. In Rome, Cicero had urged Pompey's appointment, stressing that Mithridates' past misdeeds remained unpunished.

He who marked out citizens for slaughter has still paid nothing like an adequate penalty. He has been on his throne for over twenty-two years; not hiding himself in Pontus or Cappadocia, but launching himself from his own domains into those of our subjects, flaunting himself for all Asia to see.

Cicero *In Support of the Manilian Law* 3.7

Pompey was given almost imperial powers, and a remit to settle affairs in the East. He started with his customary energy, making an alliance with Parthia which forced Armenia from the Pontic side. Pompey also told Mithridates that he would consider negotiations if Mithridates handed over those Italians and Romans who had deserted to him. One reason why Pompey wanted these deserters was that, because of the political turmoil in Rome, there were enough of them to form the fighting core of Mithridates' army.

Using the same defence strategy as before, Mithridates fell back to the Pontic interior, where he had dispersed his treasury into various castles, and from there he harried the Romans with his cavalry. As before, this was successful until the Romans trapped the cavalry and destroyed it. Mithridates was cornered in his fortress of Dasteira, but fooled the Romans into dropping their guard and escaped with his army. But as with his escape from Cyzicus, the Romans caught up and destroyed his army, though the king managed to cut his way to safety.

This time there was no help from Armenia, whose king – under pressure from the Parthians – was finally forced to submit totally to Pompey. On hearing the news, Mithridates vowed he would not do this 'while I am still Mithridates'. So the war dragged on into 64 BC. Practically speaking, Pompey had won, but there could be no peace while Mithridates lived. As Cicero assured the Roman people, 'It is difficult to put into words how much the people of Asia hate us for the incompetence and avarice of those we have sent to govern them.' As long as these people looked to Mithridates as a liberator, he had a chance.

Pompey knew that Mithridates had retreated towards the Black Sea. Involved with other projects, Pompey blockaded the exits from that sea, and trusted in diplomacy with the northern tribes to deliver Mithridates. The king was now almost sixty-eight years old, and often bedridden with stomach ulcers. Yet, entering the area as little more than a fugitive,

Mithridates took command through sheer force of personality. Appian comments, almost with wonder:

Though he had lost so many of his children, his castles, indeed his whole kingdom, and though he himself was hardly fit to campaign, his plans had no trace of the humility one might expect of his condition … there was nothing mean or contemptible about him, even in misfortune.

Appian *Mithridatica* 15 (109)

All that this sick old refugee planned to do was to invade and conquer Italy. Aware that his time was running short, he pushed his people hard. Supplies were expropriated, extortionate taxes were levied, and unwilling soldiers were conscripted. At the end of it, Mithridates had a fleet and an army of some 36,000 men whom he planned to march along the Danube, over the Carnic Alps and into Italy.

This plan teetered somewhere on the border between boldness and insanity, and it was too much for the troops. They suspected, with reason, that Mithridates intended merely to die in his armour in a last quixotic thrust at his enemy. Then the old king, always quick to uncover treason, found a conspiracy in which the chief plotter was his own son, Pharnaces. For once, the man who had executed so many of his own kin hesitated. Pharnaces did not give him a second chance. In 63, he roused the army to mutiny and cornered Mithridates in his citadel at Panticapaeum.

Mithridates realized the game was finally up. He attempted to kill himself by taking poison – which his two daughters would not permit unless they too could kill themselves with it. The daughters died quickly. Mithridates, after years of dosing himself with potions, remained unaffected despite a brisk walk along the ramparts to speed the poison through his system. Finally, he turned to his Celtic bodyguard. Appian gives this fanciful rendition of his last words:

'Kill me, and save me from being paraded in a Roman triumph. I have long been master of a great kingdom, and now I can't even poison myself … I should have known that the most deadly poison in every king's house is the faithlessness of soldiers, children and friends.'

Appian *Mithridatica* 16 (111)

The traitorous Pharnaces did as Mithridates had expected, and handed his body to the Romans. Not unaware that the status of the conqueror was commensurate with the status of the defeated, Pompey hailed Mithridates as the greatest king of his day. His body was buried with honour.

CHAPTER 6

SPARTACUS: THE MAN WHO BECAME A MYTH

Quick, boy ... bring wine, that knew the Marsian war,
If plundering Spartacus has spared a single jar.
The poet Horace asking for vintage wine – *Carmina* 3.14

The story of Spartacus is frankly incredible. Spartacus took on Rome, the most powerful Empire in antiquity, in its homeland of Italy. No one had managed this since Hannibal, and Rome had grown more powerful in the meantime. Hannibal had the resources of Carthage and Spain and a host of Gallic allies while Spartacus started with less than nothing. He literally did not own the shirt on his back. He was a slave, a prisoner condemned to die. Even after he had gathered a band of shepherds and escaped slaves, such a rabble and their makeshift weapons should have been massacred by trained and properly armed soldiers. Instead he went on to win battle after battle.

The story begins in 73 BC in Capua in south-central Italy. There, in the school of a man called Lentulus Batiatus (or possibly Lentulus Vatia), a large batch of gladiators were being trained for the arena. Until the first century BC, gladiators had not been a major feature of Roman entertainment though they had been known since 264 BC when a man called Iunius Pera first staged a gladiatorial display. Pera took the idea from the Etruscans, an ancient people who inhabited the part of Italy just north of Rome.

Originally, the gladiatorial combats had a quasi-religious function. They were a way of doing honour to the deceased at a funeral. The idea that gladiators should fight and die to amuse the public was just starting

11 *Spartacus travelled the entire length of the Italian peninsula twice during his two-year plundering spree. His army had the chance to escape after fighting its way to the Alps, but instead decided to remain in Italy.*

to take hold during the decade of the 70s BC. Though still ostensibly a funeral rite, gladiatorial combats were now held in public, and often in the arena, whereas before they had taken place in private houses, or even (on occasion) in the Roman forum. The specialized tools used by gladiators in the imperial era were still rarer. Most gladiators fought with the weapon from which they derived their name – the sword (*gladius* in Latin).

Such combats were rare, and not always to the death, for gladiators were very expensive. They had to be fit, male, and enthusiastic participants in a highly dangerous event. Unsurprisingly, this enthusiasm had often to be coerced, and therefore the job of gladiator fell on those least able to resist coercion – the slaves. Able-bodied male slaves were sold at a premium, and it was an extravagance to risk one in the arena, where his value would drop to nothing if he was killed. But the more skilled the gladiator, the less chance that he would die, and the longer he would retain his value.

Which brings us back to the school of Lentulus Batiatus where gladiators were trained in the brutal art of surviving at the cost of their opponent's life. According to Plutarch, who wrote over a century later, conditions at the school of Batiatus were particularly harsh, and the gladiators were kept in close confinement. In defence of Batiatus, his charges were particularly dangerous men. Among them was a Thracian known as Spartacus. 'Spartakos' was a place in Thrace and since it was not uncommon for a Roman slave to be named after his place of origin it may well be that Spartacus was so named by Batiatus. Spartacus had started his career as a shepherd – and in ancient Thrace this was no rural idyll. The long hours of boredom alternated with clashes with wolves, bears and bandits. Evidently Spartacus developed a taste for fighting, for he abandoned his flocks to become a soldier.

Here, the legends diverge. Some, including the historian Appian, say that Spartacus fought against the Romans and was captured. As a prisoner and unable to ransom himself, he was sold as a gladiator. A different tradition suggests that Spartacus actually fought in the Roman army as an auxiliary soldier (auxiliaries were lighter-armed non-Romans who fought beside the legions). If this is correct, it explains how Spartacus obtained that detailed knowledge of Roman warfare which he employed so devastatingly against its practitioners.

Leaving the army (according to the historian Florus, he deserted from it), Spartacus became a bandit, preying on travellers on the lonely roads of Thrace. After one of his raids he was captured, and sentenced to die. His captors decided that justice should be combined with entertainment, for Spartacus had all the requirements of a gladiator. He was a ferocious fighter, trained in arms and – in the eyes of the law – already a dead man.

Spartacus was sold in Rome as a gladiator. According to one report, he was accompanied on his travels by his wife, who foresaw a different destiny for him.

1 (*left*) Publius Cornelius Scipio took the name Africanus after he defeated Hannibal at Zama. Cultured and fond of Hellenic culture, Scipio aroused suspicion and envy among his rivals, who eventually drove him from Rome to die in exile. Carthage was later levelled to the ground by Scipio Aemilianus, another member of the same family.

2 (*below left*) Coin of an African elephant. The elephant depicted here is not the sub-Saharan African elephant, which stands higher at the shoulder, but a species which lived on the southern Mediterranean and which is now extinct. Hannibal is shown on the obverse.

3 (*right*) A bust, believed to be of Hannibal, found at Capua. The Romans thought that Hannibal's distinguishing feature was his cruelty, which may explain the expression the sculptor has chosen to portray.

4 (*left*) Bust of Flamininus, *c.* 180 BC. The self-styled 'liberator of Greece' had to fight hard against some cities before they were prepared to be freed, since Philip V had been a relatively benign overlord. Flamininus's liberation of the Greeks once he had defeated Philip was an immensely popular, but ultimately empty, gesture.

5 (*below*) Silver tetradrachm of Philip V, *c.* 190–180 BC. Though he came to power at an early age, Philip was a competent and energetic ruler. He was among the first of the eastern monarchs to perceive that the rising power of Rome might threaten his rule.

6 The Pydna monument, erected by Flamininus to celebrate his victory against Philip at Pydna, Macedon. Though much of the sculpture is badly weathered, the characteristic spine on the shield of the auxiliary cavalryman can be clearly seen, as can the *hoplon* shield of the fallen warrior.

7 (*above*) *The Death of Viriathus*. This painting is from the Prado Museum in Spain, by the neoclassical painter José de Madrazo (*c.* 1808/18). The struggle of Viriathus against the Romans had strong resonances in Madrazo's own time, when his people had fought an equally savage guerrilla war against Napoleon.

8 (*right*) First-century BC marble bust of Jugurtha's enemy Sulla, the man who first led a Roman army against Rome itself, and who killed hundreds of his political opponents in bloody purges. Sulla had a mass of blonde hair, but his complexion went blotchy in the sun, causing the Athenians to nickname him 'mulberries on cornflour'.

9, 11 (*opposite, above left and below left*) Coin and bust of Mithridates VI Eupator. Mithridates was as much a Hellenic as an Asiatic monarch. His kingdom of Pontus represented the fusion of native and Greek culture which had been taking place since the first Greek settlements in Asia Minor over 500 years earlier.

10 (*opposite, right*) Gnaeus Pompey rose through the chaos of civil war in the 80s BC and defeated Mithridates to become the greatest man in Rome. By the time of this sculpture (*c. 50* BC), age and good living had eroded Pompey's famously good looks. These and his conquests had led to his nickname of 'The Roman Alexander'.

12 (*right*) Though gladiatorial combat as a feature of funeral games went as far back as the Etruscan civilization, it was not a major part of Roman life until the late Republic, and items of specialized gladiatorial equipment that Spartacus may have worn, like this helmet, were rare until the first century AD.

13 (*below*) Detail from the funerary monument of Lucius Storax. Though usually from the dregs of Roman society, top gladiators like Spartacus were as celebrated as the film stars of today. Such was the glamour of their brutal lifestyle that a law had to be passed to ban young noblemen from fighting in the arena.

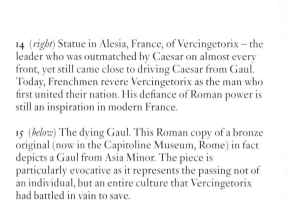

14 (*right*) Statue in Alesia, France, of Vercingetorix – the leader who was outmatched by Caesar on almost every front, yet still came close to driving Caesar from Gaul. Today, Frenchmen revere Vercingetorix as the man who first united their nation. His defiance of Roman power is still an inspiration in modern France.

15 (*below*) The dying Gaul. This Roman copy of a bronze original (now in the Capitoline Museum, Rome) in fact depicts a Gaul from Asia Minor. The piece is particularly evocative as it represents the passing not of an individual, but an entire culture that Vercingetorix had battled in vain to save.

16 (*above*) A relief of Cleopatra and Caesarion on the temple of Hathor at Dendera, Egypt. That a pure-bred Macedonian and her half-Roman son chose to depict themselves in such a completely Egyptian manner is indicative of the efforts which the Ptolemaic dynasty made to identify themselves with the culture and peoples of Egypt.

17 (*right*) Silver coin of Orodes II. The Parthian kings tried to present themselves as Hellenistic monarchs to their Greek subjects, and this has led some historians to overlook the rich native traditions and dismiss Parthian culture as a weak reflection of the Greek.

18 Bust of Cleopatra, *c.* 50–30 BC. Despite the later myths, Cleopatra was not a devastating beauty. She attracted Caesar and Mark Antony by the pure force of her personality, and because she offered them access to the wealth of Egypt.

19 (*below, left*) Bust of Julius Caesar. In fact, by his forties, Caesar's hairline had receded and he brushed his remaining hair over the bald spot. Nevertheless, the sculptor has well captured the charm and energy of the dictator.

20 (*below, right*) Bust of Mark Antony, *c.* 40–30 BC. Though dissolute and a poor administrator, Antony was a good soldier and a loyal subordinate to Caesar while he was ali

When he had just arrived in Rome to be sold, there is a story that a snake coiled itself upon his face while he was sleeping. His wife, who also later ran away and joined him, was a country-woman of his, a kind of prophetess, and one of those possessed with the bacchic frenzy. She declared that it was a sign meaning that he would gain great and formidable power but that it would end badly.

Plutarch *Life of Crassus* 8

Thus Spartacus and a bunch of similar desperadoes ended up with Lentulus Batiatus, who was preparing them to fight in a spectacle for the people of Capua. Spartacus had other plans, and began preparing the other gladiators – some two hundred in all – to make a bid for freedom. Somehow the plot was discovered. The ringleaders, Spartacus and two comrades-in-arms – Crixus and Oenomaus – had to make their break with less than half the gladiators in the school behind them. Still unarmed, they burst into the street and rampaged through one of the many eateries which were a feature of life in Roman towns. Their objective – probably pre-planned – was to seize the spits, knives and cleavers in the kitchens.

These makeshift weapons in the hands of trained fighters were more than enough to persuade the guards at the city gates not to make an issue of the gladiators' desire to leave town. On the road from Capua, the escapees discovered a waggon of gladiators' weapons and armour; perhaps even the same gear in which they were intended to die at the spectacle in Capua. Equipping themselves with this booty, the gladiators made their way up Mount Vesuvius, and set up camp in the crater.

Word of their breakout spread swiftly, and soon the small camp began to receive a steady trickle of runaway slaves who preferred life as fugitives to captivity among the Romans. Most of these new recruits were not *vernae*, as those born into captivity were called, but soldiers captured in Rome's many wars and put to work in the fields, treated little better than farm animals.

Most of them, including the gladiators themselves, were Thracians and Gauls. According to the tradition of their peoples, they elected leaders. They chose the ringleaders of the gladiators' revolt: Crixus and Oenomaus, who were both Gauls, and Spartacus the Thracian, who took overall command. This arrangement, by which the majority of leaders were Gallic, but the overall leader was Thracian, reflected both the factional stresses already developing among the runaways and Spartacus' diplomatic ability to handle them.

With Mount Vesuvius as their base, Spartacus' band turned to brigandage, and it is doubtful that they did so with either reluctance or great inexperience. Indeed, they soon became so substantial a nuisance that the Romans sent 3,000 men under the aristocrat Appius Claudius Pulcher to clear Vesuvius of their infestation. The Romans quickly penned the bandits onto the mountain, and began to close in on them.

Trapped near the crater, Spartacus showed himself to be a tactician equal to any of his era. The Romans had left one slope unguarded, since it was so steep as to be inaccessible. Using wild vines, Spartacus and his fugitives made ropes and descended the slope with these. One man remained behind to throw down their weapons and remove the traces of their escape, and then this man slipped through the Roman cordon unnoticed.

Believing their enemies trapped in the heights, the Romans were peacefully making camp when Spartacus and his men fell on their rear, killing many and routing the rest. This victory both allowed Spartacus to equip his men with Roman military hardware and brought a fresh wave of escapees to join him.

Such success was a double-edged sword. By showing that he could survive and prosper, he attracted more followers. The more followers he attracted, the more savage his predations had to be to support his men, and the more vigorous the Roman response became. It was a spiral which reflects the basic truth that Spartacus was a symptom of a wider sickness in Roman politics and society.

Whether Spartacus had failed or succeeded as a bandit, he would have quickly been forgotten by history. What turned him into a phenomenon was the huge number of people who flocked to join him. They were certainly not all gladiators. There were well under 10,000 gladiators in the whole of Italy, yet by the end of 73 BC Spartacus had 40,000 men under arms.

Spartacus' recruiting agents were the selfishness and brutality of the Roman elite. The south of Italy had never recovered from the devastation of Hannibal's war, though it had ended 125 years earlier. The war had destroyed the family smallholdings which provided recruits for the legions and now, with Rome's wars lasting ever longer, the remaining small farmers conscripted into the army remained there for years, or even decades, while their farms fell into disrepair. This suited the Roman elite, who bought up the land at bargain prices, or bullied the smallholders off their land.

The smallholdings were combined into huge farms called *latifundia*, and worked by slaves. The choice of slave labour was deliberate, as slaves did not need to be treated with even minimal decency, and could not be called into the army. Consequently, Spartacus raided lands largely populated by slaves with absolutely nothing to lose, or by the rural poor who had already lost everything and were very bitter about it. When Spartacus began attacking towns, the poor there welcomed him and enthusiastically joined in pillaging their wealthy oppressors. Spartacus always shared out the booty fairly, and this greatly aided recruitment.

Spartacus plundered his way across the countryside south of Rome, destroying rural villas and recruiting their slaves. The towns of Cora, Nuceria and Nola were sacked. The attempts of the praetors, Varinius and Glaber, to muster some resistance were hampered by complacency in Rome. Slave revolts had happened before, particularly two major revolts in Sicily (135–132 BC and 104–100 BC) which were equivalent to small wars. Each revolt had lasted for as long as it took for the legions to arrive and quash it. Lightly armed and militarily inexperienced slaves were no match for legionaries, but the praetors did not have legionaries.

[The praetor] had to make do with anyone he could quickly conscript on the way. This was because the Romans did not yet consider the affair as a war, but as something rather akin to a large pirate raid.

Appian *Civil Wars* 1.14

The Romans paid for their insouciance. Spartacus first defeated one Roman force and then the other. He caught up with Glaber at Salinae, and in his rush for safety, the praetor abandoned his official attendants, his warhorse and the fasces which symbolized his rank. Thereafter the Thracian bandit and gladiator went about with the attendants and accoutrements of a senior Roman magistrate.

Unfortunately, we have almost no information about what went on in the camp of Spartacus. Our information comes from the Romans who reported faithfully what Spartacus did, though his motives were as mysterious to them as they are to modern historians. But it seems that after his first year of freedom, Spartacus correctly concluded that he could not remain in Italy. Most of his people were captives from Gallic, Germanic or Thracian tribes, and their way home lay across the length of Italy and over the Alps. But Rome and its armies were in the way.

Spartacus got around one army by a trick which was later adopted by a protagonist of the novel *Beau Geste*.

When surrounded by the soldiers of the proconsul, Spartacus had his men put up stakes at regular intervals in front of the camp gates. He tied corpses to these stakes, and armed the corpses with weapons, so that from a distance they looked like sentries. He also lit fires around the camp, and while his enemies were deceived by this empty show, Spartacus and his army slipped away into the night.

Frontinus *Stratagems* 1.5.22

Since it was too late in the year to attempt the Alps, Spartacus went south for the winter, bringing the regions of Lucania and Bruttium almost completely under his control. Spartacus spent the winter preparing his forces – now grown to almost 70,000 men – for the confrontation with Rome. He did not allow gold and silver into towns which he controlled, but encouraged the import of iron. He actively sought out smiths to make weapons and armour for his new recruits. Spartacus had come south with a rabble, but he intended to return north with an army.

The Romans now took Spartacus seriously. In 72 BC they dispatched two consular armies and a third under the command of a praetor. Entire nations had been conquered with less. Faced with this threat, the slave army split up. Oenomaus had died in the earlier fighting, and now Crixus and his Gauls split from the main force. There may have been ethnic conflicts within the slave army, or a schism in the leadership. Or it may have been that the army was so huge it was divided for purely administrative purposes. At Mount Gorganus in Apulia Crixus' force met the army of the praetor Q. Arrius. As was to be repeatedly shown, the rebels without Spartacus were no match for the Romans. Crixus and many of his fighters were killed and his army dispersed.

Meanwhile, Spartacus took the rest of the rebels north. He reached the river Po without a serious engagement, but his huge army was far less manoeuvrable than the well-drilled Romans and he finished at a serious disadvantage. Just to the north was the army of the consul Lentulus, and to the south the other consul, Poplicola, was closing in fast. Trapped between the two, Spartacus should have been finished. Instead, he defeated first one army and then the other. It is difficult to understand how he did this, and the Romans, humiliated by defeat at the hands of slaves, remain tight-lipped about what actually happened.

In memory of Crixus and the fallen in recent battles, Spartacus made his Roman prisoners fight each other in gladiatorial combat. 'Just as though he wished to wipe out all his past dishonour by having become, instead of a gladiator, a giver of gladiatorial shows', remarks Florus, not needing to add that such treatment of its soldiers dishonoured the entire Roman state. Appian takes up the tale:

In the aftermath the Roman army retreated in confusion, while Spartacus, first sacrificing three hundred Roman prisoners to Crixus, made for Rome with 120,000 foot soldiers after burning the useless equipment and putting all the prisoners to death and slaughtering the draught animals to free himself of all encumbrances; and although a large number of deserters approached him he refused to accept any of them.

Appian *Civil Wars* 1.14

This calculated cruelty to prisoners aside, two things stand out from Appian's report. The first is that Spartacus now commanded over 100,000 men. To put this into perspective, the largest army Rome ever fielded in Italy were the eight legions and auxilia who fought at Cannae – about 85,000 men in all. Roman armies did not get larger than this simply because maintaining so large an army was a logistical nightmare. Even Spartacus, who lived by pillaging the land he passed through, felt that he could not sustain a bigger army – and Crixus had shown that the insurgents could not create another army without finding another Spartacus to lead it.

If Spartacus contemplated an attack on Rome itself he was fantasizing. Rome was defended by strong walls, and siege warfare was a complex affair requiring specialist skills and equipment. But after his most recent victories, what was impossible for Spartacus? His move towards Rome was actually a feint to draw Roman troops southward from his escape route. The strategy failed and Spartacus had to fight again, this time somewhere in Picenum. He was victorious, but another army awaited him at Mutina.

So far Spartacus had fought hastily mustered local militias, or raw recruits recently levied into the legions. The army at Mutina was a veteran army ably commanded by C. Cassius, proconsul of Gaul. Spartacus routed it anyway, in another of those victories which leaves the military historian slack-jawed with incomprehension.

Now the route over the Alps lay open. Spartacus and his people were free to go – if not with Rome's blessing, at least with a hearty good riddance. But Spartacus' followers were enjoying a standard of living higher than they had ever aspired to, and the austere forests of the north had lost their appeal. While much of Italy remained unpillaged, sanctuary in the north could wait. Spartacus, almost an unwilling prisoner of his own people, was forced to lead them back to the south.

Spartacus could probably have abandoned his army then and there. His ingenuity had already escaped a closely guarded slave barracks and defeat by successive armies. But Spartacus the freedom fighter was a nobler calling than his previous careers as Spartacus the deserter and Spartacus the bandit. Either through loyalty or lack of inclination to do otherwise, Spartacus consciously chose to continue a life of pillage and rapine.

In Rome, the people were sceptical that the consuls could defeat Spartacus, now in his third year of liberty. No one wanted the job until the aristocratic Marcus Licinius Crassus put himself forward. Crassus was among the richest men in Rome, partly through money he had gained from the death of innocent men while he was a crony of the dictator Sulla. But he was an excellent general, and the Roman people turned to him with gratitude.

Crassus was made praetor, and immediately set about raising an army large enough to match the huge numbers of his opponents. ('It is disgraceful to have to call them enemies', writes Florus – which shows that Crassus was extraordinarily patriotic in coming forward. There was little glory in defeating slaves, but the disgrace in being beaten by them was immense.)

Crassus scraped together two legions from the four defeated consular legions, and added another six by conscription and volunteers (he once said that no man was rich who could not pay for a legion from his own pocket). Spartacus served notice that he was not intimidated by this army by beating a force under Mummius, the legate of Crassus. Crassus responded by decimating the cohorts which had broken first. Decimation was an ancient punishment by which one man in ten was executed, and its revival under Crassus showed that he meant business.

Spartacus withdrew southward. At Thurii he set up camp and immediately came under siege from merchants and the agents of wealthy Italians seeking to buy back the goods Spartacus had plundered from them. Spartacus still wanted to escape Italy, even more so after Crassus pounced on a breakaway band of some 10,000 slaves and massacred them. This prompted Spartacus to move to Rhegium in the toe of Italy. If his men did not fancy the forests of Germany, they might prefer the milder climes of Sicily and the welcome from the slaves there, who had already rebelled twice in living memory.

Transport across the straits had been arranged with Cilician pirates allied to the Pontic king Mithridates (Chapter 5), who was, as has been related, no friend of Rome. But the pirates took Spartacus' money and sailed away, leaving him stranded in Rhegium, which Crassus was busily walling off from the rest of Italy. Whether the plutocrat general had influenced the pirates' decision is unknown, but this point marks the beginning of the end of the gladiators' adventure.

Spartacus and his men tried to get across the narrow straits using home-made boats and rafts, but the currents were too strong and treacherous. The alternative was to breach Crassus' barrier and head back into the Italian mainland. But the defences of Crassus were not easy to breach; Spartacus' first two attempts lost 12,000 men. Aware of the fragile and flagging morale of his followers, Spartacus employed that brutal sense of spectacle which would have served him well had he continued with a career in the arena.

In a space near the Roman lines he crucified one of his Roman prisoners. In the crucifixion of Christ, about a century later, the centurion Longinus is said to have pierced Christ's side with a spear. This would have been an act of mercy to hasten a death which otherwise took a long, agonizing time in coming. Over the days which it took Spartacus' victim to expire, it was made plain both to the Romans and to Spartacus' own followers alike that the slaves would neither give mercy nor expect any.

Perhaps motivated by this display, the slaves made their next attempt during a storm on a wild winter's night. They threw bundles of sticks into the Roman trenches, and swarmed over the walls on makeshift ladders. Within days word reached Rome – Spartacus was out. The senate did not panic, but there was a renewed sense of urgency as armies were recalled from Spain and Greece. The armies were due back soon anyway, but Rome was now taking Spartacus very seriously.

At this point Spartacus' force divided again, perhaps reflecting a division of opinion between those who wished to continue plundering and those who wanted to break out of Italy. Or there may have been ethnic tensions among the different groups who followed Spartacus. Most of the breakaway group were Gauls, and had Gallic leaders named Granicus and Castus. Crassus fell upon them near the southern town of Croton at a now-unknown place called the 'Lucanian lake'. He killed 30,000 and might have killed more had Spartacus not come to the rescue. From this engagement the Romans reclaimed the eagles and magisterial regalia which Glaber had lost for them.

No sooner had this boosted Roman morale than Spartacus threw it down again by defeating Quintus Tremelius Scrofa, whom Crassus had sent north with a strong force to prevent the slave army from escaping in that direction. Spartacus dashed through this loophole for the port of Brundisium, from where he hoped to take ship back to his native Thrace. But the army of Lucullus, summoned from Greece, had just arrived at the port, and Spartacus was forced to veer north again. It looked as though Spartacus was going to try again to take his army over the Alps since there was no serious resistance in that direction. Instead, Crassus discovered that there was no need to hurry in his pursuit – the slave army had turned and was seeking battle.

The Roman was delighted. His chief fear was not defeat by Spartacus, but that he would not get the credit for crushing the revolt. Spartacus himself was not as eager for battle as his army, and he sent messengers to Crassus to seek a settlement. These overtures were rejected with contempt; Rome did not negotiate with slaves. At the start of the battle, Spartacus sent for his warhorse and dramatically killed it in front of his assembled army. If the day went well, he said, there would be many other warhorses on offer. If it went badly he would not need a horse anyway. It was a grand gesture with an undeclared subtext. Spartacus would not flee on horseback. He would triumph or die with his foot soldiers.

The battle was a bitter one, as might have been expected against so many completely desperate men (in fact one near-contemporary estimates that Spartacus' army was still a gargantuan 90,000 men). Nevertheless, the discipline of the legions began to tell. In an effort to turn the tide Spartacus launched himself at Crassus, fighting like a berserker:

And so making directly towards Crassus himself, through the midst of arms and wounds, he missed him, but killed two centurions who attacked him together. At last when all those of his men about him had broken, he himself stood his ground.

Plutarch *Life of Crassus* 11

This last savage assault gained the reluctant admiration of the Romans. Even Florus, who generally considered Spartacus and his men almost sub-human, admitted that on this last occasion 'they died like men, fighting to the death as might be expected of those commanded by a gladiator. Spartacus himself fell, as is proper for a general, fighting most bravely in the front rank.'

The slave revolt was over. Some 5,000 rebels fleeing north ran into the returning army of Pompey which slew them almost to a man – 'tearing up the rebellion by the roots', in Pompey's own grandiloquent description. The true conqueror of Spartacus, Crassus, was as merciless as the slaves had always expected. He crucified them in their thousands – some 6,000 spaced at regular intervals all along the Appian Way from Rome to Capua.

But Spartacus himself had vanished. Oddly for a man who died surrounded by the enemy, that enemy could not find his body once the

12 *Early gladiators often fought with the armour and weapons of peoples the Romans had conquered, as on this first-century AD relief from Santa Marinella. This allowed the Romans to see their victories re-enacted in the arena, and provided a ready use for captured material.*

fighting was over. The Romans would have wanted to display his corpse to disillusion those who hoped that Spartacus lived, and would rise again. It would prevent Spartacus from becoming the legend he has undoubtedly become.

The man who single-handedly took on an Empire has inspired a ballet, books and films, though he might have been bemused by his current status as a gay male icon. His obdurate refusal to submit to slavery makes Spartacus admirable, but the evidence does not support those who see him as a Che Guevara of the Apennines. He was no campaigner against slavery. After his victory, Crassus found some 3,000 Roman captives enslaved at Rhegium. Neither Spartacus nor his followers had any programme, political or otherwise, other than the mutually contradictory desires both to escape from Italy and to remain and plunder it.

Spartacus was daring, a truly remarkable general and an inspiring leader of men. He was a brave and ferocious fighter, and dealt fairly with his friends. On this the historical sources agree. But they do not say, and we should not suppose, that Spartacus was a good man, or a particularly noble one.

CHAPTER 7

VERCINGETORIX AGAINST CAESAR: THE GRIM STRUGGLE FOR GAUL

Should Mamurra [a protégé of Caesar] take
what Long-Haired Gaul and farthest Britain once had? ...
Was it so that worn-out profligate of yours, Mentula,
could devour twenty or thirty millions in cash?
A critique of Caesar's motives – extracts from *Catullus* 29

Vercingetorix was a Gaul. He was born into the rich and ancient Celtic culture which once stretched from central Italy to northern England. Despite Roman propaganda to the contrary, the Celts of Gaul were not barbarians. When Vercingetorix was born, sometime around 78 BC, many Gallic tribes were rapidly becoming urbanized, forming into large political confederations, and changing to a monetized economy. There were signs too, of a new political maturity. The ancient kingships of many tribes were giving way to 'senates' composed of tribal leaders. In the arts, Gallic craftsmanship was of the highest quality, and Celtic metalworking was second to none. This period was the final flowering of the La Tene culture, a culture of great promise which was about to enter a time of great and ultimately fatal peril.

Gaul had fallen behind its neighbours in two crucial areas – military and political development. The Gauls had abandoned the chariots still used by the more primitive Britons, but their armies were still based on poorly organized cavalry which lacked the logistic ability to stay in the field for long. Even this premier arm of Gallic warfare was outmatched by the Germans. So much so, comments Caesar, that German horsemen habitually attacked Gallic riders on sight. Gallic foot soldiers consisted of peasants too poor to own a horse and harness; raw troops which were no match for the Romans, masters of infantry warfare.

Yet military backwardness was less of a danger than the inability of the peoples of Gaul to unite even against the most pressing threat. For most of the early first century BC, as their enemies gained in strength, the Gallic tribes dissipated their strength in fierce intertribal warfare. Vercingetorix was an aristocrat in one of the leading tribes of central Gaul, the Arverni, who had a long-standing feud with another tribe, the Aedui. In turn the Aedui dominated many of the lesser tribes of the region.

Rome, with whom the Aedui were loosely allied, had a long and uneasy relationship with the Gauls. Every Roman schoolboy knew that in the fourth century BC the Gauls had massively defeated them and looted Rome itself – a feat never achieved before, and not to be repeated for centuries. Much of the Roman legionary's equipment had evolved specifically for the difficult task of fighting Gauls. The helmets of Republican legionaries were more angular and pointed than later versions, the better to deflect the downward swing of a broadsword onto the wearer's heavily padded shoulders. The legions fought in close formation with short stabbing swords, which allowed them to bring five men to the battle line for every three Gauls. And the Roman heavy throwing spear, the *pilum*, was designed to break the force of the wild Gallic charge.

The faster evolution of Roman weapons and tactics forced the Gauls onto the defensive. By the second century BC the Romans had overwhelmed their settlements in northern Italy, taking Milan just before Hannibal arrived in the area. After the Punic wars, Rome expanded over the Alps to take its first province outside Italy: an area of Gaul called simply 'the Province', and which has that name even today as modern Provence. But most of Gallia Comata ('Long Haired Gaul', as the Romans called it) remained free and independent.

For most of Vercingetorix's childhood during the 80s BC, Rome was not an active threat. Rome's energies were absorbed in the eastern Mediterranean, and in the political struggles of the increasingly dysfunctional Republic. Of more interest to the Arverni, at this time led by

Celtillus, the father of Vercingetorix, were the ambitions of the Aedui and the expansion of the Germans over the Rhine.

This expansion was indirectly to bring the Romans back into the picture. The Roman invasion of Gaul caused one of the greatest catastrophes in the ancient world; a holocaust unmatched until the Spanish conquistadors came to the Americas in the sixteenth century. The architect of the Gallic catastrophe is also our principal source for it: Gaius Julius Caesar, the man who later overthrew Rome's failing democracy and replaced it with a military dictatorship.

Caesar has left us his *De Bello Gallico* – a history of the Gallic war probably drawn from his reports to the senate as the war took place. This is an exceptional document – an ancient war, described by its perpetrator, and drawn from contemporary material. But the wealth of this material cannot conceal that it is also a consummate work of propaganda. Caesar narrates a tale of thrilling battles and sieges. He tells of heroic deeds by 'barbarian' and Roman, and of cunning subterfuge (by himself) and base perfidy (by the Gauls). What he does not mention is that his own greed and ambition drove him to a completely unjustified war which all but wrecked Gallic civilization and led to the death or enslavement of millions.

The story begins when the Helvetii, under pressure from the Germanic people to the north and east, abandoned their ancestral homeland (which was about the same area as modern Switzerland) and migrated westward. Their path took them across the Province (Provence), the governor of which was Julius Caesar. Caesar refused to let the Helvetii into Provence. When they took another route Caesar attacked them anyway, defeating them in a series of battles which drove the survivors back to the Alps.

Now established in Gaul, Caesar turned on the Germans who had migrated over the Rhine. In a particularly shocking incident, Caesar arrested ambassadors who came to negotiate with him, then stormed the German camp that they had come from. He turned his cavalry on the fleeing women and children and afterwards noted with grim satisfaction that hardly a soul in the entire tribe survived.

This campaign gave the young Vercingetorix invaluable experience of the Roman way of war, since he probably commanded some cavalry

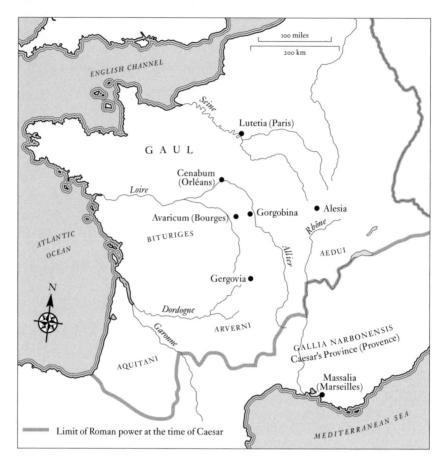

13 *Gaul, with the principal cities and tribes. Vercingetorix's attempt to unite the Gauls against the invading Romans was the first time the Gauls had felt themselves to be a single nation. Until then, inter-tribal strife had held back the development of the Gallic people.*

allied with the Romans against their joint enemies. 'Vercingetorix' is composed from the syllables of 'victor of a hundred battles', and it is probable that the skirmishes of these early campaigns gave the young chieftain his name. Knowledge of a Gaul's true name gave others power over him, so Gauls kept their names to themselves and were known only by their nicknames.

Soon the Gauls realized that their Roman protector had no intention of leaving, and his lackeys were treating Gaul as a conquered Roman province. Caesar's expeditions against Britain in 55 and 54 BC caused considerable resentment, both because they disrupted the cross-channel trade, and because Britain had a strong influence on Gaul's Druidic religion. The Carnutes tribe rose in revolt against Caesar, and were joined by the Eburones under their leader Ambiorix, who came to lead the entire rebellion. Caesar quashed them with energy, skill and savagery. The Eburones were enslaved or put to the sword, and their lands devastated so that any who had escaped Roman vengeance might perish from hunger.

Vercingetorix's Arverni did not take part in the revolt. Celtillus had been killed in a palace intrigue, and the tribe were ruled by peace-loving oligarchs led by Vercingetorix's uncle Gobannitio. Vercingetorix was outraged by the treatment of the Eburones, and the Roman assumption that his countrymen were a subject people. His fiery agitation for the pro-war party led to his expulsion from his native Gergovia (near modern Clermont-Ferrand) where the town council, if not pro-Roman, was at least thoroughly intimidated by Rome. However, Vercingetorix swiftly raised the countryside, and took power through a *coup de main*.

It helped Vercingetorix's cause that he was tall and handsome. In Gallic culture, good looks showed that a man was favoured by the gods. Vercingetorix was highly intelligent, and a powerful orator – essential in an oral culture where personal charisma counted for much. He also had a large personal following, which added to his prestige. Furthermore, Gaul was ripe for revolt. Its people were bitter and vengeful, uncowed by Caesar's demonstration against the unfortunate Eburones, but frightened enough by it to finally pull together. As an added incentive, Caesar himself had left Gaul to deal with a political emergency in Rome, leaving command with his subordinate, Labienus.

Vercingetorix struck at Cenabum (modern Orléans) early in 52 BC. His men seized the provisions stockpiled there, and massacred Roman traders and officials. News of the rebellion spread like wildfire, sped by ambassadors that Vercingetorix sent to every corner of the country. Most of the tribes of central Gaul heeded his call to revolt, the major exception being the Aedui, who chose wary neutrality. The maritime tribes of the northwest joined in the rebellion, inspired by Vercingetorix's message – 'If the people of Gaul are united and of one mind, they can stand against the entire universe.'

Soon most of Gaul was in arms against Rome. The tribes elected

Vercingetorix as commander-in-chief. He made a rapid assessment of what each tribe could supply his army, and gave its leaders a list of material and manpower required, together with a date for delivery. According to Caesar, Vercingetorix did not stop at verbal persuasion with the waverers.

To the utmost attention to detail he added the utmost rigor of authority. The severity of his punishments persuaded the wavering. For major crimes the perpetrators were condemned to every kind of torture and then burned to death. For lesser offences, he sent the offenders home with their ears cut off, or with an eye put out. The brutality of these punishments was intended as an example to frighten others, and keep them from disobedience.

Caesar *De Bello Gallico* 7.4

Caesar had retired to Provence at the end of the campaigning season of 53 BC so as to keep himself in touch with affairs in Rome. He was now caught with the uprising between himself and his troops in Gaul. Labienus, the commander of these troops, was forced into inactivity because it was now midwinter. He could not move without supplies, and vigorous guerrilla activity in the surrounding countryside denied these to him. With Vercingetorix plundering the lands of the few tribes still allied to Rome, it was vital that Caesar act fast, and he did so – leading reinforcements through the mountains into Arvernian lands, despite the fact that the snow on the passes was up to six feet deep.

The arrival of the Romans forced the Arverni to defend their homeland. Caesar wanted a pause in the campaign to muster his forces and to wait for the season to become more hospitable to his foragers, but Vercingetorix denied him this pause by besieging Gorgobina, a principal city of the Boii, a tribe allied to Caesar. Caesar had to save this town to maintain his integrity in Gaul, and he accordingly moved to defend it, making up his shortfall in cavalry with German mercenaries. He made a detour to attack Cenabum *en route*, and took it after a brief siege. He sacked the city to avenge the earlier massacre of Romans there.

Vercingetorix declined to make an issue of the siege of Gorgobina and withdrew into the lands of the Bituriges, a tribe who had initially allied themselves with the Romans, but later joined the revolt.

Caesar's earlier brutality had convinced the Gauls that painful sacrifices must be made for their freedom. Vercingetorix seems to have studied the tactics of skirmish and delay used by the British, who had been reasonably successful in coping with Caesar's expeditions to their island. After a few painful experiences at the hands of the German cavalry, Vercingetorix decided only to offer battle from an invulnerable position. This left the Romans the option of either declining battle or attacking and being defeated, losing face in either case. To contain Caesar where there was no secure position for him to hold out in, Vercingetorix adopted the British tactic of retreating from the legions while devastating the countryside to deny them supplies. Caesar gives Vercingetorix's explanation of this policy as follows:

We must try everything possible to stop the Romans from getting supplies. This should be easy since we have the cavalry to do this, and the season is in our favour. The hay has already been cut and is in the barns, and we can make sure that if foraging parties go out to get it, none of them will return alive. Furthermore, to save our lives, we have to sacrifice our private possessions – we must destroy all the farms along Caesar's line of march and within reach of his foragers ... we must also destroy all but the most impregnable towns and cities. Otherwise these will serve as refuges for our own deserters, and give the enemy sustenance when he plunders them. These measures may seem brutally cruel, but the alternative is to be conquered; to have your wives and children carried off as slaves while you yourselves are put to the sword.

Caesar *De Bello Gallico* 7.14

Thus as Caesar descended on their territory, the Bituriges destroyed their own farms, villages and cities, persuaded that if they did not do so, Caesar would do it for them. But the Bituriges could not bring themselves to destroy their capital, Avaricum (now modern Bourges), one of the most beautiful towns in Gaul. Instead the proud leaders of the tribe begged the war council on their knees to let them defend their capital. Avaricum was against the river, almost completely surrounded by marshland. It was hard to approach, and had strong walls.

Vercingetorix was sceptical. He argued that the Romans were well capable of taking the town, which should be a smoking ruin when Caesar got there, since it certainly would become one soon afterward. But Gallic commanders-in-chief were not autocrats, and Vercingetorix was forced to bow to the collective wish that the town be defended. He accordingly took up an impregnable position in the marshes some sixteen miles away and kept in touch by hourly messages.

The Gallic strategy of denying supplies to their invaders proved successful. Though Roman foragers tried different times of day and unusual routes, they were found and cut down by the vigilant Gallic cavalry. Caesar was driven to demand supplies from the Aedui and the Boii. The former were reluctant and the latter could supply little, being only a small tribe which had lately been reluctant hosts to Vercingetorix's army. The Romans had to succeed quickly or starve. One way or another, it would be a short siege.

Caesar's description shows once again that he was not dealing with savages.

The Gauls are truly ingenious at adapting ideas and putting them to their own use. They trapped our siege ladders with lassos, and then used winches to pull them within the walls. They caused our siege walls to collapse by undermining them. They are expert at this kind of work because of the numerous iron mines in their territory. And their entire wall was fortified with towers.

Caesar *De Bello Gallico* 7.22

He adds that these towers were made of an ingenious mixture of timber and masonry in such a way that the timber absorbed the shock of battering rams and the masonry made the walls impervious to fire. In the end, the Romans took the town by the same technique that they later used at Masada in Judaea – they built a massive siege mound up to the wall, and when the Gauls took shelter from a savage storm they rushed the ramparts and took them in a surprise attack. 'Our soldiers were exasperated by the labour of the siege', reports Caesar dispassionately, 'they had no thought of taking prisoners for ransom. They spared not even old men, women or children. Of 40,000 people in the town, about 800 escaped to the camp of Vercingetorix.'

The fall of Avaricum actually helped the Gallic cause. It provided further proof that the Romans conquerors were no less savage than the

Germans, and considerably better organized. It showed that Vercinge-torix had been right. His strategy would have saved tens of thousands of lives, and denied the Romans the supplies they took from the town itself. Vercingetorix's standing as a leader was greatly increased.

The Romans now turned on the Arverni. Vercingetorix kept them at bay by breaking down the bridges on the river Allier on the border to his lands. He marched along the opposite bank to the Romans, preventing them from repairing the bridges. One day the Roman army set out, shadowed as usual by Vercingetorix. What the Gauls did not see was that a large part of the army, including Caesar, had been hidden in a nearby wood. As soon as the Gauls were out of the way, they threw a bridge across the river and marched on Gergovia, capital of the Arverni.

Vercingetorix's cavalry were faster than Caesar's infantry, and the Gallic leader arrived in time to mastermind the defence of the city. Gergovia was strongly fortified and in a secure position. Though the Romans quickly seized an outpost, they were unable to take the remaining outlying forts, which meant that the six Roman legions could not form a perimeter wide enough to make a secure blockade.

The only hope the Romans had of taking Gergovia was by a surprise attack. Taking advantage of some tribal squabbling they struck swiftly at a southern fort and captured it. Then they swept on to Gergovia itself, and some Roman soldiers actually mounted the walls. Vercingetorix led a counter charge that swept away the Romans, just as a large Gallic force appeared outside the town. These were the Aedui, Caesar's wavering allies, but the Romans did not know this at the time. The Roman retreat turned into a panicked rout which was only stayed when Caesar brought up a legion which he had kept in reserve. Rather than offer battle, Vercingetorix withdrew into the city.

It was Caesar's first defeat, and he was jealous of his reputation as a general. He never forgave Vercingetorix, especially as the Roman setback pushed the Aedui into joining the Gallic revolt. The Aedui took over Caesar's supply base and handed his remounts, supplies and Gallic hostages over to Vercingetorix. A discomfited Caesar was forced to retreat across the Loire to where Labienus had established a base in what was later to become Paris. Cut off from his supply base, Caesar made good his weakness in cavalry by recruiting yet more German mercenaries.

Vercingetorix was preoccupied with politics. The Aedui had brought over a number of allies, and had encouraged other neutrals to join the cause. In return two young chiefs of the Aedui, Eporedorix and Viridomarus, felt they should have overall command of the revolt. A council was called of all the Gallic chieftains, and this council confirmed Vercingetorix's position of supreme leader. Vercingetorix celebrated his success by trying hard to stir up rebellion in Provence, the only part of Gaul under formal Roman control. He was thwarted by the resolute opposition of the Allobroges, the local tribe. They, after a previous rebellion, knew at first hand the consequences of opposing Rome and did not want to repeat the experience.

Vercingetorix remained convinced that if his troops could not defeat Caesar's legionaries, his cavalry could at least prevent them from eating. Consequently, when he heard that the Romans were on the move again, Vercingetorix concentrated on Caesar's baggage train. Summoning his cavalry commanders, he said,

'This is our moment of victory. Caesar is on the run to Provence. This will leave us free for the moment, but our future peace and security are still at threat. The enemy will return, more numerous than before, and this war will have no end. We have to strike now, while they are loaded with their baggage. If they fight to defend their supplies, their retreat will be halted. If they abandon the baggage, they will have nothing to live on, and be humiliated by a further defeat.'

Caesar *De Bello Gallico* 7.66

Vercingetorix forced a promise from his cavalry that any man who did not ride twice through the Roman column would be denied access to his home, his wife and his family thereafter. Then bringing up his infantry to make a show at the Roman front, he unleashed his cavalry on the supply train. This was one of the crucial moments of the entire war. Had the Romans lost their baggage, the campaign would have been over for the year. With his credibility damaged, and his enemies rampant in Rome, it is unlikely that Caesar would have been able to launch a further attack.

It was Vercingetorix's misfortune that he was outmatched in almost every aspect of the war. Despite Caesar's claims to the contrary, it is unlikely that the Gaul ever had any convincing numerical superiority over the Romans. His infantry was totally outclassed by the legions, and in Caesar he was facing Rome's greatest general. Now his cavalry proved yet again that they could not stand against German horsemen. After weathering the storm of the first attack, the Germans forced their way to high ground, and from there made a charge that routed the Gauls.

Vercingetorix was forced to retreat. Perhaps hoping to repeat his earlier success at Gergovia, he made for the fortress town of Alesia. He knew that Caesar would follow, and he prepared to stand siege. Because this siege was unexpected, supplies were crucial. Vercingetorix dismissed his cavalry – who were little use in siege warfare anyway – and told them to disperse to raise all of Gaul in his support. Soon after the cavalry had gone, the Romans arrived.

The following weeks saw little fighting, and a lot of engineering. The Romans threw a circumvallation around Alesia to besiege it. Then they started working even more frantically on an outward-facing wall to contain the Gallic army that would soon be besieging them. Within Alesia, the Gauls were preparing the hooks, grapnels and siege ladders they would need to attack the Roman lines once help arrived from outside. And in due course that help arrived – a Gallic host numbering a quarter of a million (says Caesar, who exaggerated the number of his enemies by at least a factor of three).

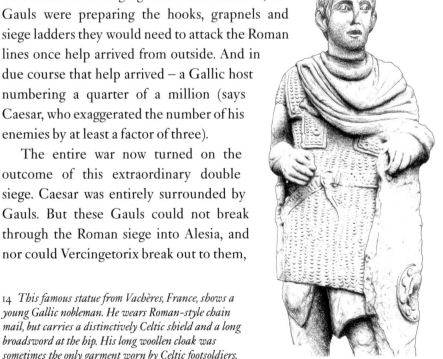

The entire war now turned on the outcome of this extraordinary double siege. Caesar was entirely surrounded by Gauls. But these Gauls could not break through the Roman siege into Alesia, and nor could Vercingetorix break out to them,

14 *This famous statue from Vachères, France, shows a young Gallic nobleman. He wears Roman-style chain mail, but carries a distinctively Celtic shield and a long broadsword at the hip. His long woollen cloak was sometimes the only garment worn by Celtic footsoldiers.*

and his supplies were running low. Finally, he was forced to turn out all the non-combatants from the town he had occupied. This mass of starving women and children made their way to the Roman lines, but the Romans would not permit them to pass through. Nor would the Gauls take them back, so these innocents were left between the lines to die miserably from lack of food, water and shelter.

Unfortunately for the Gauls, it proved impossible to co-ordinate the attacks of those within the walls with those of the force outside; or indeed for the Gauls outside to get their act together sufficiently for them all to attack at once. The most spirited attempt was made by Vercingetorix's cousin, Vercassivellaunus. He attacked the Roman lines on the outside at their weakest point, while Vercingetorix attacked at the same time and place from the inside. For almost an hour, the fate of Gaul trembled in the balance, with the Roman defenders fighting almost back to back against attacks from both sides. In the end it was the personal bravery of Caesar who led a charge at the crucial moment to turn the tide.

The Gauls were driven back, and the German cavalry made its way around the rear of Vercassivellaunus' warriors, attacking them as they fell back. Demoralized and running low on supplies, the Gallic host began to fall apart, leaving Vercingetorix stranded in Alesia with no realistic hope of rescue. His envoys to the Romans asking for terms received the uncompromising answer that nothing less than total surrender would be accepted. Now the man who had demanded so much sacrifice from others decided to sacrifice himself. Dressed in his best armour Vercingetorix set out for Caesar's camp hoping that by surrendering personally, he might turn Caesar's wrath aside from his countrymen.

The historian Cassius Dio takes up the story.

He came unannounced, appearing suddenly at a tribunal where Caesar was seated in judgement. Some of the Romans there were taken aback by this, not least because Vercingetorix was a tall man, and he looked even more formidable in his armour. When the hubbub had died down, Vercingetorix came forward without a word, and fell on his knees before Caesar, asking for mercy with just this gesture. Many of those watching were filled with pity as they compared his present condition with his previous good fortune.

Cassius Dio *History* 40.41

Caesar was not in a merciful mood. Out of respect for their former alliance, he allowed the Aedui to return to their homes. The other warriors he gave as slaves to his legionaries. Vercingetorix was thrown into chains, and sent to Rome to await his conqueror's return. He was kept a prisoner for six years, quite probably in the same Tullianum which had housed Jugurtha (Chapter 4). When Caesar was finally free to celebrate his triumph, Vercingetorix was led in chains before his chariot, living proof of the subjugation of Gaul. Then, as was traditional for an enemy leader who had appeared in a triumph, Vercingetorix was put to death.

It was a humiliating end for Gaul's greatest leader, as Caesar intended it to be. But the Gauls never forgot the time when they had united as a nation. Vercingetorix was already a cult figure by the time of the late Roman Empire, when coins were issued bearing his name. Today he is widely recognized as the first national hero of France, and his heroic defiance of the Roman superpower still has a powerful influence on French consciousness.

CHAPTER 8

ORODES II OF PARTHIA: HOW TO DEFEAT THE ROMANS

Now darting Parthia, art thou struck; and now
Pleased fortune does of Marcus Crassus' death
Make me revenger. Bear the king's son's body
Before our army. Thy Pacorus, Orodes,
Pays this for Marcus Crassus.
Ventidius in Shakespeare's *Antony & Cleopatra* Act 3 Scene 1

By the middle of the first century BC the Roman legions looked unstoppable. Spain was subdued, though defiant, Africa was a Roman province, Greece and Macedonia had been conquered, and Julius Caesar was crushing the Gauls. The Romans seemed set to bring the whole world under their sway, and now their attention turned to the former empire of Alexander in the East.

Rome already dominated most of Asia Minor, and was heartily hated there for its corruption and rapacity. But the empire of Alexander the Great had once stretched beyond Asia Minor to the borders of India. There were rumoured to be kingdoms of fabulous wealth in those uncharted lands. Did not silk come from here? And frankincense, and rare and exotic spices; for all of which Rome paid hard-won gold?

In fact these luxuries came from China, or from even further afield. But the peoples between Rome and China tried hard to conceal this fact lest the two empires start trading directly with each other instead of through them. Among these people were the Parthians. They claimed to be the direct heirs of the Mesopotamian civilization which had come down to them from the Persians who had been defeated by Alexander.

Legend claims that the first Parthians migrated eastward from the lands about the Danube. This may well be true, for even today the Persians of modern Iran have strong Aryan aspects in their language and culture.

The Roman writers Strabo and Justin say that the ancestor of the Parthian people was a Scythian called Arsaces. Arsaces later became the family name of the Parthian kings. The name 'Parthian' comes from Parthava, the province just southwest of the Caspian Sea where this people eventually settled as subjects of the Persian Empire. Their formidable armoured cavalry served with the Persian army. After a Greek victory over Persia in the 490s BC the playwright Aeschylus gloats,

Where are the high leaders of your mail-clad horse,
Daixis and Arsaces, where?

Aeschylus *Persae* 4

Conquered by Alexander the Great, the Parthians lived under Seleucid rule until the 240s BC. The Parthian leader who threw off their yoke ruled as Arsaces I from 238 until his death in 211. Mithridates I (171–138) – no relation of the king of Pontus, pp 81–93 – defeated and captured the Seleucid king, Demetrios, who remained a captive in Parthia for ten years.

With the fall of the Seleucids, Parthia became a world power. This is reflected in the kings' coinage, where Arsaces first proclaimed himself as Arsaces the King, then as King Arsaces Philhellene. The latter was to reassure the ever-increasing number of Greeks in the empire, especially after the conquest in 126 BC of Mesopotamia and the old Seleucid capital, Seleucia, on the Tigris. Under Mithridates II, Parthia dominated much of the old Persian Empire. The Parthian ruler now took the Persian title of King of Kings, with some two dozen minor monarchs under his sway.

The part of the old Persian Empire not under Parthian rule was dominated by Rome. The first formal contact between the two powers was in 96 BC, when Sulla (the same Roman noble who had captured Jugurtha and fought Mithridates of Pontus) met the ambassador of the Parthian king. The Parthian ambassador was put to death for allowing Sulla to preside over the meeting; but their agreement that the river Euphrates should mark the limit of each empire's ambitions remained in place until the reign of Orodes II.

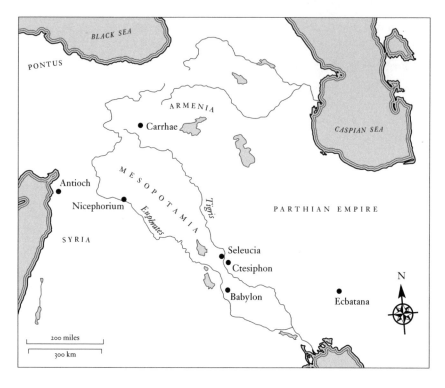

15 *The Parthian Empire. Some of the richest lands of the empire lay in Mesopotamia between the Euphrates and Tigris rivers, but the spiritual home of the Parthians lay in the austere mountains and deserts to the east, where the might of Rome never ventured.*

The Parthian Empire was organized much as the Persian Empire had been, and consequently was just as disorganized. Its ethnic, cultural, and religious diversity ruled out a one-size-fits-all government, and the semi-autonomous governors, vassal kings, and great families of the empire all had their own ideas of how to run things. The great families, the Suren, Karin and Gev foremost among them, ruled huge fiefs where their writ was law. This led to extravagant cruelty and demands for obeisance from the Parthian kings, who, being weaker, needed overt displays of power in a way that more secure monarchs did not.

The king may have been advised by two councils – one group of aristocrats called the 'synergon', and another of wise or learned men or *magi*. The empire was economically dynamic thanks to a large and energetic artisan class inspired by lax government control of their activities. Given the diversity of their empire, the Parthians had no choice but to be religiously and ethnically tolerant, as is seen clearly in their treatment of the Greeks.

The Parthian kings tried very hard to make their Greek subjects like them. They so affected to admire Greek culture that until recently scholars saw Parthian culture as a weak reflection of the Greek, ignoring a rich and flourishing tradition of Iranian art and literature outside the Hellenized areas. Although the Greeks rebelled enthusiastically every time the Romans invaded Parthia, their overlords never tried to transplant or disperse this troublesome people as the more impatient Roman Empire eventually did with the Jews.

Pliny the Elder wrote of *duo imperia summa —Romanorum, Parthorumque* ('two high empires, Roman and Parthian'), but the main difference was this: the Romans had a democratic Republic, yet mercilessly oppressed their subject peoples; whilst the absolute monarchy of the Parthians was tolerant and ecumenical. Also, as the historian N. H. Sitwell engagingly puts it, 'whereas the Romans always seem to know where they are going, even if it is to disaster, the Parthians always seem disorganized, even when they win.'

This disorganization became anarchy after the death of Mithridates II in 88 BC, when the empire plunged into a 'dark age' of revolt and civil war. When the chaos ended, the Arcasid dynasty was still on top, but it had developed a taste for patricide combined with a totally unjustified faith in the next generation. For almost the next one hundred years, every Arcasid monarch died at the hands of his son.

The trend-setter was Phraates III, who briefly restored order in the 60s BC before being killed by his sons Mithridates III and Orodes II (it is uncertain who the first Orodes was). Both sons immediately claimed the throne, and supported those claims with coins bearing the demonstrably false slogan of *philopater* ('lover of the father'). Orodes won the subsequent civil war, partly because Mithridates proved too brutally severe for his subjects' taste.

In 56 BC Mithridates fled to the Romans and petitioned Gabinius, the governor of Syria, for help. Gabinius, as is plain from contemporary Roman accounts, was not a man to let international agreements stand in the way of personal profit. He promptly advanced to the Euphrates, the border with Parthia proper, where the Roman senate forced him to pull back.

Mithridates had advanced to Babylon where he was under siege from Orodes, but his men surrendered on hearing that Rome had abandoned them. Orodes, already a patricide, did not hesitate to add fratricide to his conscience. In fact, he made a point of being present at his brother's execution. To celebrate the occasion, he issued coins of himself accompanied by the goddesses Tyche (Fortune) and Nike (Victory).

Orodes had his power base east of the Iranian plateau, where he had lived in semi-exile while his father was alive. His principal backer was the Surenas, as the head of the house of Suren was entitled. The Surenas had the hereditary right to crown the king with his own hands and to command the Parthian forces in war.

The Romans were unimpressed by a general who had (in Plutarch's words) 'delicate looks and effeminate dress … his face was painted, and his hair done up in the Persian fashion'. They took this as Parthian decadence. Certainly this was the opinion of Marcus Licinius Crassus, who replaced Gabinius in Syria in 54 BC. Crassus, the conqueror of Spartacus, was described by Plutarch as a 'superb general'. Under the dictator Sulla he had defeated tough Samnite rebels at the gates of Rome. Now a triumvir, dominating the Roman Empire with Julius Caesar and Pompey, Crassus had decided to make Parthia his latest conquest.

He had no dispute with Parthia, nor had Rome assigned that war to him. But he had heard that the Parthians were very rich, and he thought that the capture of Orodes would be easy, since he was newly established on the throne.

Cassius Dio *History* 40.12

Crassus was in his sixties at this time, and Orodes insultingly sent ambassadors to ask if Crassus was acting for the Roman state. If so it would be war to the death. But he understood that Crassus was an old man crazed by senility and greed, and therefore he would be merciful.

Orodes correctly assumed that Crassus' Parthian invasion was unpopular in Rome. One tribune had even formally cursed Crassus and his army as they went to war. Orodes also knew that Crassus had inferior soldiers – the best were campaigning with Caesar in Gaul, and the veterans were garrisoning Spain. So when Crassus told the Parthian ambassador that he would reply to his taunts in Seleucia on Tigris, the ambassador held his palm upward to Crassus and said 'hair will grow here before you see Seleucia'.

Despising an offer of passage through Armenia from its king, Crassus attacked Mesopotamia directly. He scored an initial success against Silaces, the regional satrap, and the city of Nicephorium came over to him. In response, Orodes sent the Surenas against Crassus whilst he went to punish the Armenians for their pro-Roman sympathies. Our evidence comes mainly from the Roman perspective, so we have a better account of the campaign against Crassus than against the Armenians. We are told that the Surenas was an extraordinary general.

Whenever he travelled privately, he had a baggage train of 1,000 camels, 200 chariots for his concubines, 1,000 comprehensively armed bodyguards and others more lightly equipped, and at least 10,000 servants and retainers on horseback … yet it was he who took the city of Seleucia [from Mithridates], who was the first man to scale the ramparts, and who fought hand to hand with the defenders.

Plutarch *Life of Crassus* 21

The Romans interpreted Parthian grovelling to their royalty and nobility as a sign that this was a slave nation. They were to be unpleasantly surprised by the loyalty of the king's subjects, and the personal bravery of both aristocrats and common soldiers. The Parthians were unlike any army they had fought before.

Given the Parthian character, it comes as no surprise that Parthian soldiers were unpaid, and that logistics were regarded as a black art. The bulk of the army were feudal levies, the *hamspah*, often supplemented by mercenaries. Foot soldiers were not an important component of the army, and most of those were archers. So too were most of the cavalry. These light horsemen were highly mobile – as they had to be, since on the other side of the empire they spent their time skirmishing with the nomadic ancestors of Attila the Hun.

But the Parthian army had cut its teeth on the Seleucids, and they were unimpressed by the heavy infantrymen of the legions. The Parthian heavy cavalry were cataphracts, from *cataphracti*, a Greek word meaning 'covered over'; the riders and their horses were heavily armoured. Their lances were unusually long and thick, and the combined weight of the rider and horse could skewer this lance through two opponents at once. Like any cavalry, these horsemen were next to useless against disciplined infantry in close formation, but such infantry were easy targets for the bowmen in the rest of the army. Furthermore, these archers used the compound bow – a mix of iron, horn and wood which was lighter yet more powerful than the Roman equivalents.

The Armenians were quickly cowed by Orodes. Having succeeded in detaching Armenia from Rome, the king withdrew to his new royal capital of Ctesiphon to await news of the Surenas. Crassus had played into Parthian hands by marching into Mesopotamia. On the flat plains the Romans had to choose between being tormented by archers if they stayed in close formation, or being charged down by cataphracts if they opened their ranks.

The decisive moment came in 53 BC near the town of Carrhae. Plutarch takes up the story.

The Parthians do not march to war with cornets and trumpets to encourage them. They use a kind of kettle-drum, which they beat in time from different parts of the field. They add a sort of dead hollow noise, like cattle bellowing … they know that of all the senses, hearing is most quickly confused and disordered.

… the Parthians began to shoot from all sides. They did not pick any particular target since the Romans were so close together that they could hardly miss. They simply used their great bows to fire off arrows that hit the Romans with great force. Right from the start the Romans were in a bad position. If they kept their ranks, they were wounded. If they tried to charge the enemy, the enemy did not suffer any more and they did not suffer less, because the Parthians could shoot even as they fled. This is a cunning idea – by fighting as you flee, you avoid the dishonour of running from the enemy.

Plutarch *Life of Crassus* 23 & 24

The Romans had just been introduced to the 'Parthian shot', which from that day to this has been a metaphor for damaging your opponent even as you leave the fray. The Parthians did this by turning in the saddle and

16 A Parthian horse warrior firing a 'Parthian shot' over the rump of his horse as he retreats. The Romans were bemused by this style of warfare. 'They fight even as they run away and run away as they fight', one chronicler complained.

shooting over the rumps of their horses. They cut to pieces a cavalry charge by Publius, the son of Crassus, and killed him and most of his men.

Given the inefficiency of Parthian supply chains, the Romans could reasonably have hoped that the Parthians would run out of arrows, but the Surenas had risen superbly to the occasion. He not only had camel-loads of fresh arrows on hand, but he took care that the Romans should see them re-supplying his men. The morale of Crassus' raw troops buckled. With difficulty the Romans struggled into the city of Carrhae itself. In an incident which tells us much about Parthian chivalry, four isolated Roman cohorts were surrounded and massacred. The twenty Roman survivors drew their swords and charged the entire Parthian army. Out of respect for such suicidal bravery, the Parthians opened their ranks and allowed these men to rejoin the main force.

Crassus was forced to negotiate partly by his own soldiers, and partly due to the evident hopelessness of his situation. He had little faith in Parthian promises, especially as Orodes himself had observed that 'the gods allow the punishment of treaty-breakers', but he had no choice. As the talks began, a skirmish broke out and Crassus was killed. It is uncertain exactly what happened since, as Plutarch comments drily, the Romans nearby 'had hardly the leisure to note particular details'. But one thing was crystal clear. The Surenas had a famous victory to bring back to his king.

Orodes was already celebrating a victory of the diplomatic variety. Armenian peace overtures had progressed to the point where the Armenian king had espoused his sister to Pacorus, the son of Orodes. The nuptials mixed Greek and Iranian festivities. Orodes was well educated in Greek art and literature, but his in-law, the Armenian king, wrote tragedies, orations and histories in Greek, many of considerable merit. It was hardly coincidence that the *Bacchae* of Euripides was being performed when the satrap Silaces presented the kings with the head of Crassus – at just the right moment for this gory trophy to be included as a prop in the play.

What became of the rest of the Roman army is an interesting question. Some soldiers made it back to Syria under Crassus' second-in-command, Cassius Longinus, the man who later plotted the assassination of Julius Caesar. But thousands remained prisoners, their fate of as much interest to the Romans as that of missing Americans in Vietnam has been recently. A clue as to what became of these lost legions may be some remarkably Roman-style frescos in western China, and a contemporary Chinese report of some strangely armoured soldiers manning a fort. Did the Roman legionaries end their careers serving the Parthian king on the other side of his empire? It is improbable, but not impossible. For Orodes a large body of trained soldiers was too good to be wasted. The east of the empire was restless at this time, and unlike Parthian troops, Roman soldiers certainly had no local loyalties there.

After the victory at Carrhae, the question of loyalty greatly occupied Orodes. It is a problem for the generals of tyrants that they must win, but not too well. By his magnificent victory, the Surenas had put himself on a par with Orodes himself, and this was intolerable. Within months the great general was dead, executed on the king's orders – an act of gross ingratitude which created considerable indignation in the Surenas' native East, and contributed to the unrest mentioned above.

Having deprived himself of his greatest general, Orodes had to choose a lesser man to lead the Parthian counter-attack into Syria. His own son, Pacorus, was the figurehead for the campaign, but the real commander was a general called Osaces. This Parthian expedition was more of a punitive raid than an attempt at conquest. The king's men made no attempt to hold the lands that their cavalry swept through. Nor did the Parthians try their luck against the cities they encountered, but passed them by to loot the surrounding countryside. The Parthians were poor at siegecraft; when they captured an entire Roman siege-train a few decades later, they made no use of it.

In late 51 BC their raid swept towards the city of Antioch. There it met the redoubtable Cassius and his surviving troops. It must have given these men considerable satisfaction to throw the Parthians back in bloody defeat, and to kill Osaces, their commander. At this setback, Orodes recalled his son. Either he felt uneasy about giving his offspring military command, or Pacorus was needed in the East. Pacorus was certainly not in disgrace. On the contrary – he was elevated to the rank of joint ruler with Orodes. A coin issued in the Persian city of Ecbatana at this time refers to 'King of Kings, Arsaces Philhellene [i.e. Orodes] and Arsaces Pacorus'.

With the Parthians gone from Syria, the Romans took less interest in Orodes, especially as Julius Caesar was now making his bid for supreme power. Caesar was ultimately victorious at Pharsalus in 48 BC. The defeated Pompey considered flight to Parthia, but made the fatal mistake of choosing Egypt instead.

Orodes would probably have welcomed Pompey. He was beginning to collect a corps of Roman exiles, and was quicker than the Roman senate to identify Caesar as a real danger. In 46 and 45 BC he gave substantial aid to the revolt against Caesar of Q. Caecilius Bassus, an action which spurred Caesar on in his project to invade Parthia. After Caesar's assassination in 44 BC, Orodes lent Brutus and his old enemy Cassius several squadrons of cavalry, some of whom perished with the Republican cause at Philippi.

Even with Caesar dead, Rome would not rest until it had retrieved the standards of the legions that had fallen at Carrhae. The driving force behind the invasion was Mark Antony, one of Caesar's heirs, working in collaboration with Cleopatra, queen of Egypt. Orodes had a good intelligence service, and in 40 BC he launched a pre-emptive strike against Syria. Pacorus again led the army, and this time he was no figurehead, but an able and energetic commander. We know some detail about the campaign, as Pacorus interfered in Judaean politics, and the results were recorded by contemporary Jewish writers. Booty was again a major Parthian objective.

> As for the Parthians in Jerusalem, they set themselves to plundering, and rifled the houses of those who had fled. In the king's palace, they spared nothing but Hyrcanus' money, which was about three hundred talents [Hycarnus was the High Priest]. They took other men's money also, but not so much as they hoped for; for Herod had long suspected the perfidy of the barbarians, and had taken care that his most splendid treasures were conveyed into safety...
>
> Josephus *The Jewish War* 1.268.13

Hyrcanus the high priest of Israel was chosen for the job by Pacorus, and the bribe Pacorus received for intervening included five hundred Jewish women to take home with him.

While Pacorus struck northward, another Parthian army was enjoying success to the south. Orodes had made an imaginative choice of leader for this force, giving command to Titus Labienus, a Roman. Labienus had once commanded troops for Caesar in Gaul (pp. 115–127) but had since become a Rebublican supporter. The defeat of his cause had stranded him in Parthia where he had gone to ask Orodes for more troops to join those already with Brutus and Cassius. Labienus and Pacorus brought much of Asia Minor under Parthian control, and the tide turned only when Labienus was killed in battle in 39 BC.

Worse was to follow for Parthia. The experienced and competent Ventidius took command of Roman armies in Syria. In 38 BC he defeated the Parthians and killed Pacorus, eliciting from Shakespeare fifteen hundred years later the declamation which starts this piece. Ventidius became the only Roman of his generation to celebrate a triumph for victory over the Parthians.

The death of his favourite son hit Orodes hard. He pulled his troops out of Syria and lapsed into semi-senility, compounded by failing health. He needed a replacement for Pacorus to prepare for the coming Roman assault. His frequent visits to his large harem had left him with another thirty sons to choose from. It is evidence of the failing judgment of Orodes that he picked Phraates, the eldest, as his heir.

Phraates was not a patient man. He tried to kill Orodes with aconite, using small doses of the poison to avoid suspicion. Conversely, this proved an excellent remedy for the dropsy which afflicted Orodes, and his son's ministrations came close to effecting a complete cure. When the effects of his doctoring became apparent, Phraates abandoned subtlety for the more certain technique of strangulation. To quash discussion of his conduct, Phraates purged the court of Orodes' supporters and killed his twenty-nine brothers.

As king, Phraates IV (38–2 BC) maintained the fine Parthian tradition of defeating a Roman invasion (under Mark Antony), and being killed by his son and successor. This time the assassin had help from the king's wife, who went on to marry her stepson. The wife was a former slave girl, a gift from Augustus when the two empires finally made peace.

They are truly formidable fighters; though their reputation is rather greater than their achievements. They have never conquered any Roman territory, and have lost some of their own lands. But they have never been truly beaten. Even today, they can hold their own against us.

Cassius Dio *History* 40.14

CHAPTER 9

CLEOPATRA OF EGYPT: KEEPING POLITICS PERSONAL

What of her who lately heaped disgrace on our troops,
A woman used by her own household slaves?
She claimed the walls of Rome and the Senate
Assigned to her rule as the fee for her filthy 'marriage'.
Propertius 3.11.29–32

Queens called Cleopatra were quite common in the ancient world. For example, Philip II of Macedon married a Cleopatra, which resulted in a nearly fatal estrangement from his son Alexander the Great. There were six Cleopatras of Egypt before the enigmatic and fascinating queen known to Egyptologists as Cleopatra VII. But this Cleopatra has so captured the modern imagination that she is now the Cleopatra, as much a myth as a real personality.

The Cleopatra of modern myth was a dusky Egyptian queen of devastating beauty who passed her days in languid decadence with her Roman lovers. The real Cleopatra was a Macedonian, possibly a blonde. She was hard-working, highly intelligent, and ruthless. She was not even particularly pretty. Plutarch says 'her beauty was not said to be so remarkable, or such that you would be struck by it when first seeing her'.

Yet two of the most powerful men of her day were sufficiently affected by her charms to compromise themselves politically. She bore children to each of them, threatening to create a dynasty equal to any of the great families of Rome.

And like her lovers, Caesar and Antony, Cleopatra had dynastic pedigree. She was a Ptolemy, descended from a general of Alexander the

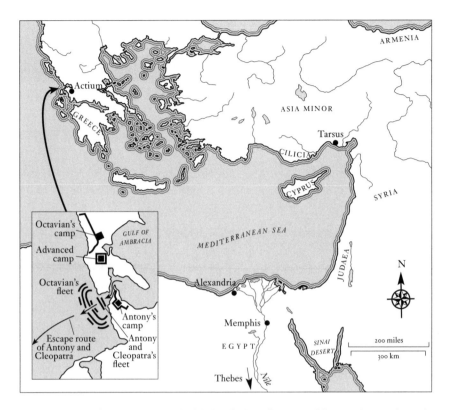

17 *Cleopatra's world. Cyprus and much of Judaea had once been part of the Egyptian Empire, and Cleopatra was determined to regain as much of her nation's ancient glory as possible. The inset shows the battle of Actium, the position of the opposing armies, and the possible deployment of naval forces.*

Great who conquered Egypt in 332 BC. Though Macedonian, Ptolemy I immediately adopted Egyptian ways to make himself acceptable to his new subjects. He also revived an older tradition of brother-sister marriage within the royal family, a practice which meant that Cleopatra was descended from her illustrious ancestor a good deal more directly than are most royalty.

Cleopatra's mother (her aunt on her father's side) was another Cleopatra, Cleopatra Tryphaena. This Cleopatra's husband (and brother) was Ptolemy XII, father of the younger Cleopatra. Ptolemy XII is sometimes called Auletes, 'the flute-player'. Ptolemy Auletes actively cultivated the friendship of Rome, partly to protect his kingdom, and partly to protect himself. By entrusting himself to his Roman patrons and by borrowing huge sums from them, Ptolemy had made some very powerful people directly interested in his personal well-being. This was necessary because Egyptian politics were conducted with the same verve as in other eastern monarchies, and murder by relative was a very common cause of death in the royal family.

Though Egypt was a rich kingdom, the cost of keeping the Romans friendly almost bankrupted the state. Nor had the mass of treasure paid to Rome prevented the Romans from seizing Cyprus from Egypt in 58 BC. This Roman land grab was the latest of a series of reverses for the kingdom, which had once dominated much of the Middle East. It was a decline which Cleopatra was determined to reverse.

We know little of her childhood. It is certain that her education was at least equal to that of her brothers. She was fluent in several languages (though apparently not in Latin, which is strange given the influence of Rome on her kingdom and her life). She was reputed to be the first Ptolemy to speak Egyptian. In all, it was probably this well-rounded mind rather than a well-rounded body which captivated Cleopatra's paramours. Plutarch speaks of her 'bold wit' and the 'charm of her company'. There is no doubt that she was quick-witted and sophisticated. According to the historian Appian, she made an early impression on the young Roman aristocrat Mark Antony, who visited her father's court when she was fifteen and Antony was on his way to the wars in Asia Minor.

Perhaps Cleopatra's father also respected her special qualities, for on his death in 51 BC she became his successor. Cleopatra made a spirited attempt to rule alone, though she was then a girl of only seventeen years of age. However, pressure from palace officials forced her betrothal to a brother who was in his early teens and who became her co-ruler as Ptolemy XIII. Cleopatra was never particularly popular with her subjects. She may at first have tried to remedy this by taking a populist, anti-Roman line and by trying to undermine her brother's standing. There are reports that she mistreated some Roman ambassadors; and some coins and official documents from this period show Cleopatra as monarch without reference to her younger brother. Cleopatra took the three-headed snake as her diadem, and adopted the cornucopia as her personal symbol, hoping that her reign would bring abundance and fertility.

This imperious young queen rapidly discovered the limits of her power. Palace officials used popular unrest caused by a drought and a famine to engineer a palace coup. Her brother ruled the country as the figurehead of a council of regents, while Cleopatra was forced to remove herself from the palace for her personal safety. She and her younger sister Arsinoe may even have fled the country for a while to take refuge in Syria.

In 48 BC the world changed. The Roman Republic was defeated at the battle of Pharsalus in Greece. One man, Julius Caesar, had made himself master of the Roman world. The defeated Republican leader, Pompey the Great, fled to Egypt. Egypt and Parthia were the last powers outside Caesar's control, and after the debacle of Crassus' Parthian expedition, Egypt seemed certain to provide a friendlier welcome. Also Pompey was the official guardian of Ptolemy XIII, an arrangement by which Ptolemy Auletes had contrived to protect his son, and which the Roman senate had seen as a means of projecting their influence into Egypt.

The council of regents, however, wanted no part of this Roman civil war, which could bring nothing but grief for Egypt. It was decided that Pompey should never set foot on Egyptian soil. As Ptolemy waited at the dock with his reception committee, Pompey was assassinated on the barge taking him ashore. This was not the end of the matter, because four days later Caesar himself arrived on the scene. Ptolemy was uncertain how Caesar would regard Pompey's assassination. Caesar had been Pompey's enemy, but had also once been his father-in-law and close political ally. Accordingly, Ptolemy withdrew from Alexandria to await events, and Caesar sailed into a town gripped by uncertainty and rumour.

Never the man to let a power vacuum pass him by, Caesar settled into the royal palace and started issuing orders. He had with him some 3,000 legionaries and several hundred cavalry, who set about restoring order. Ptolemy hurried back to Alexandria, reaching the palace just ahead of Cleopatra. The young queen had realized that the old order was changing and wanted to be a part of the new one. With Ptolemy back in the palace, she used a subterfuge to gain access to Caesar.

She took a small boat, and only one of her confidants with her – a Sicilian called Apollodorus. She landed at the palace as the evening was growing dark, but was unable to find a way of getting in undiscovered. Eventually she had the idea of lying down on a bedcover. Apollodorus rolled up the cover and tied the bundle on his back. In this way he went through the palace gates to Caesar's apartments.

Plutarch *Life of Caesar* 49

The Roman was delighted by Cleopatra's boldness. He had something of a reputation for audacity himself, and their rapport was immediate. On a political level Caesar was well aware of the antipathy of Ptolemy's regents and he urgently needed money to pay his soldiers. Cleopatra wanted to be reinstated in power, and was quite prepared to meet Caesar's needs, and other needs of a more personal nature. As one writer drily puts it, 'Cleopatra, having gained access to Caesar, was quite prepared to allow Caesar access to Cleopatra.' By the end of the night the pair had become lovers.

This was immediately obvious to Ptolemy when he saw Cleopatra with Caesar the following day. He ran from the palace screaming that he had been betrayed. Caesar's men dragged the young king back to the palace as he tried to incite the Alexandrian mob to rise to his cause, and after a 'reconciliation' Ptolemy agreed once more to share the throne with Cleopatra. But it was plain that the real ruler of Egypt was Caesar, and this was intolerable to the regents who had once ruled in Ptolemy's name.

These regents raised an army and easily persuaded Ptolemy to lead it. The war was a difficult one for Caesar. He lacked the men for a proper campaign but was reluctant to abandon either Alexandria or Cleopatra. A confused and sometimes desperate struggle followed, in which one of the principal casualties was the Great Library of Alexandria, one of the wonders of the ancient world. The library was burned in a fire which spread from the docks when Caesar torched his own ships. This did little to endear Cleopatra, his ally, to her citizens. At about this time Cleopatra's sister Arsinoe decided to join the Egyptian side, and was proclaimed queen.

It was a fateful decision. Caesar eventually overcame his enemies and Ptolemy was drowned while retreating from the victorious Romans. Cleopatra was pronounced queen of Egypt, and again married one of her

18 *Relief of Cleopatra in Kom Ombo. To her subjects, Cleopatra tried to appear a fully Egyptian queen, as shown here in traditional regalia. To the Romans she was a Hellenic monarch fully conversant with Greek culture and able to deal with Caesar and Antony on their own terms.*

younger brothers, who then became Ptolemy XIV. Arsinoe was handed to Caesar to ornament the triumph he would celebrate over the Egyptians when he returned to Rome in 46 BC. But first, Cleopatra took her lover for a trip up the Nile. The voyage mixed business with pleasure, for Cleopatra was no concubine; she was the ruler of a large and currently dysfunctional state. Caesar was often left to his own devices aboard the royal barge while Cleopatra went ashore to put her kingdom to rights.

As ruler, Cleopatra was identified with the Nile, the river which was the dominant fact of life in that country. In a land with almost no rainfall or other source of water, the flooding of the Nile's silt-laden waters fertilized and watered the fields of Egypt. The pharaohs were seen as the conduit through which the balance of natural forces was maintained by the gods and their power was theoretically absolute.

But no pharaoh ruled long without the support of Egypt's priestly class, particularly the priests of Memphis who had crowned the rulers of Egypt since the days of Ptolemy V. Alexandria was the capital of the country. At the head of the Nile delta, it was a rich and cosmopolitan port with a large Greek and Jewish population. Within Egypt's heartland, the power of Memphis had to be balanced against the traditional rights of the religious center of Thebes, principal city of Upper Egypt, where the population had never fully accepted their rulers in the north. Cleopatra was a Hellenistic monarch in Alexandria, but to the peoples of the upper Nile she was the goddess consort of the pharaoh. It may be from this trip that we can date an inscription which refers to Cleopatra taking part in a bull-procession up the river from Thebes as part of a religious rite.

Egypt had a swarm of gods, chief of whom was Amun-Ra, the god who spoke from the oracle at Siwa. Egyptian religion was both ancient and constantly adapting with relatively new gods, such as Serapis taking their place in the crowded pantheon along with Anubis, god of the dead, Apis, Horus, Osiris and others.

As well as being a religious focus for their people, the Ptolemies ruled through a firm grip on an administration that was centralized to a degree unusual in the ancient world. To ancient practices the Ptolemies added Macedonian ideas of record-keeping which proved particularly useful for taxation. The dry climate of Egypt has preserved many of these records, which were written on the papyrus which grew thickly along-side the all-providing Nile. We even have one papyrus from Cleopatra's time which deals with a tax exemption. On the papyrus, below the writing of the royal scribe, another hand has written in Greek 'Ginestho' – 'make it be so'. This is quite possibly the writing of Cleopatra herself.

Justice was dispensed directly by the Pharaoh or by his judges. There were separate legal systems for Egyptians and Greeks, and though the Greeks were undoubtedly the elite of the country, the distinction from the natives seems to have been artificial. Any person who rose to a certain level in society was probably considered 'Greek' no matter what his genetic make-up. The feudal nature of the country was emphasized by the army, for the most part Macedonian-style pikemen, who were main-tained by grants of royal land.

Caesar would have seen all this and more in his tour of the country. Things had turned out to his satisfaction. He had access to the riches of Egypt and the country's queen was dependent on him for her personal and political survival. To Caesar and Cleopatra's mutual satisfaction she became pregnant by him. Caesar left the country just before his son, Cae-sarion (Ptolemy Caesar), was born on 23 June, 47 BC.

While parted from Caesar, Cleopatra worked hard at strengthening her country. Despite her father's debts and Caesar's predations she rebuilt the economy, and concentrated her military preparations on constructing a fleet to rival Rome's. We know little of her activities at this time. Despite the later propaganda of her enemies there is no reason to believe that Cleopatra was either depraved or debauched, or indeed that she had any lovers at this time apart from Caesar. The routine business of running a kingdom is of little interest to our sources, so while Caesar was mopping up the last of the Republican resistance in Spain and Africa, Cleopatra drops out of the historical picture.

Maybe the queen also felt that she was receiving too little attention. Caesar had returned to Rome and celebrated a magnificent triumph for his various victories. Now Cleopatra turned up in Rome as well, ostensibly to negotiate a treaty of alliance. It has been speculated that Caesar had summoned her, but more probably her arrival was a huge embarrassment to the dictator. After all, Cleopatra was not Caesar's only amorous liaison.

As well as this affair [with Servilia in Rome] Caesar had many love affairs in the provinces ... including with several queens. These included Eunoe, wife of Bogudes the Moor ... but the most famous of these queens is Cleopatra.
Suetonius *Caesar* 51–52

Cleopatra was accompanied by her family. Ptolemy, her husband-brother, probably could not be left at home unsupervised, and little Caesarion was with her to remind Caesar of how much the couple had in common. Fortunately for Caesar, an ancient statute forbade monarchs from entering Rome, so Cleopatra was accommodated in a villa of Caesar's just outside the city and from there tried to win over the Roman senate. Caesar did his best to help, putting a golden statue of her in the temple of Venus Genetrix, but the snobbish Romans were unswayed by the propaganda of the 'New Isis', as Cleopatra had taken to calling herself. A letter by the orator Cicero sums up the reaction of the Roman aristocracy:

I dislike Her Majesty. Ammonius, who guaranteed her promises, knows that I have the right to do so. These were promises concerning literary matters, not unbecoming to my position – I should not mind telling them to a public meeting ... The arrogance of the Queen herself when she was living on the estate across the Tiber makes my blood boil when I recall it.

Cicero *Letters to Atticus 15.15*

If Cleopatra failed to impress the senators of Rome, Caesar had even less success. A group of them assassinated him on the Ides of March in 44 BC. In the ensuing chaos, Cleopatra slipped away to Egypt. She was aware that her prestige and entire position were again at risk. It is evidence of her insecurity that she now killed off her husband-brother, and ruled instead as the consort of her infant son Caesarion.

During the civil war which followed Caesar's death, Cleopatra's diplomatic skills were strained to the uttermost. She would be condemned by the eventual winner if she did not lend her support, yet supporting the wrong side would be disastrous. At one point Cleopatra sent her fleet, though it was never quite certain which side she had sent the ships to aid since it was driven back to port by a suspiciously fortunate storm. The four legions which Caesar had left in Egypt were allegedly sent to aid Dolabella, one of Caesar's generals, but eventually ended up in the hands of Cassius, the leader of the assassins.

It must have come as a relief to Cleopatra when the war ended in 42 BC, and the victors were Caesar's heir, Octavian, and two of Caesar's generals, Mark Antony and Lepidus. These men divided the Roman world between them. As the strongest triumvir, Antony chose to rule the more populous and prosperous East, leaving Octavian with the war-wracked West, and Lepidus with the province of Africa (which was mostly the lands once held by Carthage and the Numidian kings). Since Egypt was seen as a part of the eastern Mediterranean, Cleopatra would have to deal with Antony. Where Caesar had been abstemious, Antony was a drunkard. Caesar was cultured, Antony was uncouth. Caesar regarded food as fuel, Antony revelled in gastronomic excess. But Caesar and Antony had two things in common. They both had some of the bluest blood in Rome and they both had a taste for women with extremely strong characters.

Caesar's taste in royalty has been noted. Antony was married to Fulvia, a woman of whom Plutarch remarks, 'she was not one to rule a household if she could rule an empire instead'. Later Roman historians felt Cleopatra owed Fulvia a debt of gratitude for teaching her husband to take orders from a woman. Leaving Fulvia in Rome (where she began to incite a rebellion against Octavian), Antony hastened to the East. It was his intention to execute Caesar's plan to invade Parthia and avenge Crassus' defeat of a decade before (p. 135). The men, money, and material assembled by Caesar had been consumed by Cassius and Brutus in their war against the triumvirs, and work on the invasion had to begin anew.

In 41 BC Antony set up his base in Tarsus in Asia Minor and began to muster his forces. Cleopatra was summoned, firstly to answer charges that she had assisted the triumvirs, and secondly because, if vindicated, Cleopatra would be expected to contribute to the war effort, as befitted Rome's leading ally in the region. Cleopatra took her time in answering the summons, partly to tantalize Antony, and partly because there was a lot to do at home. Egypt had not been well administered during her absence, and there had been a succession of poor harvests. Also, she wanted time to prepare her entrance. Finally, she came to Antony,

… sailing up the river Cydnus in a barge gilded to the stern with gold. The sails were purple, and the oars were silver. They rowed to the sound of flutes, harps and pipes. Cleopatra lay dressed as Venus under a canopy of cloth of gold, fanned by beautiful boys dressed as cupids who stood on either side of her. Her maids at the rudder or working the ropes of the sails were dressed as sea-nymphs, or as the Graces. Exotic perfumes wafted to the masses on the river bank; some of whom followed the progress of the galley up the river, whilst others ran from the town to see the sight. Antony was left by himself, sitting alone on his tribunal in an empty market place.

Plutarch *Life of Antony* 26

Cleopatra had studied reports of Antony's character and correctly decided that taste and refinement could be omitted from this lavish display. She capped it off by inviting Antony to dine with her that night at a feast of sumptuous luxury. Antony was spellbound. Here was a woman of breeding and distinction who could match him in coarse soldierly repartee; a partner in his private pleasures and the sovereign of an allied state. Cleopatra was every woman Antony could wish for:

Plato says there are four kinds of flattery – Cleopatra had a thousand. Whether Antony was in a serious or frivolous mood she had some new charm or amusement tailored to his desires. She was with him all the time, never letting him out of her sight by day or by night. She played dice with him, hunted with him, and came to watch when he practised his swordsmanship.

> Plutarch *Life of Antony* 29

Leaving his subordinates to continue preparations for the Parthian campaign, Antony went to Egypt with Cleopatra. There has been considerable speculation as to why Antony seemingly abandoned affairs of state to gambol with his Egyptian queen. Infatuation might have played its part. So too might have been a desire to move to a port within striking distance of Rome, where Octavian faced mounting political problems. But there was another reason. While Antony was good at fighting, the administration and logistics of generalship bored him to distraction. The years leading to 41 BC had been violent, hectic and dangerous. So Antony used the lull before his Parthian campaign to take a holiday. Antony had good reasons for desiring Cleopatra's company. He may have been in love, but he also loved Cleopatra for her gold, her fleet, and the corn she could supply. Above all, Antony's affair with the last heir of Alexander the Great gave him some standing in the Greek East, where Rome was still heartily hated.

Cleopatra played up to Antony's love of excess, and the ancient sources abound with tales of their extravagance. She and Antony are said to have formed a band of companions called the Inimitable Livers, whose sworn intention was to live life to the full. Cleopatra pointed out that given her complete devotion to Antony's cause, there was no need to have an Egyptian queen kept in reserve. Arsinoe, Caesar's former prisoner, was both redundant and a threat. Antony acceded to Cleopatra's wishes and had her sister put to death.

As with Caesar, Cleopatra again fell pregnant by her Roman lover. And as with Caesar, her lover had to leave before she gave birth. Antony received news that Fulvia had finally provoked a full-blown rebellion against Octavian. He left with a fleet of ships to aid his wife if the rebellion was going well, to 'mediate' if it failed. Cleopatra was not to see Antony again for several years.

Cleopatra sent word to Antony that he had become the father of twins. He replied with the news that he had been both a widower and remarried. Fulvia's rebellion had failed, and she herself had died from the privations of the campaign. Antony had been forced to negotiate with the newly strengthened Octavian, and as a part of the settlement Antony had wed Octavian's sister. This was not good news for Cleopatra, especially if she intended, as in the words of one writer, 'to rule Rome through Romans'.

In the East Rome's affairs were going well. Ventidius rebuffed the Parthian assault on Syria, and Antony's generals Sosius and Canidius had successful campaigns in Armenia and the Caucasus Mountains. Antony hurried eastward – and he took his pregnant wife Octavia with him. This was a galling setback for Cleopatra, mitigated only slightly by the news that Octavia's offspring turned out to be a girl. She herself had given birth to a boy (later to be called Alexander Helios) and a girl (to be called Cleopatra Selene).

Better news was to follow. Antony left his wife in Greece, claiming that the difficulties of the campaign would be too much for her and their new child. He somewhat undid the effect of this gallantry by summoning Cleopatra, ostensibly in her role of an allied monarch, to co-ordinate the military campaign. Cleopatra was also at pains to show her people she was no camp follower. Coins of this period show her not as a beautiful queen, but as a grim matriarch totally lacking sex appeal. Antony thought otherwise, however, and the pair picked up their affair where

19 *Coin of Cleopatra. Sensing that public opinion would be firmly against her dalliance with Rome's overlords, Cleopatra on occasion tried to depict herself as a severe matriarch with the minimum of sex appeal. This changed only when Antony came fully over to her side, and the pair behaved as man and wife with their joint children acknowledged as Antony's heirs.*

they had left off. Another son, Ptolemy Philadelphos, was to be born from this meeting. In return for her efforts, Cleopatra received lands in Syria, Cilicia (which provided timber for the growing Egyptian fleet) and Judaea; all of which had once been parts of the ancient domain of the Ptolemies.

As Antony went off to war, Cleopatra toured her new acquisitions. This brought her into contact with the Jewish king from whom some of the lands had been taken. He was Herod the Great, the king of Israel who ordered the massacre of the innocents in Bethlehem when the baby Jesus was born. His meeting with Cleopatra was a splendid affair in which each tried hard to outdo the other with affectations of goodwill. Herod actually loathed Cleopatra for her expropriations, which included his personal olive groves in Jericho. Cleopatra regarded Herod as a squatter on lands that were rightfully hers. She was also jealous of his friendship with Antony and used her trip to stir up intrigues within Herod's family, where relationships were already fraught. Unsurprisingly, a major effect of the tour was to convert Herod into a secret partisan of Octavian.

Antony's Parthian campaign did not go well, in part because the Armenian cavalry deserted soon after it began, leaving the Romans exposed to the Parthian horse archers. The Romans had learned enough since the debacle at Carrhae for Antony to win several battles and afterwards manage a fighting retreat. But he still lost almost 25,000 men and had very little to show for it. The vengeful Antony later tried to regain some credit by plundering Armenia and capturing its faithless king.

In late 36 BC he arrived in Syria where Cleopatra met him with pay and supplies for his exhausted army. The next year the couple returned to Egypt where Antony celebrated a triumph for his victory in Armenia. This aroused unease in Rome where triumphs were traditionally held. The Parthian campaign had damaged Antony's credit, and Octavian argued that Antony was 'bewitched by that accursed Egyptian' (Cassius Dio I.26). Antony wrote a pamphlet entitled 'On his drunkenness' to counter Octavian's propaganda that the East had ruined his character. In a snide attack on Octavian as Caesar's heir, Antony proclaimed Caesarion as Caesar's son. Octavian claimed in return that Cleopatra was scheming to become queen of Rome. Allegedly one of her favourite oaths was 'As surely as I shall yet dispense justice on the Roman Capitol.'

20 *Coin of Mark Antony. Only in the last generation of the Roman Republic did the Romans start putting pictures of living persons on their coins. The bull neck of Antony shown here appears to have been a distinctive family characteristic.*

If this had not alienated the Romans, Antony's arrangements for his offspring seemed calculated to do the job. In Alexandria crowds beheld Antony and Cleopatra seated on golden thrones, calling themselves incarnations of the god Dionysus and goddess Isis. Antony proclaimed Cleopatra 'Queen of Kings', and she in turn promoted Caesarion to 'King of Kings'. Cleopatra Selene was to become queen of Cyrene, and Alexander Helios king of Armenia, and heir to the Seleucid Empire. His younger brother received the lands to the west.

There was outrage in Rome at what became known as the 'Donations of Alexandria'. Octavian demanded indignantly that Antony explain exactly which 'lands to the west' young Ptolemy Philadelphos had been given. Antony's will was seized from the Temple of Vesta in Rome, revealing that Antony wished to be buried in Egypt and had made to his children by Cleopatra further bequests of land that the Romans had thought belonged to them. To complete the rift, in 32 BC Antony divorced Octavia, and proclaimed Cleopatra his wife. A silver denarius with the faces of Antony and Cleopatra was already circulating in the East, and Octavian fanned fears that Antony and Cleopatra were setting up themselves and Alexandria to replace the Republic of Rome.

War was inevitable. Octavian declared it against Cleopatra, calculating rightly that Antony would stand by his woman. Domitius Ahenobarbus, Antony's leading general, was offended by Cleopatra's personal interest in the war. When she began to dictate strategy, he deserted to Octavian. Cleopatra was furious, but Antony good-naturedly sent Domitius his servants and baggage after him. Some believed that Cleopatra wanted the war fought at sea so that her navy could share in the victory. But Antony had a large army, well organized by Canidius, and he intended to fight the war out in Greece. In Greece, things did not go well. Though an indifferent soldier, Octavian knew how to pick competent subordinates, while Antony's side suffered from bickering and divided command. Eventually Octavian managed to cut the water supply of Antony's army while it was encamped near a promontory called Actium.

Cleopatra brought her navy up to evacuate the troops. Her ships were joined by those of Antony and his allies, whilst Octavian and his admiral Agrippa likewise prepared for naval action. On 2 September 31 BC the battle of Actium was fought. According to the ancient historians, Actium was a straightforward sea battle in which the forces of East and West came head to head to decide the future of the Roman Empire. The struggle was evenly balanced when suddenly Cleopatra's nerve broke and her fleet piled on sail and broke for the open sea. Torn between staying with his men or following his queen, Antony opted for the latter and abandoned his army and fleet. The fleet fought doggedly until about four o'clock in the afternoon, but demoralized by the loss of their commander they eventually surrendered. The army on the shore, still without water, held out until Canidus abandoned them.

Modern historians have queried this story. Ancient warships did not fight under sail. They were usually beached overnight, and loaded with essential supplies and soldiers on the day of the battle. Sails would not have been loaded unless they were going to be used. Since Cleopatra's ships were indeed carrying sails, this suggests that her decision to flee was not spontaneous. It seems rather that an elaborate plan broke down in the chaos of battle, leaving Antony cut off from his main force and with little choice but to follow Cleopatra.

The flight to Egypt was a disaster. Antony and Cleopatra had no army and no fleet. All they could do was wait for the inevitable arrival of Octavian – a man not known for his mercy. Their despairing offers to resign their offices and live as private citizens were rejected. Octavian was delayed by the need to set his new Empire to rights, but eventually he arrived in Egypt. The forces Antony had been able to muster crumbled at the first sight of the enemy. Word reached Antony that Cleopatra had committed suicide, and he did the same by falling on his sword.

Antony had been misinformed. Cleopatra still lived, and almost her last act before becoming Octavian's captive was to give her lover a magnificent funeral. Cleopatra knew Octavian would spare her life – at least for a while. Her sister Arsinoe had been paraded through Rome before Caesar's triumphal chariot, and Octavian intended Cleopatra to share the experience.

After crowning Antony's funeral urn with flowers she had a bath and ordered a magnificent meal to be prepared. When a peasant came with a small basket he was stopped by the guards at her door. The man moved aside the leaves which covered the top of the basket and invited the guards to try one of the beautifully large ripe figs within. The guards declined and allowed the fellow to enter. ... Cleopatra took away some of the figs and saw the asp which she had arranged to be brought in. 'So here it is', she said, and held out her arm to be bitten.

Plutarch *Life of Antony* 85, 86

Plutarch adds that we cannot be certain exactly what happened within the chamber. At the end, Cleopatra shut herself in with her servant girls. Octavian, suspecting that something was amiss, arrived and had the doors broken down. Too late.

Cleopatra was completely dead, lying on a bed of cloth of gold and arrayed in all her royal ornaments. Iras, one of her women, lay dying at her feet and Charmion, on the verge of collapse, was making a last effort to adjust her mistress' diadem. Someone asked her angrily, 'Do you think you did the right thing for your lady, Charmion?' She replied, 'It was exactly the right thing to do, for she was the descendant of so many kings', and as she said this, she too fell dead.

Plutarch *Life of Antony* 85

Cleopatra had tried to get her son Caesarion safely out of the country, but on the way he was betrayed by his tutor. Octavian reflected that 'it is possible to have too many Caesars', and had the boy killed. He was more merciful with the rest of Cleopatra's offspring. His sister – Antony's widow – took the children into her own household and brought them up with her own.

With Cleopatra's death Egypt fell into Roman hands. Her statues were left standing while those of Antony were thrown down. Her life, and her death, captured the imagination of the Roman world. While her relationship with Antony may have been political liaison with sex thrown in, it soon became the stuff of legend. Over the centuries Cleopatra has been commemorated in books, plays, operas and more recently in the cinema. It is said that when she knew the end was near, Cleopatra experimented to find a suitable poison. In Egyptian folklore the bite of an asp was meant to confer immortality. In Cleopatra's case, it appears to have worked.

· PART III ·

ARMINIUS

BOUDICCA

JOSEPHUS

DECEBALUS

Pax Romana

With the victory of Augustus at Actium, Rome's government entered a new phase. Democratic elections for Rome's top magistracies continued, but the results were largely irrelevant. Augustus had gained so much power and prestige that he was able to influence the government of Rome in almost any way he wanted. Nevertheless, Rome's first emperor was mindful of the fate of his adoptive father, Julius Caesar, who had been assassinated after he lost the support of the senate. In consequence he trod carefully in his relations with that august body. At one point Augustus offered to give up all his powers and become a private citizen. The senators, well aware of the dangers of accepting this offer if it was not sincerely meant, pleaded with Augustus to change his mind. For even without constitutional authority, Augustus possessed boundless *auctoritas*, the power that comes with respect and prestige, and this could not be stripped away by any constitutional declaration. Such dominance had existed briefly at other periods in Roman history, and the senators who had achieved it were called *principes* – the first among the equals of the senate. Augustus formalized this position, and from this we get the word for the early period of imperial rule – the 'principate'.

Though a consummate politician, Augustus was less skilled as a general and preferred to command his armies by proxy. Augustus adopted the name by which soldiers hailed a successful general (*imperator*, from whence we get the name 'emperor'), and he was jealous of those who attained military glory in the tradition of the Republic. When the general Crassus won a stupendous victory in Macedonia, Augustus blocked some of the honours Crassus was entitled to and pushed him out of public life. Another general made too much of a military success in Egypt and so great was the force of Augustus' displeasure that the unfortunate commander was forced to commit suicide. The message to Rome's generals was clear. Succeed, and the credit went to the emperor. Fail, and the blame was all theirs.

The first to fail was Varus, kinsman to Augustus by marriage, and governor of that part of Germany which the Romans had brought under their control. Varus believed his province to be peaceful, and he totally failed to notice seething German resentment at their loss of freedom. The Roman attempt to conquer Germany had two motives – firstly, even the primitive maps of ancient geographers showed that the Roman frontier would be considerably shortened if it ran along the river Elbe rather than the Rhine. Secondly, whilst the peoples of Germany remained outside the Empire they threatened not only the newly conquered provinces of Gaul, but also Italy itself.

The initial phases of the Roman conquest went well enough to lull the Romans into a false sense of security. Varus believed that he had the support of a young German nobleman called **Arminius** (Chapter 10) who had once served in the Roman army. In fact, Arminius' experience as a soldier of Rome was probably the catalyst which turned him into an ardent advocate of German liberty. Arminius kept Varus' trust while weaving about him a conspiracy which was to lead to one of the greatest debacles in Roman military history.

The Romans campaigned repeatedly to avenge the treachery of Arminius, but it slowly became apparent that the conquest of Germany would have to be postponed indefinitely. Part of the reason for this was economic. Most Roman wars of conquest paid for themselves with booty and later taxes from the conquered. The German forests and their ferocious warriors offered stubborn resistance for little financial return. Among the first to see this was Tiberius Claudius, the gloomy but efficient administrator whom Augustus chose as his successor. Tiberius had frequently campaigned in Germany, and when he decided that his kinsman Germanicus was expending money and manpower to little effect, he had him recalled to Rome.

With the accession of Tiberius to power, a flaw in the Augustan system immediately became apparent. The system required a political genius of Augustus' stature to control it properly. Senators began to understand that the loss of their hereditary power was permanent, and they bitterly resented the fact. Tiberius withdrew to the isle of Capri near Naples, and from there terrorized the Roman senate by a series of treason trials that wiped out both potential enemies and potential rivals.

One survivor of this purge was a young man called Gaius, the son of the great general Germanicus. Gaius had grown up in his father's camp, and the soldiers had affectionately nicknamed him 'Little Boots', or 'Caligula'. Caligula lost much of his family in the Tiberian purges, and must have felt himself in deadly peril when he was summoned by Tiberius to Capri. But Caligula managed to insinuate himself into the favour of the ageing emperor, and was eventually made his heir.

Caligula lacked both the political experience of Augustus, and the military reputation of Tiberius. He correctly divined the hostility of the senate and tried to enforce respect through fear. Since most historians of the period were senators, it is no surprise that they reported Caligula to posterity as a monster. Certainly, Caligula was a sadist with a twisted sense of humour who caused many innocent people to be killed. But some of the wilder claims are disputable or wrong. These include total insanity, incest with his sisters, the murder of Tiberius, and making his horse a consul of Rome.

What is noticeable, both in the case of Caligula and later 'tyrants', is that the weight of their tyranny fell squarely on the senate. The common people enjoyed the games, gossip, and imperial extravagances while the provinces continued to send in their taxes in return for reasonably competent governance. When Caligula was assassinated, the common people genuinely mourned him. The senate was in favour of returning to a Republic, but public opinion demanded an emperor and Claudius, an elderly relative of Caligula, was pressed into service.

Surprisingly, Claudius was rather a good emperor. He maintained cordial relations with the senate, and even garnered himself considerable military prestige by the invasion of the distant and fabled island of Britain. Like the Germans before them, the Britons were sufficiently unimpressed by the benefits of Romanization as to rise up in rebellion during the reign of Nero, Claudius' successor. We have only accounts of this rebellion from Roman historians, but they make the case for the rebels very clearly. In part the problem was Roman arrogance and misgovernment. In many frontier areas the Romans ruled by proxy through kings who were dependent on them. When the king of the Iceni in East Anglia died the Romans decided to make their rule more direct, and did so in the most brutal and tactless way possible.

The revolt was led by the queen of the Iceni, **Boudicca** (Chapter 11), priestess and warrior queen. That one woman with a grudge was able to bring almost the entire native population of southeast Britain over to her cause tells us much about how thoroughly the Romans were hated. As with Spartacus a century before, what should have been a minor difficulty for the local authorities became the focus of burning popular resentment of Roman rule. Britons destroyed the cities of London, Colchester and St Albans, and for almost a year it seemed as though Boudicca would drive the Romans from Britain. Like Spartacus, Boudicca's doomed revolt against tyranny has made her an iconic figure in modern times. Partly as a result of the restiveness caused by her rebellion, for centuries afterwards Britain was one of the most heavily garrisoned provinces of Rome's Empire.

Hardly had rebellion been stamped out in Britain than it flared up in Judaea. The Hebrews had never been contented subjects of Rome, and what the Romans saw as their idiosyncratic religion made them particularly hard to govern. Judaea bordered the strategically important province of Syria. With the hostile Parthians on the other side, the Romans were determined to keep Judaea peaceful. Signs of rebellion were harshly suppressed by the authorities, and this harshness created greater resentment which encouraged further government brutality. High taxation and banditry in the countryside damaged agriculture, and the weakening economy caused yet more unrest.

The revolt that finally flared up in AD 66 was less surprising than the fanaticism of the rebels who launched it. The Zealots espoused a heady mixture of political and religious extremism, though even they paled before the excesses of the Sicarii, a group whose practices were basically those of terrorists. Moderate Jews such as **Josephus** (Chapter 12), commander of the province of Galilee, eventually decided that even the Romans were preferable and took the first opportunity to surrender to the Roman army of reconquest. The war was finally won by two famous sieges. The first was of Jerusalem itself, where the rebels fought the Romans and rival factions with equal vigour. Eventually Jerusalem was taken and the Romans stormed and burned the temple where the last of the Zealots had made their stand.

The second siege was of the supposedly impregnable fortress of Masada to which the Sicarii had retreated. The general commanding the Roman army of reconquest was called Vespasian. Word reached Vespasian in AD 69 that Nero had been overthrown and that the imperial succession was in turmoil. Urged on by his soldiers, he decided to claim the imperial purple for himself and left the army in Judaea under the command of his son.

Vespasian was the first emperor to take power with the support of an army from the provinces. The historian Tacitus called this 'a secret of Empire' – that emperors could be created other than in Rome. Now the secret was out, Vespasian's feat would be regularly attempted by would-be emperors for the rest of Roman history. In another departure from tradition, Vespasian was not of the Julio-Claudian family which had ruled Rome from the foundation of the Empire. Indeed, his origins were not particularly aristocratic. These two breaks with precedent meant that any senator could dream of establishing himself or his sons on the imperial throne. This went some way towards reconciling the senate with the emperor, even as it wound up imperial paranoia another notch.

After the brief reign of Titus, who succeeded Vespasian, the throne fell to Vespasian's younger son Domitian. Domitian was in many ways a good emperor. Under his rule the provinces were well governed, and Domitian's grasp of economics was in some ways ahead of his time. When Dacian raiders troubled the province of Moesia in the AD 80s, Domitian may have calculated that it was cheaper to buy off their king, **Decebalus** (Chapter 13), than to fight a war against him, especially as Rome was already hard-pressed on the Rhine frontier. But Decebalus was no mere raider. Dacia was often troubled by civil wars and foreign invasions, yet it was a powerful state with a warrior ethos. Decebalus and his immediate predecessors had largely united the country under their leadership and Dacian power was extending towards the Black Sea and probing the Roman defences along the Danube frontier.

Domitian's settlement with Decebalus was never going to do more than buy time before another confrontation and was deeply unpopular with the senate, who also loathed Domitian for a number of other reasons. It is a notable feature of imperial history that those emperors who alienated the senate failed to live to a ripe old age, and Domitian was no exception. Though he purged the senate as bloodily as he dared, he still felt insecure. He complained that no one would believe his life was in danger until he was actually assassinated, and that assassination duly took place in AD 96.

Though Domitian would hardly have appreciated the fact, his death brought in a golden age for Rome. The elderly Nerva who succeeded Domitian ruled for two brief years and then was succeeded by the youthful and vigorous Trajan.

Trajan began his reign by settling accounts with Decebalus. This was partly because a confrontation was inevitable, and partly because the new emperor wanted to start his reign in a burst of military glory. The Dacians fought hard in both conventional battles and guerrilla warfare, but Trajan's well-organized campaign was irresistible. Decebalus' kingdom was made a Roman province. We have a fragmentary account of the war by a later historian, but the best record is visual. It is recorded in a spiral of pictures up the column which Trajan erected in Rome, where it can still be seen today.

Trajan went on to campaign against the Parthians, and pushed the Roman frontier beyond the Euphrates. This was combined with sound government at home and a balanced imperial budget. The arts flourished, and the historian Tacitus and the writer Pliny the Younger had nothing but praise for their new ruler.

Under Trajan, Rome's Empire reached its greatest extent. Trajan's successor Hadrian retrenched somewhat, and under his reign the Empire adopted a more defensive posture. Rome was to enjoy almost unbroken peace for almost a century, but the crisis that would follow nearly destroyed the Empire.

CHAPTER 10

ARMINIUS: THE MAN WHO KEPT ROME AT BAY

There can be no doubt that Arminius liberated Germany. Other kings
and generals had challenged Rome, but when the state was still young.
Arminius did so when Rome was in the full flower of its strength.
The battles were indecisive, but in war he was undefeated.
Tacitus *Annals* 2.88

According to Julius Caesar, the Germans were a much tougher proposition than the largely civilized Gauls. Like the Gauls, the Germans were ferocious fighters and, like the Gauls, some tribes made a habit of collecting the heads of those they had slain. But the Gauls were an agricultural people skilled at metalwork and masonry. Caesar tells us that the Germans despised agriculture and ate mainly meat, milk and cheese. Unlike the Gauls, to whom the accoutrements of Roman civilization were familiar, Caesar said that 'the Germans live in the same state of deprivation and poverty as before, with little change in their diet or clothing'.

The German peoples think that their greatest glory is the amount of land that can be kept uninhabited about the boundaries of each tribe. For them it shows the quality of a people that they can drive their neighbours from their homes and terrify anyone from settling near them. They also think that this gives them some security against surprise attacks.
Caesar 'Customs of the Germans' *De Bello Gallico* 1.2

Archaeology has confirmed this description to some extent, but it shows a more nuanced picture. The eastern Celts seem to have been little different – either physically or culturally – from the western Germans. Rather the two cultures seem to blur into one another along the river Main. Some of the best-preserved evidence from this period is the body of a German found in a peat bog in 1950. Unfortunately it appears that he was killed ritually, so his dress and diet may not have been those of everyday Germans of his day. But his death does confirm the opinion of the ancient writers that German justice and religion was a bloody affair, and that German gods were well pleased with human sacrifice.

We know these Germanic gods much better than we suppose since they have given us the days of the week. Caesar tells us that the Germans did not practise Druidism but worshipped those things they could see or experience directly. This is reflected in the nature of the German gods. We have Saturday from Saturn; Sunday and Monday, from the sun and the moon respectively; Tuesday is from Tiuw, god of war; Wednesday from Woden; Thursday from Thor; and Friday from Frigga, goddess of fertility.

The average German soldier of the first century AD was not well equipped. He carried a rudimentary shield and was considered well dressed if he went into battle wearing trousers. (And in fact, for those who did not own armour, fighting naked was the better option. In an age before antibiotics, many soldiers died of infection from dirty clothing forced into their wounds.) Swords were carried only by the elite, and horsemen were even rarer. The average warrior fought on foot using a *framea*, a long spear which sometimes had simply a sharpened wooden tip.

21 *A German warrior ready for battle. Although trousered here, nudity was usually preferable to dirty clothes which could infect a wound if fibres were forced into it. This warrior has his hair in a top-knot, a style favoured by several tribes.*

The Roman historian Tacitus puts this description of German military prowess into the mouth of the general Germanicus:

The German has neither cuirass nor helmet. His shield is simply woven branches or a thin, painted board without reinforcement of either leather or steel. The first line may have spears, but the rest have cruder weapons. Though their bodies are frighteningly large, and though they are formidable in their first assault, they can't endure it when they are wounded. If there is a disaster they forget divine or human commands and run from the field without paying the slightest attention to their leaders, and nor do they feel disgraced for having done so.

Tacitus *Annals* 2.14

There were tribal variations in armament such as the Frankish throwing axe and the Saxon 'scramasax' (a short dagger-like sword), but the German fighting character and rough native terrain contributed much more to their military effectiveness than did their weaponry.

The forests had (and still have) a powerful role in the German psyche. 'The country either bristles with forest or festers with swamps', comments Tacitus. The swamps were considered suitable only for drowning criminals, but the forests provided the Germans with fruit and game, with pasture for their cattle and security from attack. Groves (or even entire woods) were held sacred to various gods, and less sanctified areas provided fuel and building materials.

In the first century AD there were some dozen or so major German tribes and many minor ones. On the Roman border, the Marcomanni dominated the east, and the Chatti, Cherusci and Chauci those areas west. Another western tribe, the Batavi, supplied the Romans with mercenary soldiers and were to stage a troublesome revolt in AD 69. But in 12 BC the Batavi were allies of Augustus when he sent his legions across the Rhine to invade Germany. Under their commander, Drusus, they advanced as far as the river Weser in 11 BC and by 9 BC the Romans were ensconced in the tribal capital of the Ubii (which later became Cologne). Drusus then advanced through the territory of the Cherusci, and reached the Elbe. In AD 4 the future emperor Tiberius advanced even deeper into Germany and forced Maroboduus, leader of the Marcomanni, into an alliance with Rome, though soon after that Tiberius' campaign in Germany was cut short by a revolt in Pannonia.

At the start of the first century AD, it seemed that the conquered part of Germany was well on the way to eventual Romanization. Roman historians congratulated themselves on the way that the disciplined, organized Italians were imposing order on the feckless, passionate Germans.

The Germans combine great ferocity with mendacity so immense that those who do not know them would hardly believe it. They are natural-born liars, constantly involved in trumped-up litigation, and they expressed gratitude for Roman justice to settle these disputes. It seemed [at the time of Varus] as though this strange new concept of settling disputes with law rather than weapons was beginning to calm their barbarous nature.

Velleius *Paterculus* 2.108

Archaeology shows that Roman traders had pushed well beyond the frontiers and established trading posts the size of small towns. There was a fashion for young German nobles to serve in the Roman army, and these men brought Roman habits home with them on their discharge.

Among these soldiers were the sons of Sigimer, a chieftain of the Cherusci. We know only the Romanized version of the names of these young men. One brother was called Flavus, which unhelpfully translates into English as 'Blondy'. The other was called Arminius by the Romans. Later German nationalists have re-Germanized this name to Hermann, but this is almost certainly mistaken. It is possible that Arminius' name was derived from that of the god Irmun (as is the Roman road Ermine Street), but following German convention Arminius' real name should have been based on the Sigi- root of the paternal patronymic. We have this description of Arminius:

A young nobleman, strong of hand and quick of mind and far more intelligent than your average barbarian. ... the ardour of his face and eyes showed the burning spirit within. He had fought on our side in previous campaigns and earned the right to become a Roman citizen; indeed, he was even elevated to the rank of Equestrian.

Velleius *Paterculus* 2.108

Arminius was less than impressed by Drusus' drive through the lands of his native Cherusci, and he was deeply disgusted by Roman civilization. In his *Germania*, Tacitus gives us an idealized description of the German peoples. While deploring their violence and drunkenness, Tacitus nevertheless portrays them as noble savages, simple and chaste with unsophisticated virtues and close, supportive kinships. Much of this may have been true, particularly to the patriotic perceptions of a young German nobleman who strongly agreed with Tacitus' views on Rome's sophisticated vice and decadence. Nor, to a man of the Cherusci, was Rome's treatment of his people less than insufferable. One barbarian leader had already rebelled because 'You Romans bring it on yourselves. You don't send dogs and shepherds to guard your flocks – you appoint ravening wolves.' (Cassius Dio 56.16.)

Which brings us to Quintilius Varus, the new governor of Germany. One ancient historian summarized his previous governorship of Syria thus: 'He entered a rich province as a poor man and left a poor province as a rich man.' Varus owed his career to the favour of the emperor Augustus, whose grand-niece he had married. While in Syria he had dealt firmly with some Jewish insurgents, but he was not really a military man. Peacefully romanizing Germany had no need of a general and, if there was fighting to be done, Varus could call on three legions (the Seventeenth, Eighteenth and Nineteenth), as well as a host of auxiliaries and cavalry.

He had also Germanic allies on whom he felt he could rely, among them young Arminius. Varus was unaware that from almost the moment he had returned to Germany, Arminius was plotting feverishly against Rome. The nature of Germanic society worked against Arminius' scheming, for the Germans were an essentially democratic people who tended to elect their leaders ad hoc from the leading members of their local clan. Furthermore, the Germans felt that really big decisions should involve large-scale meetings with rousing speeches, and (hopefully) the consumption of large quantities of food and alcohol. As a result of these cultural failings, Arminius did not have either the pyramidal social hierarchy nor the inherent talent for plotting in the shadows which made the life of Roman conspirators so much easier.

Instead, each tribe and sub-tribe had to be persuaded to set aside local feuds and rivalries and act in a moderately synchronized manner. The first step in the conspiracy was for diverse communities to ask Varus for Roman garrisons – here for protection against robbers, there for guards for the supply columns, and another for protection against civil unrest. Later historians made much of the oppressive rule of Varus as one of the major factors in the revolt of the Germans, but in fact Varus seems to have had the best of intentions. He readily dispersed his troops into small, vulnerable detachments as the Germans requested, and spent much of his time dealing with lawsuits and administration.

In the autumn of AD 9 reports of serious trouble some distance away finally roused Varus from the comfort of his camp and set him and his legions on the move. Arminius enthusiastically offered the support of the Cherusci. Segestes, another tribal leader, came to Varus begging him not only to refuse Arminius' offer, but to throw the man in chains as a traitor. Arminius, Segestes assured Varus, was preparing a trap that would bring Varus and his legions to their doom. Segestes had refused Arminius the hand of his daughter Thudsnelda, and undeterred, the young nobleman had gathered a warband of followers and abducted his far from unwilling bride. Because of this family feud, Varus felt that Segestes was being less than objective and his advice was ignored. The legions ran into problems almost immediately.

They wandered into the middle of an almost impenetrable forest ... there were jagged mountains and high, dense groves of trees. Even without being attacked the Romans were having a tough time cutting trees and building roads, even bridges if required. They had many wagons with them. It was as though they were travelling in peacetime, for indeed they had more than a few women, children and servants with them.
    Cassius Dio 56.20–21

It may be (the accounts are conflicting) that Varus intended his march to finish at the Roman winter quarters, and was therefore transferring his whole camp and dealing with the local disturbance on the way. Arminius truthfully informed Varus that he needed to organize his own forces and left the Romans to it. Unknown to Varus, Arminius' forces included not only his own tribal confederation, the Cherusci, but also most of the nearby Chauci. Maroboduus and his Marcomanni remained warily neutral.

What happened next must always be to some extent conjectural.

Deep in the Teutoburg forest the Germans fell upon the Romans and destroyed them. This was one of the decisive moments in German history, yet until the last decade even the site of the battle has been a mystery. A huge monument raised by nineteenth-century Germans to Arminius' victory has since turned out to be some thirty miles out of position.

Research by Major Tony Clunn, a British amateur archaeologist, led to the discovery of a large number of iron artifacts, many of them Roman, at Kalkriese on the fringes of the Wiehengebirge hills north of Osnabrück. Professional archaeologists under Professor Wolfgang Schlüter soon confirmed what Major Clunn had suspected: this was the site of the Varusschlacht – the killing fields for Varus' legions. The evidence tells us that there had been a running battle of several days as the Romans strove to extricate themselves from the forests. When the Romans returned to the site of the battle several years later, they found the remains of 'a fallen rampart', says Tacitus. Modern archaeologists found this rampart, but were puzzled by the fact that it was more of a fence than a wall, and that most of the Romans appear to have fallen outside it.

Further investigation made it clear that the fence was of the type that the Germans wove about the edge of their pastures to stop their cattle from straying. In this case though, the creatures being herded were human. Arminius penned the confused and poorly led Romans between the forest and a nearby marsh, never giving them time to rally or organize until the entire army of some 30,000 men was utterly destroyed. Most of the legionaries were massacred on the spot, though some unfortunate senior officers were led to the sacred groves to be messily sacrificed. One god, Donar, was given special thanks for a series of thunderstorms which had slowed and demoralized the benighted Romans, most of whom were left to lie where they fell, their bones whitening in the forest clearings for the next six years.

Varus himself either died fighting or fell on his sword. Tacitus tells us that this was a family tradition, as Varus' father and grandfather had done the same (Varus' father had been on the wrong side in one of Rome's civil wars; why the grandfather committed suicide is unknown). Arminius had his men hunt through the corpses until they found Varus' body. Arminius sent Varus' head to Maroboduus of the Marcomanni, hoping that this would shift his fellow chieftain from his stubborn neutrality. But Maroboduus was not interested in this grisly trophy and sent it on to Rome to be decently interred.

News of the disaster struck Rome as devastatingly as one of Donar's thunderbolts. With Varus' legions gone, only the Alps stood between the Germanic hordes and the defenceless city. A few generations earlier, tens of thousands of the Germanic Cimbri had swarmed into northern Italy and had only been defeated by the last-ditch heroics of the generals Marius and Lutatius Catulus. Now, the emperor Augustus ordered an emergency levy and hastily ordered the elite legion V Alaudae north to fill the gap. According to his biographer Suetonius, Augustus was deeply affected by the disaster. Even months after, he would bang his head against the wall shouting 'Quinctilius Varus, give me back my legions!' I Germanica and the Sixteenth Legion were later moved to complete the repair of the Roman lines, but the Seventeenth, Eighteenth and Nineteenth Legions which Arminius had destroyed were never reconstituted and their ill-omened titles never used again.

With the frontier secure, Roman thoughts turned to vengeance. Having formerly served under the eagles, Arminius knew the resilience of the Romans in defeat and the bitter tenacity with which they pursued their enemies. The months after the battle in the Teutoburg forest saw frantic diplomacy as Arminius sought to unite the tribes against Rome, and the Romans promised, very credibly, that those who did not help against Arminius would share his fate. As soon as the campaigning season opened in AD 10 Tiberius, the heir-designate of Augustus, led the Roman counter-assault.

His recent victory had given Arminius no illusions about the ability of his men relative to Tiberius' legionaries, and he adamantly refused to face the Romans in the field. Instead he retreated ever deeper into the forests. This tactic effectively baffled Tiberius, for Roman military policy was to advance directly on whatever their enemies held dear and then to defeat whatever army came to defend it. But Germany had no cities to capture, and precious few crops to pillage. Over the next few years, the Romans made repeated shows of force, but no serious effort at conquest. Their incursions into German lands were fruitless but were intended to show that, despite the failing health of the emperor and problems elsewhere on the frontier, Arminius had not been forgotten. The reckoning was merely postponed.

In AD 14 Tiberius became emperor. He had already boosted the garrison on the German frontier to six legions, and one of his first acts as emperor was to unleash them across the Rhine. They were commanded by the son of that Drusus who had first invaded Germany. This young man had already taken the name of Germanicus, both from his father's exploits and as a statement of intent.

The relative failure of the Romans before AD 14 had rallied more tribes to Arminius. He was joined even by those Cherusci led by his uncle Inguiomer who had formerly been hostile. Another family member, Segestes, had remained loyal to Rome, at great cost to his personal popularity with his tribesmen. These men, incited by Arminius, finally penned Segestes in a woodland fort and laid siege to it. Segestes sent his son Segimundus to ask for help from the Romans. The son did so with great reluctance, because he had once been a priest in the Roman religion but had abandoned his calling to join Arminius, though he appears to have subsequently returned to his father's side.

Germanicus was well aware of the importance of encouraging deserters, so he welcomed the young man into the embrace of Rome and hurried to the relief of Segestes. His sudden arrival led to the capture of a number of young German noblemen and also of Thudsnelda, the wife of Arminius. Thudsnelda was pregnant with Arminius' child, and not best pleased at being reunited with her father Segestes.

She showed her husband's spirit more than her father's. Not for her tears or the pleas of a supplicant. She tightly clasped her hands to her chest and fixed her gaze on the swelling of her child in her belly ... the wife of Arminius later gave birth to a male child who was brought up in Ravenna.

Tacitus *Annals* 1.58

Arminius was beside himself with fury. Tacitus has him exclaim:

'What a noble father! What a mighty general! That's a heroic army which needs all its strength to abduct a single pregnant woman. I personally have seen the

fall of three legions and their commanders. I have fought my war against men
in arms, not with treachery against women with child. Look in our sacred
groves and you will find the Roman standards which I dedicated to our
German gods. Let Segestes and his priestly son live among the conquered –
they have countenanced the symbols of Roman domination between the Rhine
and the Elbe, and for that they should never be forgiven. … We have shaken off
Augustus and his heir Tiberius. Why should we cower from an inexperienced
teenager and his mutinous army? If you choose your fatherland, your ancestors
and your ancient way of life over Roman settlements and tyranny, then follow
me to glory and freedom – otherwise join Segestes in humiliation and slavery.'

> Tacitus *Annals* 1.59

Germanicus now sent a flying column to plunder the Bructeri, a tribe
allied to Arminius, and pushed towards the site of the Varian disaster in
the Teutoburg forest.

In the field, the bones of the soldiers lay scattered about, each where he had
fallen either standing his ground or trying to flee. There were bits of weapons,
and the bones of horses amongst them, and human heads had been nailed to
the trunks of the surrounding trees. In these groves stood the barbarian altars
where the tribunes and leading centurions had been sacrificed.

> Tacitus *Annals* 1.61

Germanicus gave a decent burial to the fallen (archaeology has found
where bones weathered by the elements were later solemnly interred).
Then his army turned with redoubled fury to the pursuit of Arminius.
Arminius, as always, fell back deeper into the forest as the Romans
advanced, once turning to savage a column of cavalry which advanced
too carelessly. When the Romans were deep in the forests, he struck. As
always he chose to let the terrain fight for him. The Romans were caught
on boggy ground, unable to use their cavalry and floundering through
the soft mud in their heavy armour. Finally the Romans managed to
throw up an earthwork and made camp behind it. Arminius was prepared
to accept this modest success, and perhaps ambush the Romans as they
withdrew. His uncle Inguiomer had other ideas. He hoped to inflict a last,
crushing blow on the Romans which would drive them from Germany
forever. The tribesmen were persuaded to attack the Roman camp

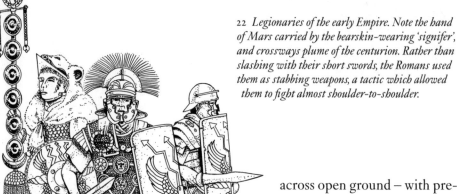

22 *Legionaries of the early Empire. Note the hand of Mars carried by the bearskin-wearing 'signifer', and crossways plume of the centurion. Rather than slashing with their short swords, the Romans used them as stabbing weapons, a tactic which allowed them to fight almost shoulder-to-shoulder.*

across open ground – with predictable results. Delighted to have their enemies in the open where their superior arms and discipline could tell, the Romans chopped the German attack to pieces and chased its remnants deep into the forest.

This brief victory gave the Romans breathing space in which to make a dignified retreat to the Rhine. They did not return for another two years, but in AD 16, Arminius received word that the Romans had appeared in force on the banks of the river Weser. Arminius hastened to the river, and asked the Romans on the other side if his brother Flavus was among them. For though Arminius had broken with Rome, his brother remained a loyal and apparently trusted officer in the legions. Flavus came to the river bank, and an extraordinary conversation followed. Arminius asked how Flavus had lost an eye and was told it was in one of the early excursions of Tiberius into Germany. Arminius asked what compensation Flavus had received for his injury and was told of various decorations and a pay rise. Flavus then urged his brother to ask for Roman mercy, pointing out that his wife and son were unharmed in Italy. In response, Arminius urged Flavus to return to 'the fatherland, his ancestral freedom, the gods of his homeland; to hear the prayers of his mother that her son would not desert and betray his family, his tribe and his people.'

The conversation became a shouting match, and Flavus had to be physically prevented from taking his horse and sword across the river to deal with his brother, who stood on the other side hurling curses and abuse at Flavus as he was led away.

Arminius mustered his forces, and sent envoys to see whether all of his opponents were as resolute as Flavus. Horsemen rode to the gates of the Roman camp and offered any deserters wives, lands, and pay of 100 sesterces per day for the duration of the war. The offer was made in fluent Latin, so that the Romans would know that some of their erstwhile comrades were already in service with Arminius.

At Idistavisus, near modern Minden, the two sides met in battle. Arminius had chosen his ground well, with a slight slope favouring his soldiers, and the woods at his back. The Germans fought with their normal impetuous fury, but this was the kind of warfare at which the Romans excelled. The Germans were driven back until Arminius himself was at bay and almost captured.

The Cherusci were being pushed back from the hills. Arminius was conspicuous among them, striking out, and though wounded, sustaining the fight with hand and voice. He threw himself at the archers, but was thrown back.... But by a violent physical effort combined with the weight of his horse he burst through. Some say the Chauci among the Roman auxiliaries recognized him even though he had smeared his face with blood to prevent this. These men opened their lines to let him through.

Tacitus *Annals* 2.18

Despite their defeat the Germans were determined to continue their resistance. Again they made a stand, this time choosing a site between a treacherous bog near a river (probably the Aller) and some woodland. It appears that they also constructed a fence of the same type that was used to trap Varus. Germanicus was happy to fight the Germans anywhere that they were prepared to make a stand, and a further grim struggle found the Romans with the river at their backs fighting the Germans who had the bog to theirs. In the end, the huge mass of the German warriors told against them. Their smaller opponents were much better at fighting at close quarters, and had the arms and tactics to do so. It did not help that Arminius played only a minor part in this battle, probably still disabled from his recent wound. His uncle Inguiomer took command and made a fair fist of it, but finally, says Tacitus, 'fortune rather than his courage abandoned him'. The Germans broke, and with nowhere to run they took heavy casualties before nightfall came to their rescue.

This victory brought the tribe of the Angrivarii over to the Roman side, and it is probable that others were wavering. But Germanicus over-reached himself. He had decided to outflank the German army by going around them by sea. More than a thousand transports laden with soldiers sailed from the mouth of the Rhine and proceeded northward up the coast. The campaign against the Cherusci was deemed a 'success', but it was not conclusive enough for Germanicus to establish a permanent base. He re-embarked his men and set out to campaign nearer Gaul. The idea of moving the army by sea was a bold one, for the Romans were not naturally a seafaring nation, and they had already suffered for their lack of seamanship on the outward journey, when a storm had destroyed some ships. They proved themselves landlubbers once again by being totally unable to cope with a massive summer storm that rolled in from the North Sea. The local tribe, the Marsi, reported that their beaches were strewn with debris and corpses from the disaster, which claimed a sub-stantial part of the Roman army.

Undeterred, Germanicus prepared to invade again, though this time by land. But the emperor Tiberius had had enough. The ghosts of Varus and his lost legions had been appeased by the Roman victories. There was no point in expending further valuable armies and gold in the tem-porary conquest of forests and swamps. If the recidivist Germans were so opposed to Roman civilization, they did not deserve it. Germanicus was ordered back to Rome. There he celebrated a triumph for his victories, parading before him the young son of Arminius, born in captivity and who had never seen his father. But after the year AD 17 the Roman con-quest of Germany effectively ceased as an active enterprise, and in AD 19 Germanicus was dead, possibly from poison. Arminius had won.

Arminius celebrated by turning on Maroboduus and defeating him in battle. As Tacitus commented in his *Germania*, a sure way to defeat the Germans was to accommodate their vices. As soon as the threat of Roman occupation was lifted, tribal feuding began again in earnest, and Arminius found himself pitted against his uncle in a power struggle. He won by recruiting the powerful Langobards and Semnones to his cause, but his position was by no means secure. Tacitus comments,

I find in the writings of some senators at that time that a letter was received from chief Adgondestrius. He promised to kill Arminius if the Romans would send him poison for that purpose. He was told in reply that 'Rome is revenged on her enemies in the open by military force, not in the dark by treason.'

Tacitus *Annals* 2.88

This relaxed attitude was almost immediately justified. In AD 19, when he was just thirty-seven years of age, Arminius was killed by his own relatives who claimed – how justly will now never be known – that he was attempting to set himself up as overlord of all Germany. Rome was to derive one further crumb of satisfaction from their German setback. By AD 47, the Cherusci were so reduced by internal feuding and endless warfare with the Chatti that they asked the Roman emperor Claudius for a king. Claudius sent them the grandson of Sigimer, and the nephew of Arminius. The new king of the Cherusci was Italicus, son of Flavus, the Roman officer and brother of Arminius.

CHAPTER 11

THE TERRIBLE REVENGE
OF BOUDICCA

*She was a very tall woman, and she looked terrifying. Her eyes were fierce,
and her voice was harsh. Her tawny hair fell to her hips in a great mass.
For her clothing she invariably wore a great golden torc around her neck
and a multi-coloured tunic. A thick cloak was thrown over all this and
fastened with a brooch. As she spoke, she grasped a spear to aid her
in terrifying everyone who saw her.*
Cassius Dio *History* 62.2

To rule her subject peoples, Rome relied on the projection of power and
the support of local aristocracies. A Roman army could fight in only one
place at a time, but if correctly positioned it could cow several different
places into submission. Likewise, if the local elites had more to gain than
to lose from aligning themselves with Rome, then the hearts and minds of
their people would follow. Rome lost Germany after losing the support
of the German nobility. They learned nothing from the experience and
proceeded, through criminal greed and stupidity, to come within an ace
of losing Britain as well.

Even before the revolt of Boudicca, Romans and Britons were thoroughly disillusioned with each other. The emperor Claudius had
launched the invasion of Britain in AD 43. He hoped for military glory to
boost his reputation, and for the reputed riches of the island to replenish
the level of imperial coffers diminished by his profligate predecessor
Gaius (better known to posterity as Caligula). For their part, some
Britons, for example the Trinovantes, had turned to Rome for relief from
the oppression of other tribes. Some petty kings, looking across the

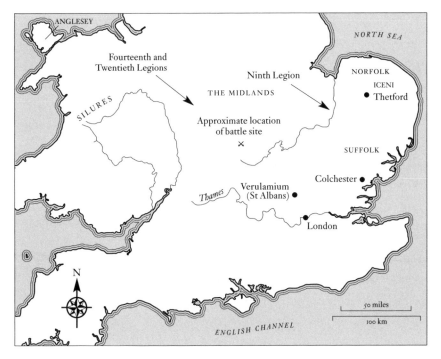

23 *Britannia. Boudicca's horde swept from Thetford to London by way of Colchester before being drawn by Paulinus to a decisive battle somewhere in the Midlands. Even today archaeologists can find traces of the devastation the avenging Britons left in their wake.*

channel, had seen that the Roman occupation of Gaul had brought peace, wealth and even high political office to those noblemen quick enough to adjust to the changed conditions.

Now, almost twenty years later, the Romans invaders were still fighting. They had found the reputed wealth of Britannia was largely an illusion, and the gold, furs and pearls which the island did produce could be found with less trouble elsewhere. The leadership of the indomitable Caractacus inspired resistance from the fens of East Anglia to the mountains of Wales, and even long-conquered areas had a tendency to flare up in renewed revolt. The governor Ostorius Scapula had died in harness, worn out by continual and often fruitless campaigning. His successor, Suetonius Paulinus, cared less for the Britons than to establish a high military reputation. He had campaigned successfully against the Silures of Wales, and now turned his attention to the Druidic cult on the island of Anglesey. The Druids were a focus of religious life in Britain and they actively encouraged resistance to Rome. But Paulinus' attempt to destroy the cult root and branch further alienated Britons who already considered the Romans intolerant and arrogant oppressors.

Tension ran particularly high in the land of the Trinovantes, unwilling hosts of the provincial centre of Colchester. The emperor Claudius himself had come to Colchester to mark the climax of his campaign of conquest, and Colchester was the only city in Britain to enjoy the status of *colonia*. The retired Roman veterans who had settled there felt they had earned the right to help themselves to the lands, possessions and women of the local tribesmen.

A splendid temple had been raised to the imperial cult (at the expense of the locals, naturally). It was customary to appoint local dignitaries to priesthoods in the cult as a way of binding them closer to Rome. In Colchester the custom had been perverted so that the unfortunate priests were required to pour out their personal fortunes to perform their duties for the benefit of Roman tradesmen and moneylenders.

The historian Dio said Boudicca claimed that the Britons felt 'despised and trampled underfoot by men who know nothing else than how to secure gain'. The Romans thought so little of the boggy island and its recalcitrant inhabitants that the emperor Nero seriously considered abandoning Britain altogether.

Some time in AD 60, events came to a crisis. Paulinus launched his attack on Anglesey, with the scene splendidly described by Tacitus:

In order to cope with a difficult and treacherous shore, he had constructed a number of flat-bottomed boats. These took over the infantry, while the cavalry crossed partly by fording the shallows, and partly by swimming their horses, and in this way they gained a beachhead on the island. On the opposite shore the Britons stood, gathered close together and ready for the fight. Women were seen running through the ranks in wild disorder; wearing funeral clothing and their hair streaming in the wind, whilst they waved flaming torches. Their whole appearance was that of Furies in a frantic rage. The Druids were drawn up in their ranks, hands uplifted, invoking the gods, and pouring forth horrible curses. The unfamiliarity of the coming combat struck the Romans with awe and terror. They stood in stunned amazement as though paralyzed, unmoving and easy marks for the enemy.

Tacitus *Annals* 14.30

Strange and unnerving as the scene may have been, the warriors on the island were no match for the disciplined legionaries once they had mustered their nerve. Superstition turned to horror as the advancing troops found 'groves devoted to inhuman rites … altars covered with the blood of captives killed by a people who considered it their duty to consult their gods through human entrails.' When the Romans left, they had done their best to purge Anglesey of all life, human, animal and – in the case of the sacred groves – vegetable.

Worse was to come. On the other side of Britain the king of the Iceni had died. Tacitus gives this king's name as Prasutagus, but apart from his single mention, this name is not substantiated. It was long thought that coins bearing his name had been found in East Anglia, but modern research has disproved this. What is certain is that this king was one of those who had thrown in his lot with the Romans. He was appointed king of the Iceni in 47 after a Roman attempt to disarm the tribe provoked an unsuccessful revolt. (It was Roman policy at that time to rule difficult and isolated parts of their frontiers through kings dependent on Rome; such rulers being known as 'client kings'.) The Iceni had profited greatly from Prasutagus' loyalty. In 1981 the site of a very well-appointed building at Thetford was excavated. This was possibly Prasutagus' royal residence. His kingdom occupied much of modern Suffolk and Norfolk and was well situated to trade with Roman Gaul.

As far as we can determine from archaeology and our sources, Prasutagus left a peaceful, prosperous and modestly contented kingdom. He left it partly to his daughters, and partly to the Roman emperor, believing that this would secure the future of his kingdom.

Within days of the will becoming known, the Iceni were visited by emissaries of the imperial procurator Catus Decianus. Just as it was the job of Suetonius Paulinus to oversee the military and legal affairs of Roman Britain, it was the concern of Decianus to look after the financial affairs of the emperor.

It seems that Decianus also had orders to reclaim a substantial debt owed by Prasutagus to Seneca, a Roman philosopher who was also one of Nero's most favoured advisers. What happened next is uncertain. One interpretation is that the Romans either wilfully misread Prasutagus' intentions and treated the lands of the Iceni as now being Roman property, or they believed that the terms of the will gave them considerable latitude in selecting what had been given to them. Another possibility is that when Prasutagus' widow could not raise the coin to repay Seneca's debt, the remainder of the kingdom was seized as surety. A third possibility is that the Romans simply got carried away.

It was as if Rome had received the whole country as a gift. All the chief men were stripped of their ancestral possessions, and the king's relatives were enslaved… whilst the centurions plundered the kingdom, their slaves pillaged the royal household as though these were the spoils of war.

Tacitus *Annals* 14.31

Prasutagus' queen protested bitterly, and for her pains was taken outside and publicly flogged as a defaulting debtor. Then, in violation of decency, law and basic common sense these same Roman officials raped Prasutagus' two young daughters, the heirs to the kingdom. (This latter act was more than mere lust – it probably made the daughters unmarriageable, and thus destroyed the royal line.) Had Decianus spent months working out how to change a basically contented people into rabidly vindictive and violent foes, he could hardly have done better.

The outraged Iceni turned to their queen. It is possible that the patriarchal Romans failed to see how much authority the widow of Prasutagus still wielded. Modern reading of the sources suggests that this woman was also one of the chief priestesses of the kingdom. Her name, Boudicca, may be related to the Celtic goddess Boudiga, and may even have been the title of her office. The prayers and rites she performed for the goddess Andraste, suggest a certain familiarity with ritual. As we have the name of the queen from Tacitus, it may even be that he mistakenly reported the queen's job description as her name. What is certain is that her name was not Boadicea as once rendered; this dates back to an error in a medieval text.

Cassius Dio puts a long speech into the mouth of Boudicca which, though an invention, does give some idea of how the British perceived Roman rule.

'Is there any treatment so shameful or hurtful that we have not suffered it since the Romans came to Britain? Isn't it true that they have taken almost everything that we own, and then forced us to pay taxes on what remains? Don't we have to pay tax for our bodies themselves, and have to put these same bodies to Roman service to plough and tend their fields? It would have been better if they had made us slaves at once, and at least put an end to our having to ransom ourselves every year. Or better still, they should have killed us at once, and put an end to it.'

Cassius Dio *History* 62.3

As soon as they heard that the Iceni were up in arms, the neighbouring Trinovantes made common cause with the rebels, and both tribes descended with a single purpose upon Colchester. Colchester was swept by conflicting rumours and alarms, but with the army in Wales, the local authorities could hardly muster two hundred lightly armed men for the city's defence. Efforts to prepare fortifications were hampered by the tribesmen in the city, who sabotaged work in every way they could. Consequently, when Boudicca launched her attack on the city, the Romans had not yet prepared even a defensive ditch or wall. Some of the veterans retreated within the Temple of Caesar, and from there saw their wives and children massacred. They themselves held out for two days before their redoubt too was taken. Archaeology shows that Colchester was literally levelled to the ground. After burning everything combustible, the Britons systematically flattened every structure of brick or clay, leaving the foundations shorn away at ground level.

From here the army turned south towards London, centre of Roman commerce in Britain. On their way they met their first Roman opposition. The general Vespasian (who was to become emperor after Nero) had also campaigned in Britain, and he had there a young relative, Petillius Cerialis. Petillius was to gain a reputation for harebrained military escapades, of which this was the first. Some detachments of the Ninth Legion were in southern Britain on special duties (such detachments were called *vexillationes*). Petillius gathered these together and confidently marched to meet Boudicca. He was stunned to find that support for the rebel queen had snowballed along the way (not least because the rebels arbitrarily dispatched those who were reluctant to join them), and his small army was easily outnumbered one hundred to one. Petillius' rudimentary force was routed, and only he and a small force of cavalry survived the subsequent massacre.

Meanwhile Suetonius Paulinus had hastened to London, no easy feat given the hostility of the population he had to hurry through. He discovered that the guilty procurator Decianus had formed his own conclusions about the Roman army's chances and already taken ship to Gaul. Reluctantly, Paulinus was forced to concede that London was undefendable and he pulled his army back, fully aware that many of the city's inhabitants would be unable to evade the British nemesis closing in on them.

Boudicca was not interested in taking prisoners or ransoming them, or any of the commerce of war. The enemy were set on slaughter, with scaffolds, fire and crucifixions, like men taking what vengeance they could before retribution came down on them.

Tacitus *Annals* 14.24

Cassius Dio was even more graphic in his account:

Those who were taken captive by the Britons were subjected to every known form of outrage. The worst and most bestial atrocity committed by their captors was the following. They hung up naked the noblest and most distinguished women and then cut off their breasts and sewed them to their mouths, in order to make the victims appear to be eating them; afterwards they impaled the women on sharp skewers run lengthwise through the entire body. All this they did to the accompaniment of sacrifices, banquets, and wanton behaviour, not only in all their other sacred places, but particularly in the grove of Andraste. This was their name for Victory, and they regarded her with most exceptional reverence.

Cassius Dio *History* 62.7

From these descriptions it is evident that neither Britons nor Romans regarded this as an ordinary war. The sheer visceral hate that the Britons showed their conquerors is a testament to the failure of Roman rule in the province, a failure which is tacitly acknowledged by even the Roman historians themselves. Like Colchester, London was burned to the ground. The fire was so hot that it formed a layer of baked clay about the houses, and this stratum still remains, now some thirteen feet (four metres) below the streets of modern London.

All this is not to suppose that Boudicca was no more than at the head of an unruly mob. She controlled her troops with surprising skill and generalship, and made sure that her conquests were well looted before being razed. The silver thus won was made into coin to finance her revolt. She also did commendably well in keeping her huge force intact and preventing it from breaking into smaller groups of looters.

She now turned on Verulamium (the modern St Albans), which went the way of earlier conquests. By now an estimated 70,000 Romans and Roman sympathizers had been killed, some of them horribly. Revenge may have been satisfied, but the revolt now had its own momentum. In taking up arms, the Britons had failed to sow their crops for the coming year; therefore they had to either provision themselves from captured Roman storehouses or starve. Nor was Rome likely to forgive. Either the legions would be thrown from Britain once and for all, or inevitably, the Britons would come under the yoke of the vindictive Romans.

Paulinus had the Fourteenth Legion, veterans of the Twentieth who were again under arms, and whatever other men he had been able to gather as auxiliaries. His force numbered less than 11,000 men. It desperately needed reinforcement by the Second Legion commanded by Poenius Postumus. But Postumus was encamped in the west and obdurately refusing to move. Postumus may have felt he was doing better service where he was, holding down the dangerous tribes of the west, or maybe the surrounding countryside was too hostile to permit him to break camp. (The fact that Postumus, the camp prefect, was in command tells us that something bad had already happened to the legion's legate.) Paulinus needed every man he had to stop Boudicca and was in no mood for excuses. Postumus would not be forgiven for disobeying orders.

The Britons whom Paulinus was fighting were not very different from the Celtic warriors of Gaul who had opposed Caesar. They were lightly armed, mainly with spears. Swords and armour were for the rich. Unlike the Gauls, the Britons mainly fought on foot, though the aristocracy formed an elite cavalry force. They were also one of the last armies of antiquity to use light chariots, though these were used to move small bands of men quickly around the battlefield rather than as fighting vehicles. Dio reports these as charging the Romans, but they would have been little use in this capacity. Despite popular legend, the chariots did not have scythed wheels and would have been a major hazard to their own side had they been so equipped.

The Britons kept huge mastiffs which made superb hunting dogs. A number of apocryphical sources report that these were also trained to fight alongside their masters in battle. As these animals were almost the size of a modern St Bernard, they must have been rather disconcerting opponents. Another offputting habit of the Britons was that they painted themselves blue with woad before going into battle. Apart from terrifying their enemies, the Britons benefited from the antiseptic qualities of the woad, which helped to prevent wounds from becoming infected.

The main strength of the British army lay in its numbers. The Romans, who were always inclined to exaggerate the numbers of their enemies, put Boudicca's forces at 230,000 men. Even if the British queen had half that number, they still massively outnumbered the Romans. We know almost nothing of how Boudicca's army was organized. British society had been undergoing wrenching social changes. The old system was of separate tribes ruled by kings (or queens; Tacitus tells us that 'the Britons do not discriminate with regard to the sex of their rulers'). These rulers had the aid and counsel of a band of nobles who, like their followers, lived in villages, where much of the land was held in common as pasture for the villagers' flocks.

The Britons shared the religious beliefs of the Gauls; indeed Britain was something of a religious centre to the Gauls, and the potential this gave Britain as a focus for revolt was one of the reasons why the Romans had originally invaded the island. It was also why the usually tolerant Romans were determined to exterminate the Druidic cult.

Paulinus may have taken advantage of Boudicca's religious office to bring the Britons to the battleground of his choosing. We only know that this was somewhere in the Midlands. It is believed that Paulinus devastated British religious shrines in the area, knowing this would draw Boudicca to him. The Romans were drawn up in a defile with steep slopes protecting their flanks, and a gentle slope running away from them. At their backs was a dense forest. Paulinus had chosen carefully. His position meant that the Britons could not surround his men, but it also meant that the Romans could not escape unless the Britons were defeated. It was time to do or die.

The Britons entered the battleground in disorganized groups each clustered about local chiefs or nobles according to their prestige, the crowd steadily pooling into a huge mass at the bottom of the slope on which the Romans waited. The British army had brought with it a horde of women and children who drew up their wagons in a line across the rear of the army. The women then chose comfortable positions and settled down to cheer their menfolk on to victory. The British army was in constant motion, with trumpets being blown and challenges and abuse being hurled at the Romans. The warriors wore coloured plaids and were mostly bare-chested.

Boudicca was among them, her two daughters accompanying her in her chariot. The Romans watched her go from tribe to tribe, urging them to make this one final effort, while (says Tacitus) she also assured her troops that it was quite proper for British warriors to go into battle under the leadership of a woman. Tacitus has given us a stirring speech on Boudicca's behalf with the general theme of 'give me liberty or give me death'. This speech included the observation that the Britons were so numerous that Boudicca doubted that the Romans would be able even to withstand the clamour and war cries of so great a host. One legion was already defeated (a reference to the men of Petillius) and another was afraid to move. For herself, Boudicca was not fighting for her lands or from the pride of her ancient lineage. She was there to avenge the rape of her daughters and the whip marks on her own body. And like every Briton, she was there to defend her freedom.

'Look round, and see how many you are. Consider our proud, warlike spirit
and think of all the reasons for vengeance for which we have taken up the
sword. Right here is where we have to win or die gloriously. There is no choice.
I am a woman, and I am certain of what I should do. You men must choose
whether you wish to live in disgrace and die as slaves.'
Tacitus *Annals* 14.36

In her role as priestess, Boudicca prayed to the goddess Andraste for the victory, and then released a hare from her cloak and watched its course as it ran between the waiting battle lines. This was for purposes of augury, as the hare had strong religious connotations for the Britons (rabbits on the other hand were unknown, as they were only introduced to Britain by the Normans 1,000 years later).

Paulinus is given different speeches by Dio and Tacitus, but both have common themes which Paulinus undoubtedly stressed. First, their opponents were only Britons. Second, victory was always sweeter against overwhelming odds. Dio includes a colourful description of the tortures awaiting any Romans who were captured, and Tacitus finishes Paulinus' speech with a hint that, if victorious, his soldiers had licence to do as they wished in the lands they had reconquered.

Thereupon the armies approached each other, the barbarians with much shouting mingled with menacing battle-songs, but the Romans silently and in order until they came within a javelin's throw of the enemy. Then, while their enemies were still advancing at a walk, the signal came for the Romans to charge. They rushed forward and hit the enemy at full tilt so that at the clash they easily broke through the opposing line. The immense numbers of the enemy meant that thereafter they were surrounded on all sides and the fighting took place everywhere at once. Their struggle took many forms. Skirmisher contended with skirmisher, heavy infantry fought similarly armed opponents, while cavalry clashed with cavalry. Another contest put the Roman archers against the barbarian chariots. The barbarians would launch their chariots at the Romans, throwing them into disorder; only themselves to be forced back by arrows, since the charioteers fought without armour. Here a horseman cut down foot-soldiers, there a troop of foot-soldiers hauled down a rider. Some Romans would advance against the chariots in close formation, and others would be scattered by them; sometimes the Britons would close with the archers and rout them, while others skipped aside from the arrows at a distance.

Cassius Dio *History* 62.12

From this report, and from that of Tacitus, we can get a rough idea of the battle. It would appear that the Romans first launched their heavy throwing spears (*pila*) and then hit the disorganized British before they could prepare their own charge. The cohorts struck the British in wedge formation and ploughed almost through their army. Though surrounded by the mass of Britons, the army kept its momentum, aided by the cavalry who charged to break the enemy where the resistance was stiffest. No Celtic army was at its best going backwards, and soon the Britons were faced with another problem. Deserters at the rear and warriors falling back were both crushed against the wagons that had brought their wives and families to the battlefield. For the Britons, who needed a frontage of at least four feet (just over one metre) to use their long spears or swing a broadsword effectively, this was a disaster. The Romans fought in close formation and stabbed rather than swung their short swords. For them, a congested battlefield was an opportunity rather than a problem. The almost defenceless British warriors were massacred, and their wives and children after that. Before the day was out, 80,000 Britons had died for the loss of 400 legionaries. The rebellion was effectively over.

Boudicca survived the battle, but she was living on borrowed time. The massacres in Colchester, London and St Albans had sealed her fate, and she would not have surrendered even if offered mercy. Instead she retired to her ancestral home and there took poison. The fate of her daughters is unknown, but they probably died with her. Dio tells us that the Britons gave her a magnificent funeral, as befitted a warrior queen. The later legend that her bones now lie under one of the platforms of King's Cross railway station is highly improbable.

Many Iceni who survived the battle did not survive its aftermath. Archaeology shows that the Romans systematically devastated their lands, even diverting watercourses away from their fields. This was a dubious tactic to employ in rainy East Anglia, but many Iceni died anyway since they had sown no crops that year. Any tribesmen captured by the Romans were either butchered or arbitrarily enslaved. It seemed that Paulinus did not aim to cow the Britons by terror – he seemed set on exterminating them altogether. His policy brought him into conflict with Julius Classicanus, the procurator who had replaced Catus Decianus. Classicanus had the job of making Britain pay its way in the Empire, and this was hard to do in a country with devastated fields and a fugitive population fighting a sullen guerrilla war. To British derision, a freed slave and a favourite of Nero was sent from Rome to arbitrate between governor and procurator, 'the Britons marvelling to see a general and his victorious army cringing to a slave'. They applauded the final decision though. Paulinus was replaced, and the Roman authorities wisely embarked on a policy of peace and rebuilding; which included rebuilding their relations with the British elites they needed to sustain their rule.

In the ensuing centuries of prosperity, the story of Boudicca was largely forgotten. In the nineteenth century it was recalled that the name Boudicca meant 'victory', and that the queen of the Iceni shared the name of Victoria with the queen who ruled over an empire more vast even than that of Rome. The warrior queen's unsavoury habits of wholesale massacre and torture were forgotten, and she became a national heroine. A statue of her, triumphant in her chariot (see plate 24), now looks over the Thames in London, the city she burned to the ground.

CHAPTER 12

JOSEPHUS: ROME'S RELUCTANT ENEMY

Vespasian came into Galilee. As to this coming of his ... and how he fought his first battle with me near the village of Taricheae, and how from there he went to [besiege me in] Jotapata, and how I was taken alive, and bound, and how I was afterward released ... I have accurately related.

Josephus *Autobiography* 74

Often all that we know of Rome's enemies is what the Romans themselves have chosen to tell us. Sometimes we are fortunate enough to have events described by those who witnessed them at first hand, as Caesar does with his Gallic campaigns, but this too is Roman history. The story of Josephus is uniquely different. He tells us, in his own words and from personal experience, what it was like to encounter the Roman army from the sharp end.

If this was not enough, Josephus later goes on to describe, in considerable detail, a major siege from the point of view of a close companion to the Roman general conducting operations. And still he is writing from personal experience. In short, Josephus had an extraordinary life, and we are fortunate that his writings have survived to tell us about it.

Josephus was a Jew, and a proud and practising member of that faith. At the same time he was an admirer of Rome, and deeply embarrassed by the rebellious habits of his countrymen. In part Josephus' writings attempt to prove to both Jews and Romans that he was an upstanding member of each culture; no easy feat given that Jews and Romans despised each other, and this caused Josephus no little soul-searching in his work.

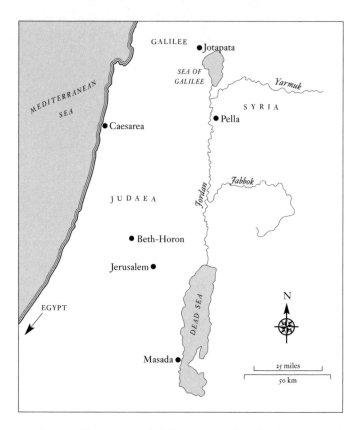

24 *Judaea at the time of the Jewish revolt. The Jewish people at this time were a majority only in the area around Jerusalem, while there was a particularly high proportion of Gentiles in Galilee. Masada had recently had its fortifications strengthened by Herod the Great.*

For example, he protests that the Jews who inspired the revolt of AD 66 were fanatics. Had they not led his people astray, claims Josephus, they would have remained loyal subjects of Rome. But the truth was that the Jews bitterly resented Roman rule, which had begun in AD 6, and were constantly ripe for rebellion. Certainly this had happened before. The small but proud Jewish nation sat at a nexus in the Middle East and had spent centuries rebelling against conquerors who swept across their lands from (for example) Babylon, Assyria, Egypt and Macedon. During periods of independence the Jews often rebelled against their own rulers. Even David, the great Jewish king who united the rival kingdoms of Israel and Judah, came very close to losing his throne to his rebellious subjects.

Nor were the last kings of Israel, Herod the Great (73–4 BC) and his hapless sons, popular with their subjects. Herod had come to power in the confused years where the Romans first seized suzerainty of Palestine. With shrewd diplomacy Herod rode out the political storms which accompanied Rome's transition from Republic to Empire, and left an indelible imprint on his country with a huge building programme in Jerusalem (where he began the reconstruction of the temple), at Jericho and elsewhere, where he built stadiums and theatres, and the fortress of Masada, which he strengthened to near-invulnerability.

Despite this, and some enlightened land reforms, Herod was a harsh ruler who was never truly accepted by the Jewish people. After his death in 4 BC, his son Archelaus was deposed as ruler of Judaea after ten turbulent years. Another son, Philip, inherited Galilee and Peraea. Philip was more successful, and ruled for thirty-three years. About the time of his death, and in the first year of the reign of the emperor Caligula, Joseph ben Matthias was born, scion of an ancient priestly family and son of a mother descended from Israel's Maccabean kings.

We know that Josephus was a gifted child, for he was far from bashful about it.

I made mighty progress in improving my learning, and quite evidently was superb at both memorizing and understanding my work. Therefore, when I was a child, and about fourteen years of age, I was greatly admired for my love of learning; and for this reason the high priests and chief men of the city frequently came together to me, in order to consult my opinion about the accurate understanding of points of the law.

Josephus *Autobiography* 2

Josephus studied under masters of each of the major Jewish sects, the Sadducees, Pharisees and Essenes, before finally deciding to become a Pharisee. This was almost the same thing, he assures his Roman readers, as becoming a Stoic (Stoicism was a respected and popular philosophy in Rome at that time).

In the year AD 64, with the emperor Nero ruling in Rome, Josephus travelled to that city as leader of a deputation seeking the release of some Jewish priests who had fallen foul of the Roman authorities. The Romans were well aware of the touchiness of the Jews, and also aware that they needed a stable Palestine on their eastern frontier, beyond which lay the rival power of Parthia. But this did not make them any fonder of either the Jews or their religion, which may have been what led to the arrest of the priests in the first place. The near-contemporary historian and senator, Tacitus, sums up the attitude of some Romans.

This worship, however introduced, is upheld by its antiquity; all their other customs, which are at once perverse and disgusting, owe their strength to their very badness ... among themselves they are inflexibly honest and ever ready to show compassion, though they regard the rest of mankind with all the hatred of enemies .... Those who come over to their religion have this lesson first instilled into them, to despise all gods, to disown their country, and to set at nought parents, children and brethren .... The Jews have purely mental conceptions of Deity, as one in essence. They call those profane who make representations of God in human shape out of perishable materials. They believe that Being to be supreme and eternal, neither capable of representation, nor of decay. They therefore do not allow any images to stand in their cities, much less in their temples. They do not flatter their kings with statues, nor honour our emperors in this way... the Jewish religion is tasteless and mean.

Tacitus *Histories 5*

Tacitus was writing after the Jewish war of AD 66, but there had been friction with the Jews before that. In AD 41 Nero's tolerant and liberal predecessor, Claudius, was forced to issue an edict recognizing that the Jewish people were different from Rome's other subjects.

Tiberius Claudius Caesar Augustus Germanicus, pontifex maximus, proclaims:... 'Therefore it is right that the Jews, who are in all the world under us, shall maintain their ancestral customs without hindrance. I now also command them to use this, my kindness, reasonably and not to despise the religious rites of the other nations, but to observe their own laws.'

Rome's suspicion and dislike were heartily reciprocated. While young Josephus was awed by the majesty of Rome, and flattered by the interest of Nero's wife Poppaea (who was instrumental in securing the release of the imprisoned priests), the Jewish people as a whole were less impressed. Apocalyptic writings were a popular genre at this time, and in the best-known of these, the Hebrew writer of Revelations effortlessly outdoes the calumnies of Tacitus.

I will show unto thee the judgment of the great whore that sits upon many waters: With whom the kings of the earth have committed fornication, and the inhabitants of the earth have been made drunk with the wine of her fornication … I saw a woman sit upon a scarlet coloured beast, full of names of blasphemy, having seven heads and ten horns. And the woman was arrayed in purple and scarlet, and decked with gold and precious stones and pearls, having a golden cup in her hand full of abominations and the filthiness of her fornication: And upon her forehead was a name written, 'Babylon the great, the mother of Harlots and abominations of the earth.'

In case his readers are having trouble with the analogy, the writer continues helpfully:

And here is the mind which hath wisdom. The seven heads are seven hills on which the woman sits. And the woman is that great city which reigns over the kings of the earth.

Revelations 17, passim

When Josephus returned to Palestine, it was to a land seething with plots and incipient rebellion. The rural poor had suffered a series of famines, and many of those unable to work their lands had taken to banditry, adding a further level of unpleasantness to country life already strained by the demands of Roman taxation. Relations between the Jewish elite and the Roman authorities had never recovered from the unsuccessful procuratorship of Pontius Pilate (AD 26–35) or the attempt of the emperor Caligula to have his statue installed in the Temple in Jerusalem; and a series of successive ineffectual procurators had failed to restore trust.

In these circumstances, the philosophy of the Zealots appealed to many. It combined religion with violent nationalism and had been about for decades (it is possible that two of the disciples of Jesus – Judas Iscariot and Simon were Zealots). Mostly their activities had been limited to attacks on Roman outposts and attempts to disrupt the tax collection, but a new generation of leaders, including the charismatic Eleazar bin Jair, advocated ever more open resistance. Yet more extreme and violent than the Zealots were the Sicarii, who were not only anti-Roman but equally opposed to any Jews whom they suspected of collaborating with the Romans. This latter group were more vulnerable, and accordingly made up the bulk of the Sicarii's victims. The name of this group came from the short curved knife, the *sica*, favoured by the assassins. Often victims were killed in the middle of a crowd and the assassin, his knife tucked under his tunic, made his getaway in the confusion. Among the Sicarii's victims was Jonathan, the High Priest, whose murder heightened the atmosphere of fear and tension.

In a manner reminiscent of modern terror groups, the Sicarii kidnapped leading Jews to extort the release of their members that had been captured. Their conduct led to a ferocious purge by the procurator Albinus, and as is often the case with such purges, the innocent suffered with the guilty. But for the Jewish people, the final straw came with the replacement of Albinus by his successor Gessius Florus in AD 64. It is hard to reconstruct exactly what happened, as we have only the account of Josephus to go by, and he was not an impartial witness. He despised and feared the Zealots, and becomes positively poetical in his loathing for the Sicarii. He was no admirer of Florus either, and says that the first years of Florus' rule were marked by shockingly blatant misgovernment and corruption. Eventually (says Josephus), Florus decided that the only way to conceal his crimes was to hide them in a more general conflagration, and he set about deliberately provoking the Jews into revolt.

For he expected that if the peace continued, he should have the Jews for his accusers before Caesar; but that if he could procure them to make a revolt, he should divert their laying lesser crimes to his charge by a misery that was so much greater. He therefore did every day augment their calamities, in order to induce them to a rebellion.

Josephus *The Jewish War* 14.3

When the Jews protested their mistreatment, Florus had the protesters arrested. When crowds gathered in a peaceful demonstration they were attacked. Accusing the Jews of perpetrating the very violence of which they had been victim, Florus ordered the Jewish community leaders to present themselves to him at the city gates for an explanation. When they gathered,

The soldiers surrounded them and struck them down with clubs. As they fled, they were ridden down by horsemen. A great many were killed by Roman blows, but more died in the violence of the crush, for there was terrible crowding about the gates, with everybody trying to get away before anyone else, and as a result no one escaped quickly. There was a virtual massacre of anyone who had fallen down, for they were suffocated, broken to pieces by the multitude trampling over them; so much so that almost no one could be identified with certainty by the relatives who came to bury them. The soldiers fell on anyone that they caught up with and beat them mercilessly.

Josephus *The Jewish War* 15.5

It was the very last straw. Alone of all the people of the Empire, the Jews had the right to sacrifice to their god for the emperor of Rome, whereas other peoples performed sacrifice directly to the emperor. But now they refused to do even that. This effectively signalled the start of a general revolt. Thus goes the account of Josephus.

We must treat this account with great caution. With Josephus stuck firmly on the fence between antagonistic Jews and Romans, we can hardly expect him to blame the war on either party. Instead he alleges that a rapacious Roman administrator (something of a stock figure in anti-Roman revolts) and a mixture of fanatics and religious charlatans dragged a well-intentioned majority to war between them.

In fact, a cycle of Jewish xenophobia and Roman over-reaction which had been escalating for several years now finally boiled over. The spark may have been an incident which Josephus mentions in passing. Nero himself handed down a judgment in favour of a Gentile who owned a building used as a synagogue. The Gentile and his friends indulged in an unseemly display of triumphalism, and the procurator used considerable force to suppress the subsequent disturbances. Tacitus confirms that religious sentiment was a powerful factor:

Most people were quite convinced that the ancient writings of their priests predicted that at this time a great power was to grow in the East, and that rulers from Judaea would attain universal sovereignty. In fact these strange prophesies pointed to Titus and Vespasian, but the people, blinded by ambition, had decided that this great destiny was meant for themselves, and no disasters would persuade them otherwise.

Tacitus *Histories* 5.13

What does seem certain is that the rebellion of AD 66 was not a smoothly planned coup but rather an unplanned sequence of events which rushed all concerned willy-nilly into war. Consequently, arrangements among the newly liberated Jews had a definitely ad hoc nature. While various factions contended for control of Jerusalem in general and of the temple in particular, leaders from the foremost Jewish families were sent to control outlying areas of Palestine.

Thus it came about that Joseph ben Matthias, later to be known as Flavius Josephus, found himself military commander of Galilee and regarding the future with considerable apprehension.

At this time the Jews were not the only people in Palestine; indeed, they predominated only in a relatively small area centred on Jerusalem. Galilee was more demographically mixed than most areas, and in fact the name comes from a Hebrew phrase meaning 'circle of foreigners'. Josephus had his work cut out handling this mixed population whose sentiments ranged from rabidly anti-Roman to vigorously pro-peace.

We accept Josephus' claim that he successfully handled these various factions for the simple reason that he was still in his job when the Romans arrived in AD 67. By this time Rome was taking the Jewish war very seriously. They had already paid once for underestimating the fanaticism which drove the lightly armed Jewish rebels against the legions. The Roman general Cestius Gallus had been defeated at Beth-Horon and the Twelfth Legion cut to pieces, losing its prized eagle to the rebels.

Despite the victory at Beth-Horon, the Jewish army was no match for the Romans in the field, and the arrival of the legions in Galilee sent Josephus' main rival, John of Gischala, speedily packing to Jerusalem.

Galilee became a scene of fire and blood from end to end; it was spared no misery and no calamity; the one refuge for the hunted inhabitants was in the cities fortified by Josephus.

Josephus *The Jewish War* 3.4.1 63

25 Jewish light infantry on the walls of Jerusalem. What the rebels lacked in equipment they made up for with fanatical determination. Slings were a favoured weapon of shepherds, and military slingers often used pellets of lead which could be hurled at lethal velocities.

Josephus now took advantage of his own precautions and retreated to the hill fortress of Jotapata, which had already successfully repelled one Roman assault. There he was besieged by three legions commanded by the future emperor Vespasian. This extract from Josephus' own account of the siege gives a flavour of the hard fighting and stratagems and counter-stratagems which took place over the next forty days.

Vespasian then set his siege engines to throwing stones and darts all over the city. There were 160 of these machines and their principal task was to clear defenders from the ramparts. Some of these engines were designed to throw long spears, which they did very noisily. And other machines had been designed to throw stones weighing a talent, or fire or a great mass of arrows. So effective was this bombardment that the Jews not only kept off the ramparts, but also avoided those places within the walls which were within reach of the engines. At the same time as the engines, a multitude of Arabian archers plied their trade, along with slingers and dartsmen. Yet the Jews were not quiescent under this attack. When it was impossible to hurl missiles down on the Romans they sallied out of the city like robber bands and in groups they pulled away the barriers that protected those working on the siege trenches, and killed them while they were thus exposed; and when those workmen gave way, they destroyed the embankment, and burnt the wooden parts of it, including the barriers themselves.

Josephus *The Jewish War* 3.7.9

Despite the vigour of the defence, Josephus realized that the fortress was doomed. He was already making plans to abandon the place when it was betrayed to the Romans by a deserter. The Romans stormed into the town and massacred its inhabitants. But Josephus and forty companions escaped to take refuge in an underground shelter. This security proved ephemeral, as one of the women with them then ventured out and was captured.

Once discovered by the Romans, those within the shelter faced surrender or death. Josephus was all for surrender, but his companions were prepared to die, and determined to take Josephus with them. In his own words, Josephus relates what happened next.

'And now,' said Josephus, 'since we are all certain to die, come on, let chance decide our common fate. We will draw lots, and the first person who draws the lot will be killed by the second, and so on. That way fate will choose the sequence of our deaths, yet we shall be spared from killing ourselves'…. This proposal was considered reasonable; so after persuading everyone to take a lot, Josephus took one for himself also. Each man then killed the other in the determined sequence, each supposing their general would die with them and thinking that death shared with Josephus was sweeter than life. Yet at the end it turned out that Josephus and one other man were left! Who can say whether this happened by chance, or by the goodness of God?

Josephus *The Jewish War* 3.8.7

Readers may speculate on other ways this miracle might have come about. Especially as Josephus then persuaded his surviving companion that it was equally undesirable to die by the lottery or to kill a fellow countryman. The pair surrendered to the Romans. The Roman soldiery were all for adding Josephus to Jotapata's already impressive body count, but Vespasian ordered that he be spared. Josephus attributes this to a

21 (*above*) Arminius on his warhorse bursts through the Roman lines. With his name 're-Teutonicized' to Hermann, Arminius became a national hero to the German people who were rediscovering their sense of national identity in the nineteenth century. The above painting, *The Battle of Hermann in the Teutoburg Forest* (*c*. 1846) by Wilhelm Lindenschmit, is one of many examples of idealizing art from this era.

22 (*right*) A bust possibly of the young Arminius, *c*. 16 BC – AD 21. The identification is doubtful, since the Romans seldom depicted enemy leaders in sculpture, and even more seldom the few who bested them in war. However, the earnest, troubled-looking man here may well look as Arminius did while he was in Roman service.

23 (*left*) Stele of a Roman centurion, AD 49–50. Many of the Roman tombstones in Colchester were preserved by being thrown face down to the ground before they had the chance to become weathered. Note the vine rod of office in the centurion's right hand, and the details of his career inscribed on the stone below.

24 (*below*) Boudicca as the Victorians saw her. This statue by Thomas Thornycroft (erected 1902) on the Thames embankment in London shows a noble-looking warrior queen with her inexplicably bare-breasted daughters in an implausibly scythed chariot.

25 (*above*) The spoils of war. In this scene
from the Arch of Titus at the entrance to the
Roman forum we see some of the booty from
the sack of Jerusalem, so vividly reported by
Josephus, including the distinctive Judaic
candelabra.

26 (*right*) Bust of Titus. The older son of
Vespasian, Titus was left to finish the war in
Judaea after his father's departure to seize
supreme power in Rome. Titus later had an
affair with the Jewish queen Bernice which
set Roman tongues wagging.

27 (*below, left*) Probably Decebalus, king of Dacia, shown here in Trajan's column. Note the distinctive headgear of those about the king, and the typically ornamented Dacian shield.

28 (*below, right*) The Adamklissi frieze, Romania (AD 108–109), is much less sophisticated than the sculpture on Trajan's column, but in many ways more realistic. Here the Dacian warrior wields his battle scythe (*falx*) two-handed, and the extra armour on the forearm of the legionary is not recorded for any other campaign.

29 (*above*) The Palmyran theatre, with the castle in the background. Unlike many ancient cities in the Middle East, Palmyra does not have a modern city built upon it, and the ruins attract a stream of tourists drawn by the legend of Zenobia.

30 (*right*) Bust of a wealthy Palmyran woman. Both the features and clothing of this lady show that Palmyra was as much of the East as of Rome, yet the wide-eyed frontal stare of this statue is typical of late-third-century Roman sculpture.

31 (*left*) Shapur I, depicted as a mighty hunter on the interior of this silver bowl. Shapur built on the work of his father to create an empire which outlasted the western Roman Empire by several centuries. Some features of Shapur's reign, especially in religion and architecture, are still powerful influences in the Middle East of today.

32 (*below*) Victory relief of Shapur at Naqs-i Rustam. The cloaked figure kneeling before the king is the captured emperor Valerian, and from this pose it is easy to understand the tradition that Shapur was in the habit of using him as a human mounting-block to get onto his horse.

33 (*above, left*) The emperor Honorius. This ivory portrait is a mixture of traditional and contemporary styles. His dress is that of an old-fashioned general, yet the banner has a Christian message and he wears a tiara, which earlier emperors did not.

34 (*above, right*) Ivory relief of Stilicho, *c.* AD 400, one of the last great generals of Rome. The influence of the Germanic tribes can be seen in Stilicho's weaponry, his long cloak, and the fact that he appears to be wearing trousers under his tunic.

35 (*right*) Seal of Alaric, *c.* AD 410. Despite the crudity of the carving, the style is contemporary Roman and the lettering around the side in Latin. Alaric did not see himself as one of Rome's destroyers, but rather sought to find a place within the Empire for himself and his people, while enriching himself at every opportunity.

36 In this detail from Raphael's *The Meeting of Pope Leo the Great with Attila* (1514), Attila the Hun is awestruck and amazed by the heavenly admonition to cease his attempted invasion of Rome. In reality, Attila's men were low on supplies and smitten with the plague, and Attila was looking for an excuse to make a dignified exit from Italy.

miraculous prophecy which he uttered that Vespasian and his sons would become masters of the world. More realistically, it is probable that Josephus' pro-Roman sympathies were known to Vespasian, and by sparing one aristocratic prisoner, he might inspire others to defect.

The same problem was occupying the Zealots who had seized control of much of Jerusalem. They had conducted a purge of their enemies, including the chief priest, and ordered that the relatives of 'traitors' should leave their bodies unburied on pain of death. Now almost anyone found outside the walls of Jerusalem was assumed to be going to join the Romans and summarily executed.

Keeping Josephus as something between a prisoner and a guest, Vespasian set out to take Jerusalem while its affairs were unsettled. He rapidly took control of the surrounding countryside, including Pella, a Gentile city whose inhabitants had been slaughtered by the Jews at the start of the revolt. But at Caesarea in AD 68, word reached him of the death of Nero. The Julio-Claudian dynasty was now extinct, and the imperial throne waited for anyone with the determination to seize it.

In Judaea, Vespasian consulted the oracle of the God of Carmel and was promised that he would never be disappointed in whatever he wanted or planned, however high his ambitions took him. Furthermore, a distinguished Jewish prisoner of Vespasian's, called Josephus, insisted that he would soon be released by the same man who had just put him in chains, and who would then be emperor.

Suetonius *The Twelve Caesars, Vespasian 5*

In 69 Vespasian left his son Titus to finish the Jewish war, while he left for Alexandria and later for Rome where, victorious in the civil war, he took up the reins of Empire.

In Judaea, it must have seemed to the bewildered Josephus that the Jews in Jerusalem were trying to do the Romans' work for them. The victors of the battle of Beth-Horon had fallen out with the Jerusalem Zealots, who were already divided among themselves. Even before the Romans reached Jerusalem the city was riven by a vicious three-way civil war which had destroyed much of the temple and almost all the grain supplies put aside for the coming siege. Only the arrival of the Romans forced the warring factions to unite. The Romans, despite their formidable discipline, were shocked by the savagery of the Jewish sallies which succeeded several times in driving them from the city gates. 'The attacks were made with a mad impetuosity that resembled the charge of wild beasts', reported Josephus, now watching events from the Roman side.

Incredibly, between their united attacks on the Romans, the Zealot factions resumed their internecine strife, so that on any given day a Zealot defender of Jerusalem had a choice of three separate sets of enemies to contend with. Despite this lack of unity, the strong walls of Jerusalem, combined with the natural advantage of its position and the ferocity of its defenders, were enough to keep the Romans at bay. Josephus was on occasion called to talk to those who offered to parley, but Titus soon discovered that such 'parleys' were intended to delay the Romans while positions were fortified, or defenders rushed up.

But the Romans were masters of siege warfare, and having wantonly destroyed their own food supplies, the defenders were in dire straits. The Romans forced the walls, and moved their attack onto the temple itself. Here the resistance was at its most fanatical, and the defenders were only slowly driven back until one of the attackers decided to speed the process by using fire. Soon the entire temple was ablaze.

Caesar [i.e. Titus] called to the soldiers that were fighting and indicated with his right hand that they should try to put out the fire. But though he shouted loudly, he went generally unheard amid the greater din. Nor were the hand signals much heeded, some soldiers being occupied with the more pressing business of fighting, and others preferring to be commanded by their own passions. For as the legions came rushing up, each man was in the grip of his own fury; they all crowded into the great temple together, some trampling on the others. Many fell among the ruins of the outbuildings where there were still masses of smouldering cinders and died the same miserable death as those whom they had just defeated. ... The rebels were already too far gone to be able to do anything and were beaten and cut down on all sides. Many ordinary people, weak and unarmed, had their throats slit wherever they were caught. Dead bodies lay heaped high on the altar, their blood running in rivulets down the steps, and every now and then another body toppled down the steps from the pile above.

Josephus *The Jewish War* 6.3.6

26 *A coin struck to commemorate the end of the Jewish war. The legend on the coin reads* Judaea capta *('Judaea captured'). Judaea is symbolized by the captive beneath the palm tree, while the letters S. C. below the coin signify that the issue was authorized by the senate.*

When the Romans burst into the inner sanctum, the Holy of Holies, and still no divine intervention came to aid the defenders, the heart went out of the Jewish rebellion. Jerusalem was sacked and razed. Josephus did what he could for his friends, persuading Titus to save their lives and free them without ransom. On one occasion he found three of his friends already crucified, and at his pleading Titus had them taken from their crosses. Two survived.

The Sicarii neither expected nor wanted mercy. They retreated to the supposedly impregnable fortress of Masada to make a last stand. The Romans followed. With the rest of the revolt over, there was no reason why the defenders of Masada could not have been starved out with a leisurely siege. But Titus wanted to make the point that once Rome had been sufficiently provoked, there was no place so remote, nor fortress so secure that Roman vengeance could not reach. The Romans built a siege ramp up the side of the mountain on which Masada stood (this ramp can still be seen today). The day before the Romans were set to storm the fortress its defenders committed suicide to a man, woman and child, gaining a moral victory which eclipsed that which the Romans had wanted to win.

Josephus accompanied Titus to Rome, not least because he now had a formidable crop of enemies in his homeland. He witnessed the triumph with which Titus celebrated his victory, and took the name Flavius in tribute to his imperial patrons (who were of the Flavian house). Then he settled down to lead the cultured life of a Roman gentleman. His literary works aimed to reconcile Romans with Jews. The *Antiquities* reminded the Romans that the Hebrew culture was considerably older than theirs, and his *Contra Apionem* was a solid defence of Judaism against the attack of a Hellenistic writer. His *Jewish War*, which has been quoted extensively here, probably relied on the campaign notes of Vespasian and Titus as much as his own recollections; and as already mentioned, this too was persuasion written as history.

Josephus was married three times and had two sons, Justus and Simonedes. The date of his death is unknown, but it was probably in the early years of the second century AD. What seems certain is that he died peacefully in his own bed – a rare achievement for the protagonist of a war against Rome.

CHAPTER 13

DECEBALUS OF DACIA: THE BRAVEHEART OF THE CARPATHIANS

This man was a master of both the theory and the practice of warfare; he was an expert judge both of when to attack and of picking the right moment to retreat; he was skilled at both ambuscades and pitched battles; and he knew well not only how to follow up a victory, but also how to handle a defeat.

Cassius Dio 67.6 *Epitome*

For more than a century before Decebalus came to power in Dacia the Romans had been uneasily aware of the threat from the wild lands across the Danube. Ancient Dacia lay at the point where the more settled Germanic and Celtic peoples met the nomadic horse tribes west of the Black Sea – peoples such as the Roxolani and Sarmatians. The people of Dacia were numerous and imbued with a warrior culture. Rome too was a militaristic society, so its senators were well able to judge the danger Dacia posed to their provinces of Moesia and Dalmatia.

The people of Dacia had long been known to the civilizations of the Mediterranean. The Greeks called them the Getae and had fought and traded with them since the seventh century BC. Though the Dacians are sometimes considered to have been a north Thracian people, their culture had borrowed from Celts and Greeks, and also possessed original aspects of its own. The constant interaction of different peoples contributed much to the vitality of Dacian culture, but it also meant that warfare was frequent to the point of being endemic. When not under attack from neighbours, Dacia was often riven by civil war.

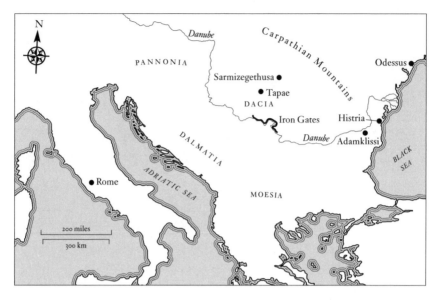

27　*The northeastern Mediterranean. From this map it can be seen that Dacia was a threat to the Roman provinces across the Danube, and that only Pannonia and the Alps lay between the kingdom of Decebalus and Italy itself.*

Nevertheless, the Dacians certainly did not deserve the title of barbarians, which the Romans so freely used to describe the unconquered peoples outside their Empire. The Dacians had a sophisticated understanding of architecture and metalwork, and their merchants were shrewd enough to deal on level terms with the Greeks. But the Roman Empire was reaching its limits at the end of the first century AD, in part because the Romans found the peoples of northern Europe hard to conquer, difficult to control once conquered, and seldom worth the financial effort. Rather than admit their limitations, the Romans convinced themselves that it was not worth conquering barbarians who lived in useless swamps and forests.

This attitude can be seen in contemporary sculptural depictions, especially Trajan's column. This shows the spoils heaped up after each battle, including rather sophisticated armour and weapons – yet in the battles themselves the 'barbarians' are shown as wielding considerably more primitive armaments. Likewise, the Romans portray Decebalus as a brave and skilled war leader, but pass lightly over his administrative and diplomatic ability. If, as recent evidence suggests, Decebalus attempted to co-ordinate his military initiatives with those of Parthia, Rome's great rival to the east, then his breadth of vision and grasp of great power politics far exceeds that of the leader of a tribal warband.

The Dacians constantly feuded with a tribe called the Bastarnae which had migrated from the Baltic region in about 200 BC. Their wars also took in the Dardani and other southern tribes, and this led to several sharp clashes with the Romans as they extended their influence across the Adriatic Sea in the late second century BC. Even then Dacia was well civilized, but we know little of the state at this time other than that its central government was headed by a king, possibly called Oroles.

Bruised by their contact with Rome, the Dacians withdrew, probably relapsing into internal strife. The country re-enters the historical record in the 70s BC under a formidable leader called Burebista. There are indications that this king re-organized the army, and during the course of his long reign he pushed the Dacian frontiers to their greatest-known extent. He subjugated the Bastarnae and the Boii (another Germanic tribe), and Greek colonies around the Black Sea, finally reaching as far as Odessus (Odessa). To the north, the kingdom extended into the Carpathian Mountains, and to the east to the river Dniester, which is now the border between Moldavia and the Ukraine. There are conflicting accounts of the extent of the western boundary, and this probably fluctuated considerably according to the country's fortunes.

The drive to the east brought Dacia into renewed conflict with the Romans. In the early 60s BC an army commanded by Antonius Hybrida was defeated by the Dacians near Histria (another Greek Black Sea colony). This clash evidently led Burebista to take a keen interest in Roman affairs. He so enthusiastically supported Pompey in his civil war with Caesar in 48 BC that Caesar contemplated invading Dacia once he had seized power in Rome.

Caesar's plans were cut short by his assassination in 44 BC. Burebista was unable to exploit the chaos into which Rome was thrown, as he was soon afterwards assassinated as well. Burebista's kingdom was divided into at least three or four parts. One fragment, led by a chieftain called Cotiso, established good terms with Augustus. The poet Horace talks of the army of Cotiso being overthrown (*Odes* 3.8) from which we may infer that the Dacians made a token obeisance to Rome. The 'overthrow' was certainly not complete since another tradition suggests that Augustus contemplated linking the Dacian leader with his family through marriage.

Marcus Crassus of Rome's great Licinian family led a campaign against the Dacians in 29 BC, but they were certainly not subdued. For most of the first century AD they enlivened the long winter nights by raiding into Moesia whenever the frozen Danube gave them the opportunity.

During the reign of the Flavian emperors the Danubian frontier became increasingly dangerous. Not only the Dacians, but also their neighbours the Roxolani, launched ever larger and more ferocious raids. Vespasian fortified the borders and sent more troops to the region, but this brought only a respite. The storm broke in AD 85, during the reign of Vespasian's son Domitian. The Dacians swarmed over the Danube and began vigorously pillaging Moesia, destroying farms, forts, and whatever resistance the Romans were able to muster. The provincial governor Oppius Sabinus was killed, and the sheer numbers of the enemy forced the Roman legions to bunker down in their camps and await reinforcements.

When reinforcements came, they were led by Domitian himself, though the emperor left the actual campaigning to the veteran Cornelius Fuscus who had served the Flavians well in the civil war of 69. Fuscus made short work of clearing the Dacians from Moesia; but as the Dacians were after plunder rather than conquest, they were probably ready to go in any case. Domitian decided that these cocky barbarians needed a lesson, and he ordered Fuscus into Dacia on a punitive expedition.

It is uncertain who was leading the Dacians at this point. They had a king called Douras, but his influence was overshadowed by the talented and warlike general Decebalus. This Decebalus, the subject of this chapter, was one of several persons in Dacian history with the same title, which was probably a nickname rather than a given name. It translates roughly as 'Brave Heart' and suggests that Decebalus liked to lead from the front. It is quite possible that he led the raid on Moesia, and the kudos thus gained forced Douras to abdicate in his favour. The historian Cassius Dio seems reasonably sure that Decebalus was in command by AD 86, and completely uncowed by the threat to his country.

Domitian prepared an expedition against this people [the Dacians], but refrained from being an active participant. He preferred to remain in the cities of Moesia indulging his taste for decadence. He was not only physically lazy with the spirit of a coward, but also a promiscuous seducer of both women and boys. He sent others to fight the war in his place, and by and large, they did a bad job.

Decebalus, the king of the Dacians, sent ambassadors to Domitian, offering peace; but instead Domitian sent Fuscus against him with a large force. When he heard about this Decebalus sent more ambassadors. This time his peace offer was a studied insult. His terms for peace were that every Roman should pay him an annual tribute of two obols. Failure to pay up would provoke war and unleash a torrent of misfortunes upon the Romans.

Cassius Dio 68.6 *Epitome*

Decebalus' cavalier attitude was inspired by his mastery of his own terrain of steep hills, thick woods and rapid rivers. Furthermore, at some point between the reign of Burebista and Decebalus, the Dacians had built a redoubt in the Orastie Mountains. This was a complex series of fortresses, watchtowers and walls spread out over some 193 square miles (500 square kilometres). Modern archaeological research on these structures confirms that the Dacians were excellent architects and engineers, and their forts must have seemed secure against the worst the Romans could do.

It is uncertain exactly what happened to Fuscus, for the Romans were always reticent about their defeats. We know that the Dacians killed him in battle, and the Fifth 'Alaudae' Legion was badly mauled, perhaps even losing its eagle. The rest of the expedition struggled back to Moesia, its punitive purpose abandoned. The blow to Roman prestige inspired a revolt in the nearby province of Pannonia. Tacitus describes the event only in very general terms, but leaves no doubt of its severity.

Item by item the news came in, the loss of all those armies in Moesia and Dacia, in Germany and Pannonia. The reckless stupidity or the cowardice of our leaders, our cohorts overwhelmed and their commanders captured. Now it was not a question of maintaining the frontiers, but the upkeep of Empire itself, and the bases of the legions ...

Tacitus *Agricola* 41

Rome reacted swiftly. The calumnies of Dio and Tacitus about Domitian's strategy were inspired by the mutual antipathy of Domitian and the senate (both Dio and Tacitus were senators). In fact, Domitian had prepared his Dacian campaign in depth. The Fourth Legion, the 'Flavia Felix', was probably already on its way, and in 88 it crossed into Dacia at a point called the Iron Gates. At nearby Tapae on the plain of Caransebes they avenged the death of Fuscus with a resounding victory. Vezinas, the second-in-command to Decebalus, is said to have escaped only by feigning death on the battlefield.

Fortunately for Decebalus it was already late in the campaigning season, and the Romans were unwilling to winter in hostile territory. They were prevented from returning the following spring by Saturninus, a provincial governor whose revolt marked the beginning of the end of the Domitian's reign.

With revolts against Rome breaking out across the Danube frontier, and Decebalus chastened by his setback, both parties were ready for a truce. Decebalus offered to do homage to Rome, and in return received from Domitian not only an annual subsidy but also workers and engineers to bolster his kingdom's already substantial defences. Despite this warming in international relations, the Dacian king was not prepared to put his actual person in Roman hands. In his place he sent a prince called Diegis to the official peace ceremony. This prince did homage and received a diadem from the Romans as though he were Decebalus.

Public opinion in Rome was incensed at the concept of paying tribute to foreigners, and the restless spirit of Decebalus would not long remain content. Another war was inevitable. Domitian was assassinated in 96, and was succeeded by the elderly Nerva. Nerva reigned for two years and his greatest achievement was the selection of his successor, Trajan – perhaps the greatest of all Roman emperors.

After spending some time in Rome, Trajan campaigned against the Dacians; for he took into account their past deeds and was grieved at the amount of money they were receiving annually, and he also observed that their power and their pride were increasing. Decebalus, learning of his advance, became frightened, since he well knew that on the former occasion it was not the Romans that he had conquered, but only Domitian. Whereas now he would be fighting against both Romans and Trajan, the emperor.

Cassius Dio *History* 68.6

Trajan was aware, as Domitian had undoubtedly been, that the settlement with Dacia had been a stop-gap until a more permanent solution could be found. The nature of that solution became clear to Decebalus as Trajan arrived on his frontier with ten legions and began the construction of a bridge over the Danube into Dacian territory.

Sources for the war which followed Trajan's incursion are highly unsatisfactory. By a cruel coincidence, the writings of Appian, Arrian, and Ammianus Marcellinus, all historians whose work has substantially survived, have missing chapters at this point. Dio is our main source; and that only from a twelfth-century epitome. Dio is, as ever, hopeless with geography and his epitome treats readers to only a cursory description of the war itself. Few documents in ancient military history are as sorely missed as Trajan's own commentary on the war, but of this only a single sentence survives. Fortunately, to commemorate his achievement in Dacia Trajan erected a column which still stands in Rome today. A spiral running up the column tells the story of the war in pictures, though in this case historians would certainly have preferred a thousand words.

The Dacian warriors on the column have long hair and beards. Apart from their leaders they are not heavily armoured and rely on oval shields for defence. They are better dressed than Germanic warriors with trousers and tunics, and even fringed cloaks on some occasions. The Dacian infantryman had a choice of weapons. A favourite was the *falx*, a sort of war-scythe. On the column the Dacians wield it one-handedly, but other depictions show the *falx* as a much heavier and more fearsome weapon which required the use of both hands. Conventional swords and spears were also used, as well as battle-axes and wooden clubs. As might be expected of a people in contact with the horse archers around the Black Sea, the Dacians were also skilled archers.

For cavalry, the Dacians relied heavily on their allies, the Sarmatians. Sarmatian horsemen wore close-fitting chain mail that covered both riders and horses. These aforementioned cataphracts were formidable opponents, and such horsemen were later included in the Roman army.

Decebalus did not seek an immediate confrontation. He withdrew before Trajan's men, seeking a suitable point for an ambush, perhaps as he had done with Fuscus. But Trajan had strengthened his army with swarms of auxiliaries, and these lighter troops were able to move more freely across rough ground and mountainsides, and this made it hard for ambuscades to remain undetected.

When the Romans advanced as far as Tapae, the scene of the Dacian defeat in 88, Decebalus took the initiative and attacked. The battle went against him, though the result was far from conclusive. The heavy casualties on both sides gave the leaders pause for thought. Decebalus returned to his campaign of harassment while the Romans retired to their winter camp.

The winter was not to pass peacefully. Decebalus gathered his allies and launched them across the Danube at lower Moesia. His attack was effectively a large raid aimed to demoralize the Romans and encourage his supporters. It did not affect the military situation, and in the spring Trajan was on the move once more. Now seriously worried, Decebalus sought peace. He had already sent one embassy to sound Trajan out, but the approach had no serious intent. This time Decebalus showed he was in earnest by sending senior aristocrats to negotiate. Little is known of the Dacian social system, but there seems to have been an upper class whom the Romans called *pileati* after their distinctive caps, while commoners were called *comati* from their long hair.

Trajan responded by sending two envoys, Licinius Sura and Claudius Livianus. Decebalus was not prepared to negotiate personally, so the war went on. Trajan's methodical generalship gave Decebalus no opening to attack, and despite desperate efforts, his fortresses were taken one by one. At some point in this process the Romans retrieved the standards which Fuscus had lost in his disastrous campaign of 86. Finally the road lay open to Sarmizegethusa, the Dacian capital. Decebalus seems to have made a final attempt to challenge the Romans in the field, but when this failed he was forced to seek whatever terms he could get.

Because the Roman general Maximus had captured his sister and also another of his fortresses, Decebalus was in a situation where he was prepared to agree without exception to every demand which the Romans made – not that he intended to keep to any agreement, but so that he could gain time to recover from his present setbacks. So he reluctantly promised to surrender his weapons, his siege engines and engineers, to give back deserters, to demolish his forts and pull back from captured territory. He also promised that the friends and enemies of the Romans would be his also, and that he would neither shelter Roman deserters or recruit his soldiers from the Empire. This last was because he had recruited a large elite force made up of former Roman subjects. This all happened after he came to Trajan, fell upon the ground in obeisance and discarded his arms. He also sent envoys to the senate, so that they might hear of the matter and ratify the peace which had been made.

Cassius Dio *History* 68.9

Once Trajan was on his way to Rome (where he celebrated a triumph and took the name 'Dacicus'), Decebalus promptly began to rebuild his fortresses, recruit vigorously for his army and acquire the same sophisticated weaponry he had promised Trajan he would forswear.

Word of Decebalus' violation of the peace terms soon reached Rome, for Trajan had left a garrison in Sarmizegethusa to monitor the king's activities. Since a resumption of the war was inevitable, Decebalus hastened its commencement by seizing a chunk of the territory of the Iazyges, a people allied to Rome. By 106 Trajan was back where he had started – on the banks of the Danube preparing to invade Dacia. This time however, he had the advantage of a superb bridge, over 3,280 feet (1,000 metres) in length, built for him by Apollodorus of Damascus.

Trajan almost did not arrive at the Danube. Spies sent by Decebalus had come close to assassinating him as he moved his army up through Moesia, something which the emperor was unlikely to forgive. Furthermore, Decebalus had invited one of Trajan's commanders, Longinus, to a conference and then treacherously taken him hostage. Longinus was a poor choice of bargaining chip. He persuaded a freedman to bring him poison, and then sent the freedman to safety with Trajan under the pretence of petitioning Trajan for Longinus' safety. The furious Decebalus sent another of his prisoners, a Roman centurion, with an offer to give Trajan the body of Longinus and ten living captives if Trajan would hand over the freedman who had helped Longinus to die. Trajan not only would not return the freedman, but ordered the centurion sent by Decebalus to break his parole and not return. Decebalus was no longer considered an honourable opponent, and he could expect neither terms nor mercy if he was defeated.

Trajan's garrisons were under considerable pressure from Decebalus' pre-emptive strike. Many of those within Dacia had fallen, and even some forts south of the Danube were under siege. Most of the year had been spent tidying up the situation, and it was the following year before Trajan was ready to move into the interior of Dacia once more. The methodical determination shown by the Romans had its effect on Decebalus' allies. One by one they melted away or made their own terms with the Romans. This option was not available to Decebalus, and his subjects fought for him with fanatical strength.

The Dacian opposition was strengthened by their warrior religion. They held that death was merely a changed state in which the consciousness survived. Their gods welcomed those who died in battle, but rejected cowards. This included any who surrendered, so it was not unusual for Dacian warriors to commit suicide rather than be captured. Their chief god was a chthonic deity (an earth god) called Zamolxis. Archaeology at the site of Sarmizegethusa shows that this god, and his chief priest, had an important role in Dacian society. There were other gods, including a war god who accepted human sacrifice. Perhaps the most approachable member of this fearsome pantheon was Bendis, a goddess who represented fertility and healing, apparently combining aspects of the Greek cult of Artemis with the Indo-European belief in the *mater magna* (the great mother).

Even the Bastarnae, former enemies of the Dacians, resisted to the last. The historian Appian calls the Bastarnae 'the bravest nation of all'. They receive special attention on Trajan's column, where they are easily distinguished by the topknots which adorn their otherwise shaven heads.

Decebalus knew better than to make an all-out trial of strength with Trajan's massive and well-trained army. His soldiers fought a bitter hit-and-run campaign interspersed with stubborn stands at every defensible point. It appears that the Romans were advancing on Sarmizegethusa from the east in two columns (a favourite tactic that Trajan was to use again in Parthia). They reached the capital in midsummer and immediately laid siege to it. Decebalus seems to have anticipated the inevitable result, and abandoned the city for the mountain fastness of Transylvania.

Trajan took Sarmizegethusa, and proved that he was in an unforgiving mood by levelling the city to its foundations. What had been a war now became a manhunt with Decebalus as the prey. Archaeology has revealed the forts which were home to Decebalus in those days. They stood on steep outcrops, and were built partly of wood and partly of stone. Their location seldom made a ditch possible or necessary. The ramparts were reinforced with towers, and other towers stood outside the walls for additional defence. Formidable though these forts were (and Trajan's column shows the difficulty experienced by their Roman attackers), they were seldom designed to offer sustained resistance. Few had a constant water supply, and this problem was compounded by the fact that the local people who took shelter within brought their livestock with them.

It was evident that the Romans were not going to give up until they had taken Decebalus, and it was also evident that this day could not long be delayed. One tradition has it that as the Romans closed in on him, Decebalus invited his remaining chieftains to a feast. After they had consumed the last of their supplies, Decebalus cut his own throat.

According to the tombstone of one Tiberius Claudius Maximus, auxiliary cavalryman, that was the moment at which he burst onto the scene and made a desperate effort to take the Dacian king alive. It seems incredible that in a war so poorly documented we should have this piece of evidence preserved, but the picture on the tombstone so closely resembles another on Trajan's column that they undoubtedly refer to the same incident.

The death of Decebalus ended the organized resistance. With nothing to lose, the local chieftains fought a sharp guerrilla campaign, but the war was effectively over. Among those who suppressed the last flickers of

28 *A coin struck to commemorate the defeat of Decebalus. The Dacian warrior wears the distinctive cap of his people and his fighting scythe (*falx*) lies before him. The legend on the coin refers to Trajan as 'the best of emperors'.*

rebellion was a capable subordinate and relative of Trajan – Hadrian, the future emperor. Trajan returned to Rome, taking with him Decebalus' head and thousands of Dacian prisoners destined to finish their lives in the Roman arena. In Dacia Trajan's settlement exemplified Tacitus' dictum that Rome 'creates a desert and calls it peace'. The native peoples were either extirpated or driven from their lands, and settlers were brought in from all over the Empire to take their place. One consequence of this is that of all modern languages, Romanian is among the closest to Latin, and the modern name of the country reflects the extent to which Trajan's settlers made themselves at home.

Decebalus would have gained little comfort from the knowledge that his nation was among the last to be absorbed by Rome. Under Trajan, Rome's Empire reached its height. After the long peace of the Antonine rulers who followed Trajan, the enemies of Rome went on the offensive, attacking Roman lands rather than defending their own. With his raids into Roman territory and his demands for ransom and tribute, Decebalus showed many of the traits of Rome's later opponents. In that much, he was a man ahead of his time.

· PART IV ·

SHAPUR I

ZENOBIA

ALARIC

ATTILA

The End of Empire

'Our history now descends from a kingdom of gold to one of iron and rust, as affairs did for the Romans of that day.' Thus the historian Cassius Dio lugubriously begins the story of Rome following the ascension of Commodus to the imperial throne in AD 180. There can be no doubt that Commodus was a thoroughly bad emperor in the tradition of Nero and Caligula, but the rot in the Roman Empire had become established long before and was already apparent during the reign of Commodus' father, the philosopher emperor Marcus Aurelius.

During the reign of Marcus Aurelius the Roman Empire was troubled by constant incursions of Germanic tribes and devastated from within by successive plagues. Some historians have postulated that the population of the Empire now went into an inexorable decline. The main evidence for this is that Rome began to field ever smaller armies and came to rely increasingly on cavalry and auxiliary soldiers. There are other explanations for this fact, however, including that Roman citizens were increasingly reluctant to serve in the legions, and Rome's extended frontiers required a fast-moving cavalry army which could move swiftly to counter any incursions.

In AD 192 Commodus met the traditional fate of bad emperors – an assassin's knife. His death brought forth the spectre of civil war which, like tyranny, the Romans had hoped was banished forever. Over the following century Rome was at the mercy of every ambitious general with a competent army, and Rome's legions tore at each other even as they were desperately needed to defend the frontiers. The Germanic tribes in the north had forced Marcus Aurelius to spend much of his reign defending the Rhine frontier. This pressure increased under Aurelius' successors, until Rome's hard-pressed military system buckled under the strain.

The financial cost of keeping Roman armies on campaign against these incursions crippled the Roman economy. In the glory days of the Roman Republic and early Empire, Rome's campaigns had paid for themselves with the booty of conquest. Defensive wars had to be paid for by taxes, and the squeeze on Rome's finances reduced many of the middle classes to poverty. The financial crisis also sparked runaway inflation which was only halted in 309 when the Christian emperor Constantine stabilized the currency with gold stripped from pagan temples.

The century between the death of Commodus and the accession of Constantine saw the rise and fall of twenty-seven emperors and pretenders to the purple, all but two of whom met violent deaths. Sometimes the military and political situation deteriorated to the point where there were several emperors ruling different parts of the Empire, each too preoccupied with barbarian incursions and the need to eliminate their rivals to worry about civil governance.

The chaos within the Empire did not go unnoticed by Rome's rivals to the east. The Parthian Empire had grown steadily weaker until Rome's troubles had given it a chance to strengthen its western borders. But another problem soon developed from within, as the vigorous Sassanid dynasty rose from the position of provincial governors to challenge Parthia's rulers for their empire. The Sassanids saw themselves as the successors to the fifth-century BC Achaemenid Empire of Darius and Xerxes, and sought to reclaim the lands of Asia Minor wrested from their 'ancestors' by Alexander the Great, which had since passed into Roman hands. Because they had a well-administered and centralized government and an efficient army, the Sassanids seemed for a while to have this objective within their grasp, especially as the situation in the Roman Empire showed no signs of improving.

The great Persian king **Shapur I** (Chapter 14) launched a series of attacks on Asia Minor which were halfway between invasions and massive raids. He met with considerable success and even captured and plundered Antioch in Syria – at that time one of the greatest cities of the Roman Empire. But Shapur had underestimated the resilience of Rome and the flexibility of her political institutions. The Roman emperor Gallienus virtually ceded control of the region to the Palmyran leader Odaenathus. Palmyra was a semi-independent city which sat astride the fabled caravan road from the Orient. Under its capable leader and with piecemeal support from Rome, Palmyra was easily a match for Shapur's ambitions. Shapur was driven out of Roman Asia Minor and, though neither he nor his successors relinquished their claims, their best chance of realizing them was gone.

Though thwarted in the west, Shapur not only consolidated the achievements of his father, but built on them. During his reign religious thought and architectural innovation took new directions which have shaped the Middle East of today.

Palmyra, the power which had blocked Shapur's western ambitions, went from strength to strength. Its leader, Odaenathus, was assassinated, but power passed to his widow Zenobia. **Zenobia** (Chapter 15) was as capable a ruler as her ex-husband had been, but her ambitions were far greater. She saw Palmyra as a successor to the empire of the Seleucids, and envisaged her children ruling over an empire that stretched from the Black Sea to Egypt. Zenobia's vision of the future held no place for Rome in the region, and her soldiers attempted to usurp Roman authority even as Zenobia herself tried to maintain the ever more flimsy pretence that she was an ally of Rome.

But Rome was slowly recovering from her wrenching crisis. A series of strong rulers rose from the Balkan provinces to unite the Empire and a tenuous political stability returned. The emperor Aurelian (270–275) managed to fight off both usurpers and Gothic invaders and consolidate at least the central part of the Empire under his rule. With this much of the Empire reunited under his leadership he turned his attention to the East, and more particularly to Palmyra.

Zenobia did not give up without a fight. Her war with Aurelian became legend in the Middle East, and she is still remembered today as one of the great warrior queens of antiquity. Palmyra survived the experience of Roman reconquest, but was never again more than a shadow of its former greatness.

Aurelian himself, like so many third-century emperors, met his death through assassination. The leader who eventually replaced him was

Diocletian (284–305). Diocletian's name was long reviled by posterity as the most infamous of all persecutors of the nascent Christian church. Nevertheless, he was also the man who restored the Empire to something like stability and set the pattern for the remaining centuries of imperial rule. The Empire of Diocletian was not one which Julius Caesar would have recognized or particularly liked.

Diocletian gave the emperor all the trappings of an oriental monarch and required a suitably servile approach to his diademed person. Rome was virtually abandoned as the imperial capital. It was too far from the frontiers where the imperial armies could be urgently required at any moment. Having established his new world order, Diocletian also became the only Roman emperor to resign from the post and die peacefully in retirement a few years later. Diocletian had envisaged the Empire as being divided among different rulers, each with their own area of competence. Although his system did not last, this was the beginning of the trend which was to see the Roman Empire divided into eastern and western halves.

This trend was accelerated by Constantine, who was emperor from 307 to 337. As well as the stabilization of the currency mentioned above, Constantine established Christianity as the religion of the Roman Empire and built Constantinople, the magnificent city which was to rule the eastern empire for another thousand years and which is now – as Istanbul – the greatest city of modern Turkey.

Constantine and Diocletian had stabilized a sinking ship. Rome's economy became ever more sclerotic as the burden of taxes fell ever more heavily on the declining number of those capable of paying them. The population was divided into the more aristocratic *honestiores* and the humbler *humiliores*. Many of the latter were little more than serfs, unable to change their profession or change their abode without the permission of their 'betters'.

The military situation continued to worsen. The Persians to the east maintained their unrelenting pressure and the Germanic tribes to the northeast were being forced westward by the Huns migrating into their lands from Asia.

A key moment in the fall of Rome came at the battle of Adrianople in AD 398. In an attempt to relieve the pressure on Rome's frontiers, the emperor Valens had permitted a large part of the Visigothic tribe to settle within the Empire in depopulated lands near the Danube. It did not occur to Valens' officials that free peoples needed different treatment from the subject peoples of the Empire. The arrogance, venality and incompetence of those appointed to handle the Visigothic immigration promptly drove the tribesmen to revolt. Valens refused offers by the rebels to negotiate, confident that his army could win an easy victory.

He paid for his error with his life, but the consequences of the Roman defeat lived on long after him. At Adrianople, the last Roman field army was destroyed. Thenceforward, the Roman army would be an oft-derided appendix to Rome's main military arm – barbarians fighting under their own standards and officers. These soldiers were called *foederati* and enjoyed a status somewhere between allies and subjects. They were supported by the long-suffering Roman taxpayer.

It did not take long for **Alaric** (Chapter 16), the Gothic leader, to work out that nothing stood between himself and the treasure of his paymasters. What his people received as salary they were quite capable of taking as booty. All that prevented the complete Gothic domination of the Roman Empire was the great general Stilicho and the remnants of Rome's once-mighty armies. Stilicho was for a while a restraining influence on the Gothic king, but Alaric proved a master at playing off the rivalry between the eastern and western parts into which the Roman Empire was now divided. Alaric first attacked the eastern empire, and once Stilicho had been removed from the scene in Italy he turned his armies against the city of Rome itself.

By the time the horsemen of **Attila the Hun** (Chapter 17) appeared on Rome's frontiers in the AD 430s, the western Roman Empire was practically defenceless. The Visigoths were the virtual rulers of Gaul, and Africa was fast falling out of Roman control. Italy was wracked by famine and plague and the emperor was little more than a figurehead. For the beleaguered peoples of the West, the Hunnish hordes seemed unstoppable. Attila swiftly became the most important person in Europe, and both eastern and western empires anxiously sought reassurance about his intentions. After extorting lands and treasure from both empires, Attila launched a massive invasion of the West. His decision was perhaps influenced by the fact that the eastern empire was already showing signs of recovery under the competent emperor Marcian, while affairs in the West remained as chaotic as ever. In the end, the invaders who had started their journey in the northeast of

China were finally halted on the plains of France. The Huns withdrew to central Europe, and after the death of Attila never again threatened Rome.

The Roman Empire in the East recovered from its malaise, and went on as the Byzantine Empire until 1453. But in the West there was no recovery. There the Roman Empire was doomed.

CHAPTER 14

SHAPUR I: THE KING OF KINGS

The worshipper of Ahuramazda, the god Sapores, king of kings of the
Iranians and non-Iranians, of divine descent, son of the Mazdayasnian, the
god Artaxares, king of kings of the Aryans, grandson of the god-king Papak.

Shapur introduces himself in an inscription carved on rock
at Naqs-i Rustam near Persepolis

In AD 220 the empire of Parthia, Rome's neighbour and rival in Asia, was almost four hundred years old. For most of that period it had been at loggerheads with Rome. After a century of setbacks, in which the Parthian capital of Ctesiphon was twice captured and destroyed, it seemed that the Parthian king Artabanus V finally had matters under control. He had driven the Romans back over the Euphrates and re-established that river as the border between the two powers. Furthermore, he had obtained the massive sum of two hundred million sesterces from the Roman emperor Macrinus as part of the peace settlement which ended the war. With Rome wracked by constant civil wars and apparently in terminal decay, the Parthian king might have been forgiven for believing the worst was over for his empire.

King Artabanus now turned his attention to an unruly vassal called Ardashir, the father of the future Shapur I. Shapur's grandfather Papak had taken possession of the city and district of Istakhr. Istakhr's great significance was that it encompassed the ruins of Persepolis, capital of the Persian Empire destroyed by Alexander the Great in 220 BC. Ardashir had built on his father's achievements and, by a mixture of military skill and diplomatic ability, made himself master of several of the small autonomous states within Parthia.

As befitted a King of Kings, Artabanus delegated the disposal of his unruly subordinate to a sub-king. Ardashir promptly defeated him and took his kingdom before turning on Artabanus himself. The Parthian king was defeated in three successive battles, and killed in the third at Susiana in AD 224. The Parthian Empire was effectively destroyed, though remnants held out for at least another decade. In 226 Ardashir was crowned at Ctesiphon and a new empire was born. This new empire of the Sassanid Persians took its name from Ardashir's grandfather Sassan, the founder of the royal line and high priest of the goddess Ahahita (in whose temple at Istakhr the severed head of Artabanus finished up).

The kings of Armenia, at that time ably represented by Khosrau I, were of the Parthian line and bitterly opposed to the new dynasty. Khosrau put together a wide-ranging alliance which included the Romans in the west and the Kushan Empire to the east. In 227 Ardashir decided to break this diplomatic encirclement by launching a campaign of conquest to the east. For details of this war we have to rely on the Chronicle of Tabari, an Arabic historian of the ninth to tenth centuries. He informs us that Ardashir conquered distant Hyrcania, Balkh

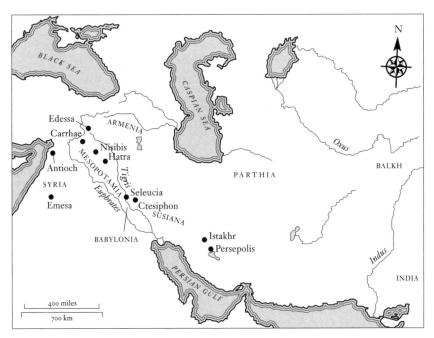

29 *The empire which the Sassanid Persians seized from the Parthians stretched from the river Euphrates to the Himalayas, an area also occupied by the Seleucids and Persians under Cyrus the Great.*

(Afghanistan), and quite probably much of modern Turkmenistan. This forced the Kushan emperor to sue for peace, leaving Ardashir free to turn his attention to the west where the Romans had taken the chance to occupy an area corresponding to modern northern Iraq.

Ardashir's counter-attack into Mesopotamia in 230 may have been spearheaded by his competent warrior son, Shapur, on whom the ageing King of Kings was increasingly dependent. Shapur had no easy task. Rome in the third century AD might be wracked by barbarian invasions from outside and civil wars within, but the once-mighty Empire was still no pushover. The young emperor Alexander Severus launched a campaign against Shapur in 232.

The fanciful and grossly inaccurate *Historia Augusta* is laudatory about Alexander's achievement:

He routed this great king [Shapur], putting him to flight, he who had brought seven hundred elephants to this war, eighteen hundred scythed chariots, and many thousand horsemen. Thereafter Alexander promptly returned to Antioch and gave his troops the booty taken from the Persians, allowing the officers, generals and even common soldiers to keep whatever plunder they had taken from the countryside. For the first time Romans had Sassanid slaves, but because the kings of the Persians think it disgraceful that any subject of theirs should be in slavery to another race, they paid ransoms which Alexander accepted and either recompensed the slave owners or deposited the money in the public treasury.

Alexander Severus, *Historia Augusta 55*

The reality is that the campaign was at best an indifferent success, though there was certainly some bloody fighting. Alexander was prevented from following this up by a German invasion to the west. While campaigning on the Rhine, Alexander was killed by his soldiers, who had taken a preference to the more warlike general Maximus. In a few busy years Maximus was succeeded as Roman emperor by Gordian II, Gordian III, Pupienus and Balbinus. Ardashir took advantage of Roman distraction with the imperial succession to take the important towns of Nisibis and Carrhae. He also took Hatra, the town which represented the high tide-mark of Roman expansion, some fifty miles (eighty kilometres) south of Mosul in modern Iraq.

Ardashir now started styling his name as Artaxerxes, after the rulers of the Achaemenid Empire. In so doing he made the explicit claim that the Sassanids were the legitimate successors of the Persian Empire which had ruled much of Asia until its conquest by Alexander the Great. This meant that Persia claimed suzerainty over all lands east of the Mediterranean, which almost guaranteed perpetual warfare with the Romans, who saw the same territory as an integral part of their eastern empire. This claim to unconquered territory was made largely on Shapur's behalf, for Ardashir himself was ailing. In either 239 or 240 he made Shapur his regent, with Shapur (as yet uncrowned) taking the reins of government. Coins from this period show father and son together, with the symbolism of the coins clearly indicating that executive power lay with the son.

Shapur's coronation duly followed the death of his father in 241, and the new King of Kings promptly set about finding new kings to conquer. He first turned on the Kushan Empire, where his onslaught destroyed the Kanishka dynasty and pushed Sassanid influence as far as the Oxus river.

Then he rapidly turned on the Romans, driving deep into Mesopotamia. Here he came up against the Roman emperor of the day, Gordian III (238–244). At the youthful age of seventeen, Gordian was no match for a seasoned campaigner like Shapur; but he was sufficiently aware of his limitations to heed the advice of Gaius Timesitheus, the Praetorian Prefect and Gordian's father-in-law. The Sassanids collided with the Romans west of the Euphrates river, somewhere near the Roman town of Reshiana, and Shapur was given a stinging setback. Fortunately for the Sassanid cause, Timesitheus died of disease soon afterwards, leaving Gordian to campaign on alone.

Shapur himself takes up the story:

When we had first become established in the empire, Gordian Caesar raised in all the Roman Empire a force from the Gothic and German realms and marched on Babylonia [Assyria] and against us. On the border of Babylonia at Misikhe, a great 'frontal' battle occurred. Gordian Caesar was killed and the Roman force was destroyed. And the Romans made Philip Caesar. Then Philip Caesar came to us for terms and to ransom their lives gave to us 500,000 denars and became tributary to us.

Shapur *Deeds of the God-Emperor Shapur*, inscribed at Naqs-i Rustam

Shapur renamed Misikhe 'Peroz-Shapur' ('Shapur is victorious'). Unsurprisingly, the Romans offer a different version of events, and present the defeat at Misikhe (less than fifty miles [eighty kilometres] west of Baghdad) as a mere setback which the successor to Timesitheus, Philip the Arab, used to stir discontent among the soldiery. Exactly how Gordian died is uncertain. Disease, Philip's machinations and mutinous soldiers have all been offered as alternatives to Shapur's claim. However, Philip needed to get to Rome very quickly to consolidate his position. He was eager to finish the war with Shapur at almost any cost, and Shapur's claim of a huge payment to accomplish this seems quite credible.

Shapur too had some consolidating to do at home, and he may have been aware that without fortune on his side things might have gone very badly for him. Certainly he treated Rome with some circumspection thenceforth, and the region remained peaceful for almost a decade. The emperor Decius succeeded Philip and reigned until 251. Decius died that year in battle with the Goths, who inflicted a major defeat on the Roman army. It was probably this which persuaded Shapur that the Romans were too weak withstand another Sassanid attempt to claim their 'ancestral' dominions.

Unusually, this time Shapur decided to forego the usual invasion route and instead move up the Euphrates into the Roman province of Syria. At a place called Barbalissos the Roman garrison of the province was destroyed in a fierce battle. Shapur claimed that 60,000 Romans were slain. This was probably an exaggeration, but certainly Shapur took control of both Syria and its capital Antioch – and Antioch was at that time the third city of the Roman world. Events were more than usually confused in another Syrian city, Emesa, where the local priest-king Uranius Antonius seized power from the Sassanids and proclaimed himself emperor of the Roman world.

Shapur's invasion and another Gothic incursion brought about a further convulsion in the Roman imperial line, and the emperors Trebonianus Gallus and Aemilius Aemilianus came and went in quick succession. When the Romans finally arrived to retrieve their lost province they were under the command of Publius Licinius Valerianus, usually rendered in English as Valerian.

As was usual when the Romans got themselves sufficiently organized to launch a serious campaign against the Persians, they did rather well. The Persian incursion may have been a large raid rather than a campaign of conquest, for Shapur fell back before Valerian's forces. By 253 the imperial mint at Antioch was again producing Roman coins; Valerian himself wrote a letter from Antioch in 255 and, according to the historian Zosimus, also helped with the restoration of the city. During this respite Valerian took to proclaiming himself *restitutor orbis* – 'the restorer of the world'.

However, a Roman emperor of the third century rarely had time for relaxation. A Scythian invasion sent Valerian hurrying north to defend the province of Cappadocia. Scenting another opportunity, Shapur invaded while Valerian's back was turned, this time taking the more conventional approach of pillaging his way through Mesopotamia.

By now Valerian had news of the situation in Bithynia, but his sphere of command was such that he could trust none of his generals with the defence of that province. He therefore sent Felix to Byzantium, and he himself went from Antioch to Cappadocia, and after savaging every city which his troops passed by, he returned to Antioch. But … at the time Shapur launched an invasion into the East, and brought most of it under his control.

Zosimus Book 1

Fortunately for Valerian, his son Gallienus was campaigning successfully in the western provinces of the Empire, so the father could wearily return his attention to the Sassanid king. The sources are spotty and vague, but it seems that Valerian won a victory of sorts outside Edessa in 260. Shapur was saved, as on previous occasions, by fortune. Plague broke out in the Roman army and with his fighting force crippled, Valerian was forced to withdraw into the city itself, where Shapur promptly put him under siege.

Mindful of how Philip had bought himself out of a similar situation, at some time in April or May Valerian offered terms. Shapur could hardly believe his luck when Valerian offered to negotiate in person, along with all his senior officers. The Persian sense of honour was as strong, or stronger than the Roman, but it did not apply to sworn enemies. The Roman negotiators were taken captive as soon as the opportunity presented itself. Of course, Shapur put it slightly differently.

During our third invasion, when we were campaigning against Carrhae and
Edessa, and were besieging Carrhae and Edessa, Valerianus Caesar came
against us ... and beyond Carrhae and Edessa there was a great battle between
us and Valerianus Caesar, and we gained possession of Valerianus Caesar ...
and we burned and devastated and took captives.

Shapur *Deeds of the God-Emperor Shapur*, inscribed at Naqs-i Rustam

While the fate of Valerian is not certain, a recurring theme is that Shapur
kept the captive emperor as a personal mounting block for his horse –
every time Shapur went on horseback he ascended to his horse by
putting his foot on the neck of his crouching former enemy. In the
inscription at Naqs-i Rustam – excerpts of which have been quoted
above – there is also a picture of Shapur receiving homage from the
defeated emperor.

Shapur put his Roman prisoners to work in Persia, and one irrigation
project on the Karun river near Shuster is still called *Band-I Kaiser* – 'the
mole of Caesar'. Valerian himself may have lived for another two years.
On his death, his skin was filled with straw to make it look lifelike, and
displayed in a Persian temple. For centuries afterwards Persian diplo-
mats made a point of displaying their trophy to Roman envoys. 'The
disgrace to the name of Rome for all future time', Zosimus calls it with
disgust.

Shapur now seemed close to his dream of extending his empire to the
Mediterranean coast. Odaenathus, ruler of Palmyra, and commander of
the last significant pro-Roman military force, sent a message to Shapur
suggesting an alliance. But hubris had Shapur firmly in its grasp. He
responded proudly that Odaenathus might be lucky to remain as a vassal
if he presented himself personally to Shapur and brought presents to
purge his insolence.

This was a mistake. At best the Persians had a mixed record against
the Romans in the field, and Odaenathus had none of the problems of
command and control that beset so many Roman emperors. His small
but highly motivated army fell on the Persians as they returned loaded
with plunder, and scattered them. Odaenathus then used his authority
as a Roman magistrate, and the prestige of his success, to rally the scattered Roman forces of the East. Suddenly Shapur found himself on the

defensive against a well-generalled army thirsting for revenge. Exact details of Odaenathus' campaigns are not known, but after five years of successful warfare he had driven Shapur from all his conquests in the Roman East and even threatened Ctesiphon itself.

Behind Odaenathus' lines, normal life in the Roman provinces seems to have resumed, though Odaenathus' wife Zenobia (see next chapter) was later to try to fill the power vacuum in the region and establish Palmyran sovereignty.

Shapur himself seems to have decided that attempts to expand his empire to the west were too costly. While he had gained prestige from his capture of Valerian, and considerably booty from his campaigns, he had been defeated as often as he had won victories and had not expanded his borders to any significant degree. He had also discovered that a well-led Roman army was still the world's finest fighting force. For the remaining years of his reign he remained in a wary stand-off against Rome; not at peace, but also not initiating hostilities. Since the Romans had their hands more than full elsewhere, this was enough to guarantee that Rome's eastern border remained uneasily peaceful for the time being.

Apart from Rome, Shapur had much to occupy him. His empire had other borders which had to be defended from wild nomads and the organized powers of ancient India. There was also the distant Chinese Empire. In his *Decline and Fall of the Roman Empire*, Edward Gibbon tells the story of a refugee who turned up in the Sassanid Empire who may well have been Xiandi, the last Han emperor of China. On receiving a brusque letter from the new regime in China demanding that this man be handed back, Shapur replied diplomatically that he had sent the man to the 'extremity of the earth where the sun sets. I have dismissed him to certain death.' Shapur had in fact sent the refugee to Armenia where he passed his remaining days in some comfort.

The main difference between Persia and the Parthian Empire which it had succeeded was that the Sassanids were more centralized and more organized. Power in the provinces was devolved to local governors (often members of the royal family) rather than local aristocrats of doubtful loyalty. In Shapur's reign, both aristocrats and monarch enjoyed considerable freedom from the plots, treasons, executions and assassinations which were the order of the day in Rome.

Shapur followed his Parthian predecessors in making his person as remote and awesome as possible. He was surrounded at all times by elaborate protocol and ceremony and wore an imposing crown and sceptre allegedly bestowed upon the line of kings by the chief of the Persian gods, Ahuramazda himself. 'The vainglorious monarchs of this people [the Persians] permit themselves to be called brothers of the sun and moon', remarks the historian Ammianus Marcellinus.

Marcellinus, sometimes called 'the last historian of Rome', gives us a good account of the Persians, though unsurprisingly he is mainly concerned with their military capabilities. When they were not in armour, Persian aristocrats wore

...shining robes of many lustrous colours, so many that though the robes be left open on the front or on the sides, the person remains covered from head to foot. They are fond of golden bracelets, necklaces and pearls.

Ammianus Marcellinus 23.6.84

In appearance the Persians were

Slender, rather swarthy with leaden features, and eyes as grim as goats' ... they have splendid beards and long shaggy hair ... they are a sensual people, seldom satisfied even by a host of concubines, though they do not indulge in boys... they also abstain from overly sumptuous feasts, and avoid heavy drinking as though it were poison. Mealtimes are not fixed. They eat when they please, and finish after a moderate meal... one might regard their fastidiousness as womanly were they not such good fighters, though cunning rather than brave, and therefore most to be feared at long range. They are vain and abrasive in their manner, no matter what their circumstances, and are generally haughty and cruel. Skinning men alive, especially slaves and peasants, is by no means unknown.

Ammianus Marcellinus 23.6 passim

While he constantly harked back to the glories of Persia's Achaemenid past, Shapur was also an innovator. He introduced new financial instruments learned from his conquests on the Indian frontiers. These further stimulated trade, which already did very well from the caravan routes which flourished between Rome and China without either party being clearly aware of the other's role thanks to the skill of the Persians as middlemen. Neither Shapur nor the Romans allowed their military disagreements to interfere with this trade which seems to have gone though Palmyra even while Odaenathus and Shapur were at each other's throats.

Both Shapur and his father were great builders. Shapur launched the construction of at least two new cities, and his interest in irrigation and infrastructure has already been mentioned. Ardashir's palace also contained an architectural innovation – the *iwan*. This onion-shaped dome capped the entrance to the palace, and this type of structure has since become a definitive feature of Middle Eastern architecture.

Another innovation by Shapur and his father was the merging of church and state into a single centralized organization. The ancient creed of Zoroastrianism now became the state religion and the different sects were united by the regularization of the Zend Avesta, Zoroastrianism's sacred texts. The king became the representative on earth of the god Ahuramazda, and attained semi-divine status himself. A holy fire was lit in the temple when the king ascended to the throne and remained burning for his lifetime. The *magi* (priests) rose to positions of influence, and their interest in astrology contributed much to ancient astronomical understanding. From their understanding and use of the supernatural come the modern words 'magic' and 'magician'.

A distinctive feature of the Persian religion was that they did not permit burial or cremation of the dead as burial would pollute the sacred element of earth, and cremation would pollute both air and fire. Consequently bodies were left for the birds, eventually to be buried in the bellies of vultures. Strange as this may seem to western cultures, this practice continues 2,000 years later in modern India.

Shapur promoted the Zoroastrian faith not least because its theme of the struggle between good and evil was suited to a warrior nation; but he was no bigot. His tolerance extended to a personal interest in the prophet Mani, whose teaching combined elements of Zoroastrianism, Christianity and Buddhism. For Mani, the Zoroastrian struggle between good and evil was transmuted to the struggle between spirit and matter. While Buddha laid out the path by which a good man should live his life, Jesus illustrated the ideal. Manicheanism's appeal to elements of some of the world's major religions gave it a following from Gaul to China. This religion too is a legacy of Shapur's time, for it survives today despite enthusiastic efforts by Popes, Mullahs and Party chairmen to stamp it out.

Persian noblemen of Shapur's time were cultured individuals who were expected to have a knowledge of literature and the arts. Many played chess, polo, or an early form of tennis. But the chief occupation of the aristocracy was war. The army was commanded by a member of the royal family, though not the king himself. The national battle standard was a massive banner called the *Kaviani*, embroidered with gems and gold and silver thread. Its presence indicated the presence of the King of Kings himself. Other soldiers rode to war under a more portable standard which displayed the orb and wings of Ahuramazda.

As with the Parthians, the main striking arm of Shapur's army was its armoured cavalry. It is unknown at what point 10,000 such cavalrymen were formed into an elite unit known as 'The Immortals', but this too might date to the reign of Shapur. Ammianus Marcellinus gives us a good description of these cavalrymen:

The Persians lined up against us, the serried ranks of mail-clad cavalrymen so closely formed that the bodies covered with close-fitting plates of armour gleamed as they moved, dazzling those who watched them, while all of the mass of horses were protected by leather coverings.

    Ammianus Marcellinus 24.6.8

The horses were also armoured, though some of this covering was only leather. The obvious disadvantage of wearing this armour in a climate where the temperature could reach fifty degrees Celsius (122 degrees Fahrenheit) meant that these troops had to be deployed with care, especially as the infantry tended to be a conscript rabble of peasants. These were reduced to the level of serfs in the Sassanid Empire and their fighting ability was about as poor as their morale, which was generally rock-bottom. They made useful camp servants however, and no Sassanid general felt his army was complete without them.

Also, as with the Parthians, the heavy cavalry were supported by a host of horse archers, both native Persians and tribesmen brought in from the steppe and the area about the Black Sea. The entire force was highly mobile and sufficiently different from the general run of Rome's enemies to make fighting them something of a specialist art.

A more esoteric addition to which the Romans had to adjust was war elephants, with which the Sassanids persisted long after they had become unfashionable as an arm of war with other states in western Asia. The elephants were not used to break infantry in Carthaginian style, but supported howdahs which acted as platforms for small groups of archers. Probably the two main purposes of Sassanid elephants in war were to overawe the enemy and discomfort their horses. Roman cavalry were not habituated to elephants and liked neither the sight nor the smell of them.

In all, the army of Shapur earned the sincere respect of their enemies, including the Romans, whose judgment in matters military was by now very well honed.

Through training and discipline, through constant drill and exercises they can, as we well know, inspire fear in the mightiest army. They depend mainly on the bravery of their cavalry into which all nobles are strictly trained ... were they not constantly plagued by revolts [in the fourth century] and border wars, they would have conquered many other peoples.

Ammianus Marcellinus 23.6.83

Shapur ruled until 272 and, unusually for an eastern monarch, he seems to have died of natural causes. After his death he was succeeded by his son Hormazd whose reign lasted less than a year. In the following centuries, the Sassanids were to face a number of challenges, not least from a resurgent Roman Empire, but the sound footing on which Ardashir and Shapur had founded their empire stood the dynasty in good stead. Shapur was a competent and far-seeing administrator as much as he was a warrior imperialist. Under his rule the Sassanid Empire reached its farthest extent. And while Shapur's wars with Rome were at best inconclusive, of all the enemies of Rome none but Shapur could claim to have literally stuffed a Roman emperor.

CHAPTER 15

ZENOBIA: RENEGADE QUEEN OF THE EAST

While Gallienus behaved unspeakably, even women ruled excellently ....
She [Zenobia] held imperial power in the name of her son ... ruling longer
than could be endured from a woman.

'The Thirty Tyrants', *Historia Augusta* 30.1

In the latter half of the third century AD, Rome had no shortage of enemies. Gaul had broken away to form a separate empire in the West. From the north, the Gothic hordes swarmed unabated, breaking through frontier defences and pillaging deep into Roman lands. Rome's desperate need for money and soldiers created unrest throughout the Empire, and usurpers exploited this unrest to claim, and often win, the imperial purple.

The Persians were arrogantly confident after their defeat of Valerian and had heady dreams of seizing control of the entire Roman East. The power that forestalled them was not Rome, but a small desert city the Romans called Palmyra, which rose briefly to dominate the entire region.

The inhabitants of Palmyra, a mixture of Syriac and Aramaean peoples, with a few enterprising Greeks, called their city Tad'mor. It was an ancient city, built around a complex of oases, with a history of settlement dating back to 7000 BC. (Damascus, to the southwest, is almost the same age, and is today the world's oldest continuously inhabited city.) Originally dominated by the Seleucid Empire, Palmyra became semi-autonomous by the late first century BC, enjoying its first contact with Roman civilization when Mark Antony tried unsuccessfully to sack the place in 41 BC.

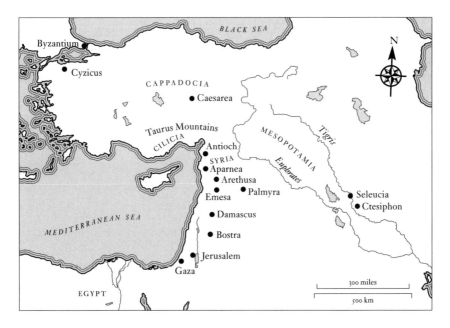

30 *The Middle East in the late Roman era. Zenobia saw no reason why Palmyra should not dominate all lands west of the Euphrates on this map, including Egypt. She legitimized this by claiming to be an heir of the Seleucid Empire which had once covered much of the same area.*

By the time of the emperor Tiberius, Palmyra was under Roman suzerainty – not through conquest, but by the Palmyran acceptance of Rome's dominance. The Romans posted troops in the city and set up a system of taxation, but otherwise Palmyra was left alone to prosper under the Roman peace.

And prosper it did. Palmyra was above all a trading city, as is shown by two of its deities, Arsu and Azizu. These gods, on camel and horseback respectively, guarded the caravans that brought wealth to the city from east and west. Palmyra was where the rival empires of Rome and Parthia did business. Palmyra traded with the coastal cities of Roman Syria, and imported spices and silks from Arabia, China and other parts of the Far East. In the other direction, it sent a steady flow of Roman gold, retaining a fair percentage for itself.

As merchants, the Palmyrenes bring the fruits of India and Arabia from Persia. These they sell in Roman territory.

Appian *Civil Wars* 5.1.9

Palmyra was built in a distinctive mixture of Hellenistic and Parthian styles, combining a Greek agora and Roman architecture with Persian bas-reliefs; one of the region's largest temples was to the Semitic god Baal. The emperor Hadrian visited the city in about AD 129 and found a thriving hybrid culture united in the pursuit of commerce and profit.

The crisis of the third century caused many Palmyrenes to re-think their allegiance to Rome. Roman taxation was a growing burden, and the peace and security offered in exchange was becoming ever more tenuous. With Valerian's defeat by the Sassanid Persians, and the Roman Empire fractured under diverse and often rival *imperatores*, the Palmyrenes sought other protectors.

The mix of East and West which typified Palmyra was personified in its leader of this time, a man called Septimius (a good Roman name) Odaenathus (an Arabic name meaning 'little ear'). Odaenathus appears not to have been a hereditary monarch, but rather the head of one of the trading houses thrown to predominance by the turbulence of the times. With the backing of the Palmyran people, Odaenathus decided to offer an alliance to Shapur, the Persian king (see previous chapter). In reply, the Persian sharply rebuked Odaenathus for his impertinence. Only absolute vassalage from Odaenathus would satisfy the arrogant monarch, so Palmyra returned its allegiance to Rome.

At that time, Rome was led by the son of the defeated emperor Valerian, Licinius Gallienus. Gallienus was struggling to hold together the central parts of Rome's dominions, and was quite prepared to cede control over outlying areas, as long as the usurpers acted in the name of Rome.

Thus Odaenathus found himself a *dux Romanorum* – a Roman military leader, and as such he took the war to the Persian enemy. Palmyra possessed two formidable arms of war: archers and the cataphracts which were a distinctive feature of eastern armies. The soldiers used another word to describe the armour that they wore in the baking desert heat: *clibanus*, the Latin for 'furnace'.

Odaenathus was a good general, with well-paid and motivated troops. He promptly retook the strategic forts of Carrhae and Nisibis, and even briefly besieged the Persian king within his capital city. After these victories Odaenathus began calling himself the 'King of Kings', probably to insult the Persian king who habitually took this title. Meanwhile, a delighted Gallienus made Odaenathus a *vir consularis* and bestowed on him the grand-sounding but basically meaningless title of *corrector totius orientis* ('supervisor of the whole East').

A sudden incursion of Goths into Cappadocia in 267 had the *corrector totius orientis* hurrying northwards to meet the new threat. Soon after, word came back to Palmyra that Odaenathus was dead. Palmyra's leader had not died in battle, but through assassination. The assassins had also slain Septimius Herodes, the son of Odaenathus, and the perpetrator was a nephew, called Maeonius. He alleged that he was avenging an insult which the king had offered him, but the assassination of Odaenathus' son shows that Maeonius had ambitions towards the royal succession.

These ambitions were short-lived. In Palmyra, Odacnathus' wife Zenobia claimed the throne for her son Vallabathus (though by some reports Vallabathus was preceded briefly by a brother called Herodianus). Acting as regent, Zenobia promptly captured Maeonius and dispatched him as a sacrifice to her husband's memory.

It has often been asked whether Maeonius was a cat's paw for one of the rival powers in the region. The Persians may have offered to look kindly on the new king if the formidable Odaenathus were removed from the scene. Or perhaps the Roman governor of Syria, Cocceius Rufinus, judged (correctly) that Palmyran power had grown to the point where it was a threat to Rome.

But suspicion has fallen principally on Zenobia herself. The murdered heir of Odaenathus, Septimius Herodes, was a son from another marriage and, until his death, the children of Zenobia were unlikely to succeed to the throne. Now, through her son, Zenobia controlled an empire that extended from the Taurus Mountains in the north to the Arabian gulf in the south, and included Cilicia, Mesopotamia, Arabia and parts of Syria.

Zenobia has fascinated historians almost from the time that she came to power. Eastern queens were rare but not unheard of. Zenobia's contemporaries would have recalled Semiramis, legendary queen of Assyria, and Artemisia, the fifth-century BC queen of Halicarnassus. Zenobia deliberately cultivated her exotic image, calling herself the 'Queen of the East'. She modelled herself on another famous queen, Cleopatra, whom

31 *Coin of Zenobia. This coin was minted during the period when Zenobia was openly in defiance of Rome, for the 'AUG' after her name proclaims her to be an 'Augusta', or mother of the emperor – the title she proclaimed for her son.*

she claimed as a distant ancestor. (A very unlikely claim, but not impossible; Cleopatra was a Hellenistic queen and Palmyra had been a part of a Hellenistic successor kingdom, albeit of Seleucia rather than Egypt.)

Zenobia would on occasion present herself to the troops in full battle armour, and address them in a loud and (by some unflattering reports) very unfeminine voice. But this same queen gathered in her court a school of leading neo-Platonist philosophers, and made one of them, Longinus, her chief advisor.

Zenobia seems to have spent her first eighteen months in power quietly consolidating her hold within Palmyran territories. She noted the death of Gallienus in 268, assassinated while he struggled against the usurper Aureolus in Milan, Italy. Gallienus' successor, Claudius Gothicus, was fully engaged with the Gothic invasion which her late husband had set out to subdue. With the Romans preoccupied elsewhere, Zenobia decided that the time was right for expansion. In early 270 her troops went into action. Their first engagements were attempts to absorb Bostra in the south, destroying the temple of Jupiter Hammon in the process.

Soon after, Palmyra took control of Antioch, which Zenobia described with some effrontery as Vallabathus' 'ancestral city'. As Antioch was a Hellenistic foundation, this relates to Zenobia's claim to Macedonian ancestry. In further pursuit of that claim she Hellenized her father's name to Antiochus, the name borne by the Seleucid kings of Syria. The Palmyrenes also attempted to extend their control toward the Black Sea, a move which caused friction and confusion among Roman officers unsure of how to handle their assertive ally.

Claudius Gothicus inflicted a massive defeat on the Goths, and stabilized Rome's northeastern frontier. What he intended to do next is unknown, since he then promptly died of the plague. Quintillus, his successor, was hardly on the throne when he was deposed by Aurelian, one of Gothicus' generals. Zenobia took advantage of the chaos to make herself queen of Egypt – not by alleged ancestry, but by conquest. This marked her decisive break with Rome. Gallienus had encouraged Palmyra, and Gothicus had tolerated it, because the city had ostensibly been acting in Roman interests. But in fomenting unrest and sending troops into Egypt, Zenobia showed that she had fatally misjudged Rome's new emperor.

Zenobia tried to pretend that she remained a loyal servant of the Empire. Coins struck in areas under her control carry the emperor's head, with that of Vallabathus on the obverse. Vallabathus wears the laurel wreath of a Roman, and not the diadem of an eastern potentate. But such protestations of loyalty could not excuse the incursion of Palmyran arms into a subject province; that was an affront Rome could not overlook.

Egypt at that time was a hotbed of unrest. A large faction, led by one Timagenes, came enthusiastically over to the Palmyran side. The history of the struggle for Egypt is confused. Our best source is the *Nova Historia* of the historian Zosimus, with some help from the *Historia Augusta*, though the latter is often a mixture of gossip and speculation. There is also an Arab tradition, preserved in the Chronicle of Tabari (839–933), which describes the deeds of one Zebba, presumed to be Zenobia, but this is too fanciful to be of real assistance. Some papyri, of doubtful veracity, also give varied – and conflicting – accounts of events.

It appears that the governor of Egypt, called Probus, responded vigorously to the Palmyran incursion. He had been fighting Gothic pirates, but now returned to Egypt and succeeded in driving the Palmyrenes out completely. According to the *Historia Augusta*, Probus followed the rebels to Gaza, where their superior local knowledge led to his being ambushed and killed. However, other sources allege that this Probus was the future emperor of the same name, so the matter is doubtful.

What is in no doubt was the reaction of the emperor Aurelian. He was one of the strong rulers from the Balkans who steadied the floundering

Roman ship of state – the men named the 'Illyrian emperors'. As testified by his nickname *Manu ad ferrum* ('hand to the sword'), Aurelian was not a patient or diplomatic man. Having stabilized the Danube frontier, he now decided to deal firmly with Palmyra's presumption of power in the East.

After consolidating the defences of Rome (including building the Aurelian walls, which still stand in the city today), Aurelian moved east in 272. As he moved through the Balkans, he gathered his army about him. There could now be no doubt that Palmyra was regarded as an enemy of Rome. Palmyran coins reflected this fact, in that they no longer displayed the head of Aurelian on contemporary issues, instead calling Vallabathus *Imperator*, and Zenobia *Augusta*, mother of the emperor.

It is not clear where Aurelian's army met the Palmyrenes for the first time. Zosimus suggests three battles, though the second may have been a continuation of the first. By this reading, the two sides met near Immae, a village on the plain not far from Antioch. Zenobia had gathered a large army and placed it under the command of her best general, a man called Zabdas. For victory, the Palmyrenes were counting on their heavy cavalry, who seemed more than a match for the lightly armed Dalmatian horsemen Aurelian sent against them. But Aurelian knew that hit-and-run tactics would rapidly wear down the Palmyran riders, already sweltering in their armour under the desert sun. With the enemy cataphracts demoralized and exhausted, Aurelian struck with the full strength of his army, sending the Palmyrenes reeling back to Antioch.

In Antioch, Zabdas gained time for an orderly retreat by parading a man whom he claimed to be the captured Aurelian through the streets. Zabdas also left a rearguard in the hilly suburb of Daphne to slow the real Aurelian when he arrived. In reply, Aurelian marched into the suburb with his legionaries in the famous *testudo* formation – soldiers in the centre of the unit covering the heads of their fellows, so that the advancing troops looked like a huge tortoise, invulnerable to missiles thrown from the heights. Daphne was captured and the rearguard killed, but Aurelian was looking for other cities to come over to him so he refrained from sacking Antioch, and even dedicated some temples there.

With the example of Antioch before them, Apamea, Larissa and Arethusa swiftly surrendered. But outside Emesa, Aurelian encountered determined Palmyran resistance. This time the Palmyran cavalry got to grips with the Roman horsemen and roundly defeated them. But before the victorious cavalry could rally, Aurelian unleashed a special corps of Palestinian warriors. These soldiers were armed with massive iron-tipped clubs which smashed through the flexible mail of the cataphracts, destroying their costly protection. The cataphracts were routed and again Palmyra's army was forced to retreat. This defeat was a particularly bitter blow for Zenobia, for at Emesa she lost her treasury to Aurelian, and with it her chance to sustain an increasingly costly campaign.

There was now no choice but to retreat to Palmyra itself, and for Zenobia to call for help from her husband's erstwhile foes, the Persians. Shapur did not rebuff her outright, and the hope of Persian intervention sustained her through her fighting retreat across the desert. The *Historia Augusta* suggests that Aurelian himself was in danger from archers and skirmishes with light horse. The same work suggests the skirmishers were with 'Syrian bandits', though it is hard to conceive of bandits bold enough to take on a Roman army in mid-campaign. In any event, both Aurelian and his army were thoroughly weary of desert warfare by the time they reached the walls of Palmyra.

Perhaps for this reason, Aurelian made Zenobia a proposal that he must have considered thoroughly magnanimous. Vopiscus, the man who allegedly wrote the history of this campaign in the *Historia Augusta*, offers this version of Aurelian's opening negotiations:

'From Aurelian, Emperor of Rome and Restorer of the Orient; to Zenobia and those fighting in this war on her side. You have failed to obey the orders I gave to you when I last wrote. Nevertheless, if you surrender, I promise that you will live. Zenobia, you and your family will be able to live in the palace which I shall ask our revered senate to grant. In return, you must hand over your jewels, your silver, your gold, your robes of silk, your horses and your camels to the treasury of Rome. The rights of the people of Palmyra will be respected.'

Vopiscus 'Life of Aurelian', *Historia Augusta* 26

If Aurelian hoped that Zenobia would eagerly accept his offer, he was to be disappointed. He did not even receive the courtesy of a gracious reply. Instead Zenobia retorted spiritedly,

'Zenobia, Queen of the East, to Aurelian Augustus. No one but you could think of asking something like this in a letter, when what is required is manly courage. Surrender myself? As if you don't know that Queen Cleopatra chose death rather than to live in any way but as a queen. The Persians have not abandoned us, and are coming to our rescue. The Saracens and the Armenians are with us. If even the brigands of Syria have defeated your army, Aurelian; what will happen when the reinforcements which come to us from all sides have arrived? Then you will change the tone that you are using to order my surrender as if you had already completely triumphed.'

Vopiscus 'Life of Aurelian', *Historia Augusta* 27

And there matters rested for the moment. The Romans were not ready to try an assault, and the Palmyrenes lacked the strength to sally out. There were some skirmishes of archery, but essentially both sides were waiting for the other's supplies or willpower to run out.

Aurelian had advertised himself as 'the restorer of the East'. If he failed to take Palmyra, his credibility would be severely damaged. He was well aware that as a usurper himself, only success could give him the legitimacy to ward off other usurpers. It would not be exaggerating greatly, therefore, to say that this siege was a life-or-death issue for him.

For the Palmyrenes, the question was what the Romans would do if their patience was severely tested. In an age before chivalry, a city received mercy for surrendering promptly rather than for resisting bravely. Aurelian had promised mercy, but the longer he waited to exercise it, the more strained that quality would be. Under the circumstances, it was not surprising that Zenobia was forced into making the next move. Desperate for Persian help, she slipped from the city, and made a dash for the Persian lands beyond the Euphrates.

It was a last-ditch gamble, and it failed. She and a band of companions on camelback had almost reached the river when they were intercepted by Roman cavalry. Zenobia was captured and, when the news reached Palmyra, the city threw open its gates to the Romans. True to his word, Aurelian spared the city pillaging and loss of life. Despite expropriating the city treasury, he was nevertheless showered with gifts from wealthy Palmyrenes who were delighted that their rebellion had ended with so little cost to themselves.

Zenobia and her closest followers were taken to Emesa for trial. Aurelian's soldiery, with memories of their hard struggle across the desert still fresh in their minds, agitated violently for her execution. Zenobia herself had abandoned the idea of dying like Cleopatra, and pleaded with Aurelian for her life.

'You [Aurelian] I know are a true emperor, because you win victories. Gallienus, Aureolus and the others, I did not think of as emperors. [The goddess] Victoria was a woman like me, and I intended to be her partner in royal power if there was enough land in which to do so.'
'The Thirty Tyrants', *Historia Augusta* 30

Rather unworthily, Zenobia tried to put all the blame for her conduct on her advisors, especially the philosopher Longinus, who withstood her accusations with a dignity that put his queen to shame.

Aurelian executed those whom he deemed as most closely implicated in the Palmyrene revolt, but he spared the life of Zenobia. He was less concerned about his prisoner's dignity: Zenobia was exhibited as a captive in each of the towns he passed through on his return to the West. According to one report, she was taken through the streets of Antioch chained to a dromedary, and then exhibited for three days on a wooden platform built especially for that purpose. This was not pure vindictiveness on Aurelian's part. Zenobia had built up a powerful personality cult, and the best way to break this was to show the charismatic Desert Queen as a debased and humbled Roman prisoner.

We do not hear what became of Vallabathus, the young king in whose name Zenobia claimed to rule. It is possible that he was killed at the time that Palmyra surrendered or, as another report has it, that he died when the ship carrying him to Rome sank off Illyria. Also, in the spring or summer of 272, the mint of Alexandria started producing Roman imperial coinage again, so Egypt too had evidently returned to its allegiance.

In 273, Aurelian turned his attention to the West and Tetricus I – a rebel senator who was now leading the breakaway rebel 'Empire of Gaul'. Zenobia's supporters in Palmyra now took the opportunity to rebel once more, overthrowing the pro-Roman faction in the city. According to Vopiscus, they also killed the garrison that Aurelian had stationed there.

As ruler, they probably chose Zenobia's father, Antiochus, though other reports refer only to 'Achilleus, a kinsman'. Aurelian had no intention of leaving the Palmyran situation smouldering behind him and promptly returned. Palmyra had failed to return the East wholeheartedly to the Zenobian cause, so Aurelian did not face heavy resistance. Nor did Palmyra itself long withstand him. Not a man to waste mercy on the ungrateful, Aurelian had Palmyra comprehensively sacked and its walls thrown down.

Though he destroyed Palmyra forever as a power in eastern affairs, Aurelian stopped short of wiping out the town itself. Palmyra continued as a modest trading centre. Under the emperor Diocletian, who came to power in 284, the walls were rebuilt. Later emperors also refurbished the city, which remained part of the Roman Empire until it was taken by the Arabs in 634.

The rebellion of Zenobia was a failure. In fact, it has often been debated to what extent it was a rebellion at all. When Odaenathus came to power, the question seemed to be whether Palmyra or Persia would rule in the East, so weak was Rome perceived to be. Gallienus positively encouraged Odaenathus to assume as much responsibility as he could handle, and rewarded his successes with honours. Claudius Gothicus, if not as effusive as his predecessor, at least tolerated Palmyra's pretensions towards being a great power, though it is not clear whether he would have continued to do so had he lived.

The fact is that the Romans saw Palmyra as a stop-gap. Palmyrenes were barbarians to be given temporary suzerainty until Rome was strong enough to reclaim it. This is not to overlook the provocation of Zenobia – by her activities in Egypt she clearly overstepped the line from over-weening ally to rebel. But one suspects that Aurelian was set to reclaim the East for Rome no matter how Zenobia had behaved toward him.

Aurelian, conqueror of East and West, died in 275 while returning to the East to do battle with the Persians. Aurelian was a hard man and when his secretary, Eros, was caught in some wrongdoing, the man was frantic to escape punishment. He drew up a list of officers close to Aurelian, and went to each of these men claiming that Aurelian believed them to be conspiring against him. These men too knew their commander, and thought their only hope lay in assassinating Aurelian, and throwing themselves on the mercy of the soldiery. On finding that they had been deceived, they slew Eros, but by then the man who had reunited the Empire was dead, killed in part by his own reputation.

And Zenobia? While her fate is not completely certain, the most credible reports say that she was exhibited in Rome at the triumph of Aurelian after his defeat of the Gallic Empire along with Tetricus, the ex-emperor of the Gauls. In one account, she was loaded with gold chains so heavy that she required the help of assistants to stay upright.

By Roman tradition, those leaders marched through the streets behind a triumphator's chariot were then led off to the dungeons of the Roman prison near the forum, and there strangled while their conqueror ate his victory banquet. No such fate awaited Tetricus. Perhaps in recognition of the timely desertion of his army, the ex-emperor was restored to the ranks of the Roman aristocracy, and even given an administrative post in Lucania.

Zenobia too was spared, and settled in a country estate near Hadrian's famous villa. Later she is reported to have married a Roman senator, and lived out her life as a Roman country gentlewoman. Unlike Tetricus, Zenobia had remained a rebel in arms until the end. That she was not executed for her treason has less to do with chivalry than with realpolitik. Aurelian had noted the pro-Zenobian sentiment which had led to fresh revolt in Palmyra, and sympathy for Zenobia remained strong in Egypt. It came down to straightforward political calculation. Were the peoples of the Roman East more likely to rise in memory of a warrior queen martyred in her fight for liberty, or for a living Roman matron, married, and currently domiciled near Tivoli?

CHAPTER 16

ALARIC THE VISIGOTH: THE BARBARIAN AT THE GATES

[The Roman ambassadors] declared, perhaps in a more lofty style than became their abject condition, that the Romans were resolved to maintain their dignity, either in peace or war; and that, if Alaric refused them a fair and honourable capitulation, he might sound his trumpets and prepare to give battle to an innumerable people, exercised in arms, and animated by despair. 'The thicker the hay, the easier it is mowed,' was the concise reply of the Barbarian.

Gibbon *The Decline and Fall of the Roman Empire*

Through a series of linguistic mutations, the word 'Goth' today refers to a fad among teenage girls for excessive make-up and dark clothing. But in the fourth and fifth centuries AD the Goths were yet more terrifying.

May Jesus in future protect the world against such savage animals! They were everywhere. Their speed was such that they arrived even before the rumour of their approach. Neither religion, rank nor age caused any to be spared. The cry of the infant aroused no pity in them.

Jerome *Letters* 60.16

The Goths fundamentally influenced the early history of Spain and France, actively participating in the fall of the western Roman Empire. Although by the time of Alaric the Empire of Caesar and Cicero was a sorry shadow of its former self and, if it did fall, it did not have far to drop. In fact, many medievalists credit the Goths with reinvigorating the ossified, sterile culture into which the Mediterranean world had declined.

The origin of the Goths is something of a puzzle. Evidence from the second century AD puts them in the area of modern Poland. The Goths believed that they had moved there from the Baltic, and some philologists suggest Gotland in Sweden as a possible homeland. The Goths continued moving south-eastward, eventually becoming two separate but related peoples – the Ostrogoths, or Eastern Goths; and the Visigoths, who settled in the now-abandoned Roman province of Dacia.

In 238 they introduced themselves to the Romans with the first of what were to become habitual incursions across the Danube. For the next century and a half the health of the Roman Empire could be roughly calibrated against the success or failure of these incursions and more than one Roman emperor died trying to prevent them. Constant friction with Rome rubbed some Roman culture onto the Goths. Ulfilas, a follower of the Arian creed, converted the Visigoths to Christianity in the mid-fourth century and gave the Gothic tongue a written form. Some has survived in a text known as the *Codex Argenteus* ('the Silver Bible'), making Gothic the best-known early eastern Germanic language.

The Gothic raids were not inspired purely by greed. The growing power of the Huns in the steppes of Asia had displaced waves of peoples westward. The Ostrogoths pressed against the Visigoths, and the Visigoths, caught between their desperate cousins and the Roman Empire, petitioned the emperor Valens for sanctuary within his borders.

Valens allowed the Visigoths to move into the depopulated regions of Upper Macedonia, there to act as a buffer against their wild cousins outside the Empire. But according to the report of the later Gothic historian Jordanes:

Soon famine and want afflicted them, as often happens to people who are still settling into a country. Those who ruled the Goths in place of kings, Fritigern, Alatheus and Safrac, began to despair of the condition of their host and begged Lupicinus and Maximus, the Roman commanders, to open a market. But is there nothing that men will not stoop to if driven by an accursed lust for gold? The administrators, urged on by their greed, sold them at a high price not only beef and mutton, but even the carcasses of dogs and polluted animals, so that a slave could be exchanged for a loaf of bread or ten pounds of meat.

Jordanes 26.134

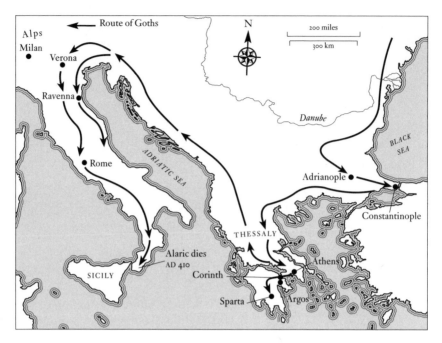

32 *The travels of Alaric and his Goths, beginning at the Danube where Alaric was born, and ending near Sicily where he died. After Alaric's death, the Goths went on to Gaul and Spain.*

The greed and stupidity of the local Roman officials caused the Goths to abandon their allegiance to the Empire. When Valens brought up his army to quell the revolt, the Goths fell upon it at Adrianople in August 378.

Scarcely one third of the entire [Roman] army escaped. Never, except in the battle of Cannae, has there been so destructive a slaughter.

Ammianus Marcellinus 31.14

What made this defeat yet more catastrophic was that those slaughtered were almost the last field army Rome possessed. From then onward, Rome depended on allies (*foederati*) and mercenaries for her defence.

Alaric was about ten years old at the time of the battle of Adrianople. His reputed birthplace was the island of Peuce (Fir Tree island) at the mouth of the Danube. His family, the Balthi (literally 'bold men'), were second only to the Amals in their standing among the Gothic people, and may have included Fritigern, the leader who brought the Goths to settle in Macedonia.

While Alaric was a youth, the Gothic leader Athanius made peace with the emperor Theodosius at Constantinople. The Goths rejoined the Empire, on condition that they could fight under their own commanders with their own military organization. Like many young men from Rome's barbarian allies, Alaric was sent to Constantinople, partly to be Romanized, partly as a hostage, and partly to acquire a military education. In Constantinople Alaric first met Stilicho, the general who, though in part a barbarian of the Vandal tribe, was the last great defender of Rome.

In 394 Theodosius led both Stilicho and Alaric west to deal with the pretender Egnatius, a puppet of the Frankish leader Arbogast. Expecting Theodosius' arrival, Egnatius and Arbogast had entrenched themselves in the eastern Alps near the river Frigidus. A frontal attack on their position was virtually suicidal, yet Stilicho and Theodosius demanded exactly that of Alaric and his Goths. The Goths fought ferociously, but were predictably and bloodily repulsed.

Despite this, skilful subversion of the enemy combined with a fortuitous storm to give Theodosius the victory. Egnatius was killed and Theodosius celebrated a triumph in Rome. There he made his son Honorius emperor in the West under the guardianship of Stilicho. Alaric and his men were rewarded for their exertions, but Alaric suspected that his men had at best been carelessly sacrificed, and at worst judiciously culled.

In 395 Theodosius died. His empire was divided between his sons, Honorius in the West and Arcadius in Constantinople. Alaric had felt undervalued by Theodosius, and Honorius showed him even less favour. Alaric did not receive the higher command he had wanted, and his Goths were not given the honorarium that usually accompanied a change of emperor.

The warning signs of impending disaster were clear. Alaric was surly and mutinous. The two new emperors were feeble and incompetent and their chief ministers loathed each other. According to the historian Zosimus, Stilicho and his eastern counterpart, Rufinus, were equally corrupt.

Therefore in their respective cities [Rome and Constantinople] iniquity of every kind ruled the day. Money flowed into the coffers of Rufinus and Stilicho from every direction; while on the other hand, poverty haunted the houses of those who had once been rich. The emperors did not really know what was going on. It was as though they assumed that all that Rufinus and Stilicho ordered was done through the force of some unwritten law. They amassed immense wealth …

Zosimus *Historia Nova* 5.130

According to Zosimus, Rufinus rapidly discerned the disaffection of Alaric, and provoked him into rebellion.

While Rufinus was working on his disreputable plots, he discovered that Alaric had become seditious and rebellious. He [Alaric] was displeased that he had not been entrusted with the command of other military forces besides the barbarians which Theodosius had allocated him when he helped to overthrow the pretender Egnatius. Therefore Rufinus sent private messages to Alaric, urging him to lead his barbarians and the allied warriors of any other nation out of Roman service, since he could easily conquer the whole country [of Italy] for himself.

Zosimus *Historia Nova* 5.133

Alaric's Goths thought the same. According to Jordanes, 'they preferred to carve out a kingdom for themselves rather than remain in sleepy subjugation to others'. Alaric was raised on a shield and proclaimed king of the free nation of the Goths. This was an innovation, for the Goths had previously been ruled by 'judges' – members of the leading families elected as war leaders or to resolve disputes.

At first Rufinus' scheme seemed to backfire. Alaric led his nation against Constantinople, either from a lingering loyalty to Honorius, or from a mercenary attraction to the eastern empire's greater riches. However, Alaric must have known that he had little chance of storming the superbly defended city of Constantinople itself.

Rebuffed at Constantinople, Alaric plundered his way through Thessaly into Greece, conquering proud and ancient cities such as Sparta, Corinth and Argos. Athens went unplundered, probably because it surrendered promptly, though Zosimus gives a more fanciful account:

When Alaric advanced with all his forces against the city, he saw Minerva …

and Achilles standing in an heroic posture, as when Homer describes him furiously fighting the Trojans to revenge the death of Patroclus. Alaric was struck with awe by this sight, and abandoned his attempt to storm the city. Instead, he sent heralds with proposals for peace. These were accepted, and mutual oaths exchanged. Alaric entered Athens with a small number of troops. There he was entertained with all possible politeness, and shown great hospitality; after which he received some presents, and departed leaving the city and all Attica unharmed. Thus was Athens alone preserved …

Zosimus *Historia Nova* 5.134

While sojourning in the regions about the Black Sea, the Goths had learned the art of cavalry warfare from the Scythians. Heavy cavalry had become the Goths' favoured arm of warfare. Gothic horsemen used a heavy lance called the *kontos* and carried several light javelins as well. Though it is highly unlikely that the Goths yet had stirrups (which would made their lances much more effective), they definitely outmatched the Roman cavalry. Few Roman infantry units now had the discipline and cohesion to stand against a Gothic charge, and once they broke they were easy meat for the pursuing riders.

Having no long baggage train, Alaric's infantry were more mobile than their Roman counterparts. They wore mail coats and often sported colourful cloaks and tunics. They were lightly armed and sometimes fought stripped to the waist. Swords were popular with both horse and foot soldiers, and that old Germanic favourite, the battle-axe, was still in use (though archaeology shows that most of these were not the double-bladed variety).

33 *Visigothic foot soldier. The main strength of the Visigothic army was its heavy cavalry, but because the army tended to live off the land which it passed through, even infantry were much swifter and more manoeuvrable than their imperial opponents.*

The infantry had bowmen in their ranks who changed to being efficient swordsmen at close quarters. Shields were painted with simple patterns in bright primary colours, and contained more than a few parts cannibalized from Roman shields picked up along the way.

The Goths ran rings around the army which Rufinus dispatched against them. Our information about the Peloponnesian campaign is confused, mostly because events were confusing. Rufinus constantly tried to bring down the Goths by treachery, while the unfortunate Greeks hosting the war deftly shifted allegiance to whomever they hoped would plunder them least.

Rufinus was killed, either by his own frustrated soldiers or through the machinations of Stilicho. Alaric terrorized Greece for two years (395–396) until Stilicho brought troops from the western empire to the rescue and soon had Alaric pinned against the borders of Arcadia. It briefly appeared that the Gothic king's career had reached an untimely end.

But somehow Alaric managed to take ship across the Corinthian Gulf and escape northwards with his plunder. This was either a brilliant military manoeuvre or part of a clandestine deal hatched with Stilicho, and neither ancient contemporaries nor modern historians are quite sure which. Certainly Alaric was deeply involved in the secretive and truly Byzantine rivalry between the eastern and western empires. On his return to Illyricum Alaric was, for some unknown reason, made the prefect of a large part of that important province by Arcadius, the eastern emperor. Suddenly, an obscure political intrigue had transformed the Gothic king from plundering barbarian to high Roman official.

The architect of this unlikely metamorphosis was probably Eutropius, the successor to Rufinus, and every bit as devious and self-interested. 'He led the emperor like a sheep', Zosimus reports scornfully.

Eutropius was intoxicated with wealth, and imagined himself so elevated as to be above the clouds. He dispatched emissaries to almost every country, to investigate both public business and the circumstances of every private individual. And from none of those things did he fail to devise some way of making a profit.

Zosimus *Historia Nova* 5.139

Relations were fast deteriorating between East and West. Eutropius declared Stilicho a public enemy at Constantinople, and Alaric became a cat's paw for a proxy war against Stilicho. So, after a suitable pause to re-stock his ranks with recruits and his armoury with weapons (the latter from of the imperial foundries which he now controlled), Alaric heard the voice of destiny.

The poet Claudian tells us Alaric was passing a sacred grove when a mysterious voice whispered, 'Stop your delays Alaric, this is the year to break through the barrier of the Alps. This is the year when you shall penetrate to the city itself.' The mysterious voice had also inspired Radagaisus, another Gothic leader, to attack Rome. If the Goths were acting in concert, their attacks were poorly co-ordinated. Radagaisus arrived in early 402, and met Stilicho.

When Radagaisus, king of the Goths, having taken up his position very near to the city, was closing upon the Romans with a vast and savage army, he was in one day so speedily and so thoroughly beaten, that not even one Roman was wounded, much less killed, whilst far more than a hundred thousand of the enemy were laid low, and he [Radagaisus] and his sons were captured and promptly put to death, suffering the punishment they deserved.

Augustine *The City of God* 23

Radagaisus was, Augustine says, 'a worshipper of demons', but Alaric was a Christian. Accordingly he held off sacking Piedmont to celebrate Easter properly. To his vast indignation the less-inhibited Stilicho descended on him with his army. Caught at a disadvantage, the Goths fought gamely. They inflicted heavy casualties on the Romans but were forced to retreat. Stilicho caught up with them at Verona and drove them over the Alps. According to one report, Alaric even had to abandon his wife as a captive to the Romans.

Though a great general, Stilicho was also a realist. The Goths were so numerous, and Rome so weakened, that some sort of accommodation was necessary. Furthermore, relations with Constantinople were now so poisonous that Alaric might be needed for a war against Arcadius. Though probably not yet a formal ally of the western empire, Alaric marched his army eastwards, to Epirus in Greece. There word reached him in 408 that Arcadius had died, and his army could stand down.

Quick to seize an opportunity, Alaric demanded huge compensation for the expense of preparing for war, and for the plunder he would now forego. To concentrate Roman minds, he left Epirus for the province of Noricum near Italy. This persuaded the emperor Honorius to retreat from the imperial capital of Milan to the impenetrable marshes around Ravenna, there (according to popular opinion) to pursue his hobby of raising chickens undisturbed by the perils and alarums of the outside world.

Stilicho turned his attention to the senate:

'Alaric has spent all this time in Epirus so as to join with me against the emperor of the East, and to take the Illyrians from his rule, and add them to the subjects of Honorius.' said Stilicho. 'This would have been done already if letters had not arrived from the emperor Honorius postponing the expedition to the East, although Alaric had spent so long preparing for it.' … Accordingly, the senate decided that Stilicho was being completely reasonable, and decreed Alaric three thousand pounds of silver for maintaining the peace, although most senators voted more out of fear of Stilicho than through their own judgment or inclination.

Zosimus *Historia Nova 5.156*

The northern barbarians were deeply feared and despised throughout Italy. The Italians relied on these *foederati* for security, but considered them fickle, violent and untrustworthy. That centuries of Roman bad faith and double-dealing had largely brought this about was beside the point. Persuading the senate to hand a massive sum to Alaric bankrupted Stilicho's political reserves just as a further barbarian incursion and the invasion of a pretender from the West further lowered his stock.

The general's enemies were quick to pounce. Honorius, who sometimes appears to have been less intelligent than his own chickens, was told that Stilicho was aiming for the imperial throne. The emperor was persuaded to sign the death warrant of the only man capable of saving his Empire. Stilicho served that Empire to the last, docilely offering his neck to the executioner to prevent a ruinous civil war. Rome's last great general died in August 408, and any hope of preserving the western empire died with him.

Stilicho's death signalled a general pogrom of Germanic peoples in Italy, and thousands of the wives and children of Rome's *foederati* were massacred by the people who had long been taxed to pay for their maintenance. No one seems to have considered the obvious consequence – that there was now nothing to stop Alaric from descending on Rome like a wolf on a herd of sheep. In 408 his army was encamped at the gates. His Goths were as bad as ever at siege warfare, but Alaric had time for a leisurely siege, and starvation would conquer Rome for him.

He blocked the gates all round the city, and having control of the river Tiber, prevented the arrival of supplies from the port to the city. … The Romans … received no relief, and all their provisions being consumed, the famine was predictably followed by a plague, and all places were filled with dead bodies. The dead could not be interred outside the city, for the enemy was in possession of all the access roads, so the city was made their sepulchre.

Zosimus *Historia Nova* 5.164

The senate blustered, then pleaded, and then – with rumours of cannibalism rife in their city – asked Alaric what it would cost for him to go away. The price was so huge that the stunned emissaries asked what Alaric intended to leave them with. The answer was curt and to the point: 'Your lives'. Eventually Alaric settled for 5,000 pounds of gold, 30,000 pounds of silver, 4,000 silk robes and other fine fabrics, and a huge quantity of pepper. This last was imported from India and beyond, and was of great value.

Alaric accepted this bribe because plundering Rome would expose his army to the plague raging in the city. Anyway, Alaric did not want the demise of the Roman Empire, but a place of honour within it for himself and his people. He repeatedly declared his friendship, and hinted that he might even cede the massive ransom from Rome in exchange for land between north Italy and the Danube.

Negotiations stalled because the court of Honorius combined traditional Roman bloody-mindedness with an un-Roman inability to do anything practical. There was some reason for their policy. The rampant anti-barbarianism which had helped to precipitate the present crisis now prevented the imperial court from making any concessions, and anyway, concessions seemed only to spur Alaric to greater demands. The death of Arcadius had brought about a certain rapprochement with the eastern empire and help was hoped for from there.

Alaric set about breaking the stalemate. He returned to Rome in 409 and, after the briefest of sieges, persuaded the senate to depose Honorius and set up a more co-operative emperor. This was Priscus Attalus, the city prefect. Unfortunately for Alaric, the Romans of Africa remained loyal to Honorius, and by the fifth century Africa was Rome's principal supplier of grain. With the weapon of famine in Honorius' hands, Alaric, ever the realist, promptly deposed his puppet and re-opened negotiations.

He now had an extra card to play, for in the second siege Gallia Placida, the sister of the emperor, had fallen into his hands. Alaric, to his credit, did not harm his valuable hostage, pretending that she was a guest staying with him until the peaceful conclusion of negotiations.

To stress his point, Alaric marched towards Ravenna, firing off protestations of friendship in advance of his army. He was ignored by the court of Honorius, which seemed determined to sit out his presence in Italy. The Romans were encouraged by the presence in Italy of one Sarus, a Visigoth aristocrat from a family traditionally opposed to Alaric's Balthi clan.

In the meantime Alaric proceeded to Ravenna to confirm the peace with Honorius; but fate invented another obstacle which no one could have expected, or ever have predicted would happen to the state. For while Sarus and a barbarian retinue had based themselves in Picenum, and were allied neither with the emperor nor with Alaric, Ataulphus [one of Alaric's Goths], who had a feud with Sarus based on some old quarrel, brought his whole army to the place where Sarus happened to be. Sarus had only three hundred men with him, and was no match for his enemy. So as soon as he saw him approaching he made up his mind to flee to Honorius, and assist him in the war against Alaric.

Zosimus *Historia Nova* 5.178

Alaric became aware of this when only a few miles from Ravenna. The gates of the city were thrown open, and Sarus' men launched a stinging attack on Alaric's vanguard. Alaric had been expecting a relatively civilized parley with the imperial court, and this sudden assault took him by surprise. To make matters worse, a herald lent by Honorius then comprehensively insulted Alaric in Sarus' name. It was quite evident that Honorius was not going to negotiate. With Ravenna strongly walled and further protected by impassable marshes, there was nothing the Goths could do to make him.

In a fury, Alaric turned on Rome, making that unfortunate city the proxy for Honorius in Ravenna. The third siege was even shorter than its predecessors. The senate attempted a desperate and somewhat pathetic defence, but in vain. The Salarian gate was opened to the oncoming army – maybe through a deep-laid plot by Alaric, or through the vindictiveness of a servant or slave. It may even have been that some Romans, remembering the horrors of the past siege, and certain of the result of the present one, simply decided to get it over with. For almost eight centuries no enemy had set foot in Rome. Now the city from whence the legions had marched to sack almost every capital in a thousand-mile radius itself faced a sack.

As sackings go, that of Rome on 24 August 410 was a polite affair. Apart from a fire in the gardens of Sallust, the Romans lost mainly their pride and possessions. (The mildness of this sack explains why thugs with a penchant for mindless destruction are referred to as Vandals – who later sacked Rome very destructively – rather than Goths.)

Our sources are woefully deficient, but probably the best account is that of Procopius of Caesarea, written over a century later.

But some say that Proba, a woman of very unusual eminence in wealth and in fame among the Roman senatorial class, felt pity for the Romans who were being destroyed by hunger and the other suffering they endured; for they were already even tasting each other's flesh; and seeing that every good hope had left them, since both the river and the harbour were held by the enemy, she commanded her domestics, they say, to open the gates by night....
And they [the Goths] set fire to the houses which were next to the gate, among which was also the house of Sallust, who in ancient times wrote the history of the Romans, and the greater part of this house has stood half-burned up to my time; and after plundering the whole city ... they moved on.

Procopius of Caesarea *History of the Wars* 3.2.30–39

Despite the alleged good conduct of the barbarians, the sack of Rome must have been nothing other than nasty and brutal. Yet Alaric found apologists, including St Augustine of Hippo.

And now these wretches do not thank God for his great mercy ... that he should decree if Rome were to be taken, it should be by barbarians who, despite the practice of all wars that have gone before, protected, through respect for Christianity, everyone who sought refuge in sacred places. These barbarians were very much opposed to demons and the rites of impious sacrifices, so they appeared to be conducting war with them which was much more terrible than their war with men. So the true Lord and ruler of all scourged the Romans mercifully ...

Augustine *The City of God* 23

A popular story of the time says that when Honorius heard the grim news 'Rome has perished', he was appalled: 'But she was eating corn from my hand, not an hour ago!' To the emperor's immense relief his courtiers explained that calamity had befallen not his favourite chicken, but the city after which it was named. This improbable tale shows the prevailing and justified sentiment that the rulers of the Empire were neither capable of, nor particularly interested in, defending their subjects.

The shock of the sack reverberated around the Roman world. St Jerome, then in Jerusalem, tells us how the news was received.

We received a terrible rumour about events in the West. They told us that Rome was under siege, and the only safety for its citizens was that which they could buy with gold, and when that had been stripped from them, they were besieged again, so that they lost not only their possessions, but also their lives. Our messenger gave the news in a faltering voice, and could hardly speak through his sobbing. The city which had captured the world was now itself captured.

Jerome *Letters* 127

Back in Italy, Alaric's problems with the grain supply had convinced him that the key to imperial power was to be found in Africa. He spent a week stripping Rome of almost everything movable, and then headed southward for Calabria to muster a fleet for the invasion of Africa. As might be expected of people from the eastern Danube, the Goths were poor sailors. Their first fleet was destroyed by a storm, and before Alaric could gather another, he was seized by a sudden illness and died.

That Rome's conqueror did not long survive his impious assault caused great satisfaction at Ravenna. Even more satisfying was the news that Alaric's successor, his brother-in-law Adolphus, intended to quit Italy and inflict his people upon the Gauls. Alaric himself was buried with his weapons and gold in true barbarian splendour.

At Cosenza in Calabria, the course of the river Busento was diverted while Alaric was laid to rest in the river bed. When the river was returned to its original course, Alaric was safe from vengeful Romans. He has remained so thereafter, despite the best efforts of treasure hunters and archaeologists.

CHAPTER 17

ATTILA THE HUN: THE SCOURGE OF GOD

Now the leaders of the various nations waited on Attila's nod like a crowd of slaves. When he indicated his wants by even so little as a glance, each came forward trembling fearfully and in any event, did as he was ordered. Attila was the supreme lord of all these kings.

Jordanes 200

Of all the horrors which accompanied the fall of the western Roman Empire, none was more terrifying then the Huns. Their westward march pushed the Ostrogoths against the Visigoths and brought the Visigoths into their fatal collision with Rome. Then, late in the fourth century, the Huns themselves arrived.

Their features are so terrible that they totally intimidate even those who are their equals in warfare. Their enemies flee in horror from their dark terrifying faces. They have, in a manner of speaking, no more than a shapeless lump for a head and tiny eyes ... they are brutal to their children from the day they are born, using a sword to slice open the cheeks of the boy-children so that they learn they must endure wounds before they receive the nourishment of milk. A face so scarred by the sword spoils the natural good looks of a beard, and the young are ugly and grow old beardless ... though they have the bodies of men, they are as cruel as wild animals.

Jordanes 127–28

The origin of the Huns lay somewhere on the steppes of Asia. The Chinese knew them as the Hsiung-Nu, and their savage raids menaced northern China for most of the millennium before the birth of Christ. At about the time that Rome was embarking on the first of its great wars with Carthage in the mid-third century BC, the Chinese were constructing their Great Wall against the Huns. Naturally, such a wall was no problem for the athletic Hun tribesmen, but it was a major obstacle to their horses.

And the Huns were almost exclusively a cavalry army. They had two kinds of horses – small wiry steeds of great stamina, and larger, specially bred chargers which were used by their heavy cavalry. Each Hunnish warrior rode with a string of horses, sometimes up to sixteen to a rider. Such a readily available change of mounts combined with the Huns' own natural hardihood made them among the fastest-moving forces in the ancient world. The Huns even cooked on the march – their staple diet while on campaign was allegedly raw meat which slowly cooked between their thighs and the bodies of their ponies during the course of a day's riding.

With their power waning in the Orient, the Huns turned westward. This was not an organized migration, for at this time each Hunnish tribe had its own leaders. As the grazing and pillage in an area declined, they moved on to fresh fields further west, and by this process of slow migration reached the great Hungarian plain, and the borders of the eastern Roman Empire.

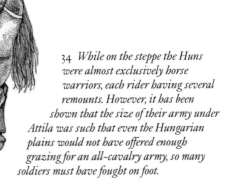

34 *While on the steppe the Huns were almost exclusively horse warriors, each rider having several remounts. However, it has been shown that the size of their army under Attila was such that even the Hungarian plains would not have offered enough grazing for an all-cavalry army, so many soldiers must have fought on foot.*

Two major changes took place during this time. The leadership of the Huns had gradually become more consolidated and monarchical, and the plains of Hungary, though vast, offered insufficient grazing for the swarms of Hunnish horses, so the army now included a great mass of infantry. Not all these infantry were Huns. The Ostrogoths had been overwhelmed in 374 and were now among the vassal soldiers of their former enemies.

At first relations with Rome were peaceful – indeed some Huns may even have fought for Stilicho in his campaign against Radagaisus in 402 (p. 263). The Danube frontier became a meeting point where Roman gold, silks and spices were exchanged for horses and barbarian slaves. It also rather pleased the Romans that a further wave of Hunnic peoples, known as the Ephthalites or 'White Huns', had ensconced themselves north of the Caspian Sea and were making life difficult for the Sassanid Persians (p. 233ff.), who were often rivals of Rome.

Theodosius II, the son of the eastern emperor Arcadius (pp. 262–63), promoted the king of the largest group of Huns, a man called Rugila, to the rank of general and paid him a subsidy of three hundred and fifty pounds of gold for securing the Empire's northern border. In 433 Rugila died. He was succeeded by two brothers, Attila and Bleda, thought to be the sons of Rugila's brother Mundzuk. Bleda makes no further mark on history. Attila is believed to have murdered him in 445, though this assumes (perhaps unjustly) that Hunnish dynastic politics were as blood-thirsty as those of 'civilized' nations to the south.

At the time of his accession Attila was already in middle age.

He had an arrogant walk, and he rolled his eyes as he looked about. The power of that haughty spirit showed through in every movement of his body. He certainly loved war, yet he was restrained, lenient to those to whom he gave his protection, gracious to supplicants and keen of judgment. He was short, with a barrel chest and a large head. He had small eyes and a sparse beard flecked with grey. His ancestry was plainly evident in his flat nose and swarthy complexion.

Jordanes 180

Attila re-negotiated relations with Theodosius, doubling his tribute and reclaiming refugees who had fled Hunnish suzerainty to the Empire. It was also agreed that Rome would not ally themselves with the enemies of the Huns and that free markets would be opened for trade between the two powers. The peace was far from perfect. The Roman town of Margus in the Danube area was flattened when its bishop gravely offended the Huns in 441, and there were clashes with the western empire. After these incidents, Attila was easily bought off with another massive ransom of gold, mainly because he was involved with the Persians and Thracians to the east, and the Burgundians and other tribes in the west.

But the Roman Empire was too large and too tempting a target for Attila to ignore forever. In 447 his Huns swarmed through the defences of the eastern empire. Like Alaric before them, they found Constantinople too tough a nut to crack and turned their attention to Greece. Theodosius once again sent his treasury into battle. The annual tribute now reached 2,100 pounds of gold (including the arrears that were not paid while Attila plundered the Empire), and now Attila also demanded and received overlordship of a huge swathe of territory along the middle Danube.

The Romans invested a further sum of gold to bribe one of Attila's lieutenants to murder him. The attempt failed without seriously upsetting Attila. We have a detailed report of a visit to the Hun leader by a certain Priscus, whose account of an embassy to Attila has survived. He tells of life among the Huns, and of Attila whom he met personally at a dinner:

A sumptuous meal had been prepared on silver plates for us and [Attila's] barbarian guests. Attila himself ate meat from a wooden platter, and was equally restrained in other ways. While the guests drank from gold and silver goblets, his cup was of wood. His dress too was simple and clean. The sword at his side, and the bindings of his Scythian shoes ... were without ornament.

Priscus *Embassy to Attila* 448

Elsewhere in his chronicle Priscus tells us that a shepherd on the Danubian plains had come across one of his flock limping from an odd wound. The shepherd had followed the trail of blood from this wound until he found the blade of a strange sword, most of which was still buried in the ground. Recognizing a good omen when he saw it, the shepherd hastened to Attila with the mysterious sword. Attila immediately identified this as the Sword of Mars, and announced that 'he had been appointed the over-lord of the world, and through the sword he was assured of victory in all his wars'.

Apart from illustrating the use of basic propaganda techniques, this story shows that Attila's religious beliefs, while otherwise uncertain, could at least stretch to accommodate a god from the old Roman pantheon. He showed wary respect for the temporal power of Christianity but was completely unembarrassed about destroying sacred buildings and taking the lives and treasures of those within.

The power of Attila's propaganda and the violence of his deeds have entrenched him in European folklore. His unearthly steed and magic sword are recurring themes in the Sagas of Norway and Iceland; and in Germany's ancient *Niebelungen Lied* Attila is Etsel, the wearer of twelve mighty crowns, who promises his bride the lands of thirty kings. Etsel's capital city, Etselenburgh, is evidently Attila's capital, the city on the site where Budapest now stands.

In 450 Theodosius died. His legacy was the famous Theodosian Code, the systematic organization of the laws of the Empire which profoundly affected the development of European legal systems. His death brought back to power the emperor's sister Pulcheria, once regent for her younger brother but recently sidelined by a palace power struggle. Pulcheria married the competent administrator and general Marcian, who gave Attila notice that payment of his tribute would now cease.

As it happened, Attila was already planning to invade the Roman Empire, but his target was the western half. He was coming to claim Honoria, sister of the emperor Valentinian, as his bride. Yet more remarkably, he was coming at Honoria's invitation. The sister of the emperor had been discovered in a clandestine affair with a palace functionary, and may even have become pregnant by him. The emperor attempted to hide the scandal and his sister from the public. Honoria was outraged by her forced seclusion and the execution of her lover, and she smuggled a ring and a message to Attila asking him for assistance.

Attila decided to treat this as on offer of marriage, and awarded himself half of Valentinian's domains as his dowry. 'A shameful thing indeed, [for Honoria] to seek licence for her passion at the expense of the public well-being', comments Jordanes sadly.

The invasion was no impulsive undertaking, and Honoria's rash gesture no more than the flimsiest pretext. Attila's massive army included hundreds of thousands of his own Huns, his vassal Ostrogoths, and elements of other Germanic tribes including the Gepids and Alans. Ancient accounts estimate that some 300,000 to 700,000 men surged over the Rhine into the poorly defended provinces of Gaul. Immediately before his invasion Attila assured the Romans that his quarrel was with Theodoric, king of the Visigoths; and told Theodoric that his invasion was a part of his quest for Honoria, reminding him of his many quarrels with the Romans. Jordanes comments of Attila's diplomacy, 'Beneath his great ferocity he was a subtle man, and fought with craft before he made war.'

The defender of Gaul was Aetius, a worthy successor to the great Stilicho. He occasionally obeyed the emperor Valentinian, but it was a sign of the increasing irrelevance of the Roman emperor that Aetius had come to power not by imperial appointment, but by defeating a rival in battle. Aetius was very familiar with the Huns, having been in exile among them during one of the low points of his political career.

Aetius scraped together the remnants of Rome's military power, but this could only augment the force needed to stop Attila – the combined Franks and Visigoths who were, in any case, the true rulers of the lands west of Rome. In the first instance it fell to the Christian bishops of the major cities to organize their defence, or to make what compromises they could with the conqueror. The prevailing mood is best summed up by a Christian hermit who boldly confronted Attila: 'Thou art the Scourge of God; the chastisement of the Christians.' Attila immediately adopted the new title. If his enemies believed him sent by their god to punish their evil-doing, then opposing him might be construed as blasphemy. Certainly it did not help Christian morale.

The historian Ammianus Marcellinus gives this description of the Huns on campaign.

They form columns to go into battle, filling the air with their wild discordant screams. Generally they have no regular battle order. They move quickly and suddenly, now dispersing, now coming together into loose clumps, now spreading havoc widely across the plain, now swarming over the ramparts and pillaging the camp almost before their approach has become known. It must be allowed they are formidable warriors. They fight from a distance using sharpened bones cunningly fixed to the shafts of their weapons. Close to, they fight with swords, and while their enemy is intent on fighting off their berserk attack they throw a net over him and so entangle his limbs that he can neither walk nor fight.

Ammianus Marcellinus *History* 31.2.9

Bolstered by promises of support from Aetius, the city of Orléans withstood a ferocious siege. Legend has it that reinforcements arrived just as Attila had breached the walls, but in fact the Hun leader was forced to abandon the siege by news that his enemies had taken the field against him.

The battle of Chalôns (more accurately called the battle of the Catalaunian Plains) was one of the decisive battles of western civilization. That is, without a victory for Aetius, there would not have been a western civilization, other than that which Attila permitted to exist.

The armies came together on 19 September AD 451, when the Franks came across a band of Gepid tribesmen who had become detached from Attila's main force. It says something of the ferocity of the following day's fighting that this clash was accounted a skirmish, though it left 15,000 dead. As the next day dawned, it became clear that whoever occupied a ridge in the centre of the battlefield would have a decisive advantage. Each side occupied their own side of the ridge, and the Romans eventually won the bitter battle for the crest. The Huns fell back in some disorder, and the Visigoths launched a series of fierce cavalry charges on the retreating enemy.

The fighting became hand-to-hand, fierce, savage, confused and without the slightest respite. No ancient saga has recorded such a conflict. Such deeds were done that no brave man who missed this incredible spectacle could expect to see anything so awesome for the rest of his life. Our elders report that the blood from the bodies of the slain turned a small brook which flowed through the plain into a torrent. Those made desperately thirsty by their injuries drank water so augmented with blood that in their misery it seemed as though they were forced to drink the very blood which had poured from their wounds.

Jordanes *History of the Goths* 207

While leading a charge, Theodoric (king of the Visigoths) was struck by a javelin, fell, and died under the hooves of his own cavalry. Few noticed at the time, and those who did were spurred to greater fury as a result. Attila had positioned himself in the midst of his army, and this core fell back on the wagons of their camp even as the rest of the Hun army unravelled about them. Nightfall brought the battle to a confused halt.

It is said that Attila remained magnificently composed even at this moment of extreme peril. He had heaped up a huge pile of horse saddles, and was determined that if the enemy broke through he would throw himself into the flames of this funeral pyre. Thus none would have the satisfaction of physically injuring him, and the master of so many different peoples would not fall into the hands of his enemies.

Jordanes *History of the Goths* 213

Aetius advised against an assault on Attila's wagons. Some felt that he wanted to keep Attila as a counterweight to the Visigoths, others thought that without an imminent threat to Rome, Aetius' position would be weakened. In fact Aetius' motives were probably less cynical. The Visigoths were weakened by the death of their king, and Aetius' army was in very poor shape. Hydatius, a contemporary historian, puts the dead on both sides at 300,000. Even allowing for exaggeration this makes Chalôns the bloodiest battle since Adrianople, and larger than any battle fought in western Europe for the next five hundred years. With Attila stopped in his tracks, Aetius could be excused for saving the remnants of his army for the multitude of other threats facing Rome.

Attila made his escape across the Rhine, never to trouble Gaul again. He spent the winter re-gathering his strength and plotting revenge. In 452 he launched another devastating attack against the western empire, and this time his target was Rome itself. In northern Italy Concordia, Altinum and Patavium (modern Padua) were rapidly conquered and torched. Hun raiders spread across Lombardy and attacked Milan, driving many north Italians to the islands of a lagoon off the northeastern coast, where they raised the city which later became Venice.

Aetius and the Roman army did nothing. Relations between Aetius and the imperial court varied between acrimony and loathing and, with his power base securely in Gaul, Aetius was not deeply inclined to come to Italy to rescue Valentinian. Nor, without the help of the Visigoths, did Aetius have much chance of stopping Attila. But more importantly, famine and plague had arrived in Italy ahead of the horsemen of the Huns. Aetius calculated that Attila's invasion would grind to a halt simply because the Huns would get through their rations faster than the plague got through their ranks. It was a sad reflection of how far Italy had fallen that in military terms the country was worth neither invading nor defending.

It was said that Attila was bent on the destruction of Rome itself, but his advisers were equally determined to keep him from the city because of their superstitious awe at the fate of Alaric, who had sacked Rome and died very soon afterwards. Then, as Attila prepared to ford the river Mincius in northern Italy, he received an unusual delegation.

This report is from the historian Prosper, writing some three years after the event:

Now Attila, having once more collected his forces which had been scattered in Gaul, took his way through Pannonia into Italy … To the emperor and the senate, and to the Roman people, none of all the proposed plans to oppose the enemy seemed so practicable as to send legates to the most savage king to beg for peace. Our most blessed Pope Leo – trusting to the help of God, who never fails the righteous in their trials – undertook the task, accompanied by Avienus, a man of consular rank, and the prefect Trygetius. And the outcome was what his faith had foreseen; for when the king had received the embassy, he was so impressed by the presence of the high priest that he ordered his army to give up warfare, and after he had promised peace, he departed beyond the Danube.

Prosper of Aquitaine *Gallic Chronicle* An.452

Later writers give more elaborate accounts of the meeting, with the apostles Peter and Paul appearing at the Pope's side, and the mighty Attila almost prostrate with awe. More probably, just as Attila had once sought any pretext to invade Italy, he now sought any pretext to withdraw. His attack had been at least in part to repair the damage to his reputation after Chalôns, and this objective had been realized at least to some extent. He departed, warning that he would soon be back unless he was followed by Honoria and her dowry.

But the defeat at Chalôns and a fruitless campaign in Italy meant that Attila was in the unusual position of having to husband his resources. His threats were rightly perceived by the court of Valentinian as little more than bluster, and Honoria remained in Italy. Attila then sent his ambassadors to the emperor Marcian in Constantinople, promising his bloodiest campaign yet if the tribute of gold he had received from Theodosius was not restored. The eastern emperor was no more moved than his western counterpart. Under the energetic and capable Marcian the eastern empire was in better shape than it had been for years. Attila refrained from invasion, probably judging that even a successful campaign would so weaken him that he would be vulnerable to his hordes of enemies and restless subject peoples.

In an attempt to reduce the number of his enemies, Attila attacked the Alans, a people he had almost brought under his control before the battle of Chalôns. But the Visigoths were now on their guard and their new young king Thorismund dashed to the aid of the Alans. Defeat followed for the Huns. The battle was a far smaller affair than Chalôns, but it cost Attila dearly. His reputation as an invincible conqueror was severely dented. Though the Huns were formidable against the remnants of Roman power, it was now evident that the Visigoths and their allies were capable of standing against them.

Attila was now forty-seven years old. Despite recent setbacks, he remained the most powerful person in Europe, and his command over his own dominions was unquestioned. Jordanes comments, 'There was no way that any ... tribe could be wrested from the power of the Huns, except by the death of Attila – an event earnestly wished for by the Romans and other nations.' No would-be rebel was ready to face the legendary wrath of Attila. It was said that he had eaten two of his own children, though his motives for doing so were unclear. One story suggested that a jealous wife had killed the children, and then fed them to her unknowing husband to revenge some insult which Attila had done her. Certainly a wife of Attila had cause for jealousy. The Huns were polygamous and Attila had a splendid collection of wives.

It was his desire to add to this collection that proved Attila's undoing. The maiden in question was called Ildico, a girl of such beauty that even today some hopeful Hungarian mothers christen their daughters with this name. At the wedding Attila abandoned the restraint reported so admiringly by Priscus. He was staggering from drink by the time he retired to his marriage bed.

The following day, not even the obvious charms of his bride could explain Attila's tardiness in leaving the bedchamber. His attendants grew increasingly alarmed and finally, amid scenes of uproar, the doors were broken down. The ruler of the Huns was found lying dead on his bed while his new wife cowered in a corner in a state of hysterics. Suspicion not unnaturally fell on the girl. However, even Hun forensic science was capable of quickly establishing the true cause of death. While lying on the bed Attila had suffered a massive nose bleed. Normally he would have rolled over and the bleeding would have passed. However, Attila was so deeply unconscious that the blood flowed into his lungs until he passed from being dead drunk to simply dead. 'His death was as squalid as his life was marvellous', says Jordanes.

Priscus believed that the death of Attila was such a blessing that the gods announced it personally to the rulers of the world. Marcian saw in a dream that some deity stood by him, showing a broken bow. This symbolized that the power of the Huns, who relied so much on the bow, was now broken.

Attila was given a fitting funeral:

His body was placed in a tent of silk in the middle of a plain, the focus of general adoration. The best horsemen of all the Huns rode around the tent in circles, as though in the games at the arena. In the place to where he had been brought, the funeral dirge spoke thus of his deeds. 'This is the lord of the Huns, King Attila, son of Mundzuk, lord of bravest tribes, sole master of the Scythians and Germans. No man has done as he. He captured cities and terrified the Romans of both East and West. Only by their supplications would he take an annual tribute and refrain from plunder. And fortune favoured him so that after all these deeds, he died not at the hand of his enemies or the treachery of his friends, but in the heart of a nation at peace, happy, joyful and without pain.'

Jordanes 257–260

His coffin had three layers. One was gold and one silver, showing that Attila had received tribute from two empires. The third layer was iron, showing how Attila had enforced the payment of that tribute. The Hun warriors cut their faces with their swords, that he might be mourned not just with the tears of women, but by the blood of men. Then Attila was buried with weapons captured from his enemies, and a substantial collection of the booty he had taken from them. The burial took place secretly and in the dead of night, and the Huns killed those who did the burying, so that no-one might know Attila's last resting place.

Perhaps even then, in 453, the Huns knew that their power was waning. Without Attila's personality to hold it together, the tribe broke into warring factions. These were headed by Attila's sons, none of whom could agree on who should lead their people. Attila's former subjects joyfully threw off the Hunnish yoke, and the Germanic tribes quickly reabsorbed his conquests. Within two generations, the Huns were a fading memory, their principal legacy to Europe being the name bestowed on the land where they had settled. In Hungary, Attila remains a national hero and, like that of his fateful bride Ildico, Attila's name is also a popular choice at christenings.

EPILOGUE

The Roman Empire in the West ended in AD 476. It finished not with a bang, but a whimper. No imperial palaces were stormed, no barbarian hordes overwhelmed the last bastions of civilization. Instead, the Roman Empire was wound up as neatly as any bankrupt business would be today.

The last western emperor was known as Romulus Augustulus (the 'little Augustus'). He was known as such because, like many emperors of preceding years, he was the puppet of the commander of the Roman army in the West. In this case, that commander was Orestes, the father of Augustulus. In 476, Orestes was overthrown in an army coup by one of his officers, a man called Odoacer, and Augustulus' tenure of the imperial throne came to an end.

Odoacer entered into negotiations with Zeno, the emperor of the eastern Roman Empire. At this time Zeno recognized another pretender to the western imperial throne, and he agreed with Odoacer that he would stop supporting his candidate if Odoacer did not claim the western imperial throne himself. The result was that Augustulus was sent into retirement in a monastery and Zeno announced himself overlord (in theory) of the entire Roman Empire. Odoacer returned the regalia of the western Roman emperor to Constantinople and got on with the business of ruling Italy.

These developments did not seem particularly extraordinary at the time. They simply continued the trend of the previous hundred years in which the Germanic peoples assumed greater political and military responsibility for the lands west of the Balkans. It must be remembered that these 'barbarian hordes' were as Christian as the Romans themselves. Many of them were well educated, and held high office in the Roman Empire even as the fabric of that Empire gently crumbled away around them. And of course, Roman and Germanic soldiers had fought side by side against other barbarian invaders, and against other Roman and Germanic soldiers in various civil wars.

Nor was the fall of the western Roman Empire a particularly unwelcome development for its former citizens. When, sixty years later, the eastern Roman Empire re-conquered Italy, the reaction of the Italians was one of dismay. Rome was seen as bringing with it corrupt government, heavy taxes and the forcible conscription into the army of anyone too poor to bribe their way out of it. The Goths who ruled Italy at the time of the Roman re-conquest promptly rebelled, and the natives complicitly supported this rebellion. Eventually, under pressure from the Persians in the East, Byzantium tacitly acknowledged that the western empire was beyond its control. This was partly because the West was now desperately poor and had little to offer the East in either trade or taxes.

Theories abound as to how the West had been reduced to this state. The historian Gibbon blamed Christianity. In fact, so did many contemporary Romans, which is why St Augustine of Hippo wrote his extraordinary apology for the Goths in *The City of God* where he pointed out that, since the new masters of Italy were also Christian, everything had finished for the best. In the year Augustine died, the Vandal tribe conquered his native city of Carthage.

Other historians blamed the fall of Rome on depopulation, pointing to references in the ancient texts to plagues and *agri deserti* ('abandoned fields'). Certainly, by the end of the Empire, a few thousand men counted as a substantial army whereas in the glory days of the Republic a single legion contained 6,000 men. The stifling weight of a corrupt bureaucracy and the diminishing returns of excessive taxation also played their part in Rome's fall. If any form of enterprise was almost impossible to launch and attracted the attention of avaricious civil servants immediately, there can be little wonder at the parlous state of the Roman economy.

A further point which has been made by modern historians is that for the first seven hundred years of its history, the Roman economy grew on the back of its conquests, with booty from the frontiers imported to the center. During the long peace of the Antonine emperors of the second century, Rome was essentially living off its fat. This system broke down in the third century under the pressure of over-centralization, economic failure and barbarian invasion. Though the East was able to sustain the settlement imposed in the fourth century by Diocletian and his successors, the economic devastation in the West proved too great, and Roman government itself collapsed, or rather, simply faded away.

Throughout its history, Rome had fought a mixture of civilized and barbarian states, and on the whole, did better when fighting civilized enemies. It was barbarian Gauls who first sacked Rome in 387 BC, and barbarian Visigoths who did it next in AD 410. It is true that Rome was not generally much superior to its barbarian enemies in terms of weapons technology. It is probable that Attila's Huns brought the stirrup to western Europe, and the Roman siege weapons which so impressed Josephus at Jotapata were widely used by all the Mediterranean civilizations, and were of limited use against barbarians.

Rome did have superb logistics and organization, but these were equally useful against civilized and barbarian enemies. However, when fighting civilized opponents, the Roman commanders could define clear objectives. Once the enemy was defeated in battle, its principal cities would be besieged, or threatened with siege, and capitulation or negotiations would follow. Otherwise the taking of the capital would generally signal the end of the war. This tactic was as effective against the Palmyrenes of Zenobia as it was against Hannibal's Carthaginians.

Far greater problems were caused by enemies who refused to play by these rules. Mithridates and Jugurtha fought on even after their principal cities had been taken and other nations, such as the Lusitanians of Viriathus and the Germans of Arminius, offered the Romans very little in terms of physical strategic objectives. In Britain it is probable that Suetonius Paulinus ended Boudicca's rebellion by bringing her to battle by threatening sacred sites in the Midlands.

During the years of the Republic, Rome had huge reserves of manpower and a steely will to win. It was these two factors which carried the state through the war with Hannibal after a series of defeats in battle which would have forced many other nations to the negotiating table. The social structure of Rome was a driving force in the city's expansion. Because military success was an important factor in political advancement, Roman commanders tended actively to seek military confrontations.

Thus Philip V of Macedon found his efforts to negotiate frustrated by Quinctius Flamininus, who went so far as to ask his friends in Rome to seek peace if his command against Philip was not renewed, but to press for the war to be continued if it was. Later, Mithridates of Pontus faced the same problem – the Roman governors of neighbouring provinces actively sought to provoke war for their own political ends. This ethos continued right to the end of the Republic when Caesar went to war with Vercingetorix and Crassus invaded Parthia.

Yet even in the first years of the Empire a more defensive mentality became evident. Emperors were less eager for their generals to win glory on foreign fields, and the expansion of the Empire became restricted to those times when the emperor was on hand to get the glory for himself. Claudius made a point of being present when the Romans established themselves in Colchester in Britain, and Trajan led his armies in person against Decebalus. When the tide turned against the Empire in the third century AD, Roman emperors fought and died with their men. Valerian was the only emperor to fall into enemy hands when he was captured by Shapur I, but Claudius Gothicus and Valens both died in battle.

While Rome was overly dependent on foreign soldiers by the fall of the western empire, soldiers of other nations had been closely integrated with Roman armies almost from the start. Jugurtha, Spartacus, Arminius, Vercingetorix and Alaric all fought on the Roman side in their early careers. Crassus took Gallic cavalry with him to Parthia, and German cavalry recruited by Caesar played a vital role in the defeat of Vercingetorix. Other units, such as Cretan archers, Palestinian clubmen and Palmyrene cataphracts, added specialist skills that the legions were unable to provide.

Yet in the end, what failed Rome was the loss of the factors which propelled the city to Empire. With her population apparently in decline, and her people bereft of their military ethos, Rome in the fifth century was ripe for conquest.

FURTHER READING

Abranson, E. 1979. *Roman Legionaries at the Time of Julius Caesar*. London: Macdonald Educational.

Adcock, F. 1957. *The Greek and Macedonian Art of War*. Sather Classical Lectures, v. 30. Berkeley: University of California Press.

Appian (trans. White H.) 1932. *Appian's Roman History Book 6, The Wars in Spain*, Chapter 12. Harvard University Press: Cambridge, Massachusetts.

Applebaum, S. 1989. Josephus and the Economic Causes of the Jewish War. In Feldman, L. H. (ed.) *Josephus, the Bible and History*, pp. 237–64. Detroit: Wayne State University Press.

Ashton, S. 2003. *The Last Queens of Egypt*. London: Longman.

Baldwin, B. 1966/67. Two aspects of the Spartacus slave revolt. In *Classical Journal* 62, p. 289ff.

Barnett, G. 1994. *Zenobia, Empress of the East*. Wide Awake Press: Alhambra, CA.

Bédoyère, G. de la. 2003. *Defying Rome*. Stroud: Tempus.

Bertrand, A. C. 1997. Stumbling through Gaul: maps, intelligence and Caesar's *Bellum Gallicum*. In: Ancient History Bulletin 11.4, pp. 107–22.

Bishop, M. and Coulston, J. 1989. *Roman Military Equipment*. Princes Risborough: Shire Archaeology.

Bohrmann, M. (trans. Lloyd, J.) 1994. *The Zealots and Yavne. Towards a Rereading of the 'War of the Jews'*. New York: Peter Lang Publishing Inc.

Bradford, E. 1981. *Hannibal*. London: Macmillan.

Bradley, K. 1989. *Slavery and Rebellion in the Roman World*. Bloomington: Indiana University Press.

Brown, P. 1978. *The Making of Late Antiquity*. Harvard: Harvard University Press.

Cameron, A. 1993. *The Later Roman Empire*. London: Harper Collins.

— 1993. *The Mediterranean World in Late Antiquity, AD 395–600*. London: Routledge.

Connolly, P. 1998. Legion vs. Phalanx, *Military Illustrated 124*, pp. 36–41.

Cook, S., Adcock, F. and Charlesworth, M. (eds) 1930. Rome and Macedon: Philip against the Romans. In The Cambridge Ancient History, ed. I, II vols, *Rome and the Mediterranean VIII, 218–133 BC*, pp. 116–37. New York: Macmillan.

Creighton, J. and Wilson R. (eds) 1999. Roman Germany: Studies in Cultural Interaction. In *Journal of Roman Archaeology Supplement 32*.

De Beer, G. 1975. *Hannibal: Challenging Rome's Supremacy*. New York: Viking.

Delbrueck, H. 1975. *Warfare in Antiquity*. Nebraska: University of Nebraska Press.

Dudley, D. and Webster, G. 1962. *The Rebellion of Boudicca*. New York: Barnes & Noble.

Ehrhardt, C. 1969. What should one do about Dacia? In *Classical World 63* no.7, pp. 222–26.

Ferrill A. 1986. *The Fall of the Roman Empire: The Military Explanation*. London & New York: Thames & Hudson.

Flamarion, E. 1993. *Cleopatra: The Life and Death of a Pharaoh*. New York: Abrams.

Foreman, L. 1999. *Cleopatra's Palace: In Search of a Legend*. New York: Discovery Books.

Furneaux, R. 1973. *The Roman Siege of Jerusalem*. New York: Hart-Davis.

Garnsey, P. and Humfress, C. 2001. *The Evolution of the Late Antique World*. Cambridge: Orchard Academic.

Gibbon, E. 1985. *Decline and Fall of the Roman Empire*. Nebraska: Bison Books. (online version http://ccat.sas.upenn.edu/jod/texts/gibbon.fall.html.)

Gilliver, K. 2002. *Caesar's Gallic Wars 58–50 BC*. London: Osprey.

Goldsworthy, A. 2001. *The Punic Wars*. London: Cassell.

— 1996. *The Roman Army at War, 100 BC – AD 200* (Oxford Classical Monographs). Oxford: Clarendon Press.

Goodblatt, D. 1987. Josephus on Parthian Babylonia. In *Antiquities Vol. XVIII*, pp. 310–79.

Grant, M. 1992. *Cleopatra*. New York: Barnes & Noble.

Green, P. 1993. *Alexander to Actium : The Historical Evolution of the Hellenistic Age*. Berkeley: University of California Press.

Halsall, P. 2003. Mithridates and the Roman conquests in the East, 90–61 BCE. In *Ancient History Sourcebook: Translated Selections from Appian and Plutarch with Introductory Material*. (e-book at http://www.fordham.edu/Halsall/ancient/asbook.html.)

Jacobs, W. 1973. *Hannibal: An African Hero*. New York: McGraw Hill.

Jones, T. 1996. Jugurtha. In *Colliers Encyclopedia*. New York: MacMillan.

King, A. 1990. *Roman Gaul and Germany*. London: British Museum Press.

Livy (trans. Yardley, J. C.) 2000. *The Dawn of the Roman Empire, Books 31–40*. New York: Oxford University Press.

MacKendrick, P. 1975. *The Dacian Stones Speak*. Chapel Hill: University of North Carolina Press.

Maenchen-Helfen, O. 1973. The world of the Huns. In *The Columbia Encyclopedia, 6th ed.* Columbia: Columbia University Press.

Marshall, B. 1973. Crassus and the command against Spartacus. In *Athenaeum n.s. 51*, p. 109ff.

Masaoki, D. 1984. On the negotiations between the Roman state and the Spartacus army. In *Klio 66.1*, p. 170ff

McGing, B. 1986. Foreign policy of Mithridates VI Eupator, king of Pontus. In *Mnemosyne Supplement 89*.

Michalowski, K. 1970. *Palmyra*. New York: Praeger.

Millar, F. 1993. *The Roman Near East: 31 BC – AD 337*. Cambridge, Mass.: Harvard University Press.

Momigliano, A. (ed.) 1987. *On Pagans, Jews, and Christians*. Connecticut: Wesleyan University Press.

Narain, A. 1957. *The Indo-Greeks*. Oxford: Oxford University Press.

Peddie, J. 1997. *Hannibal's War*. Phoenix Mill: Sutton Publishing.

Plutarch (trans. Dryden) 1962. *Life of Marius*. London: Everyman.

Pomeroy, S. 1975. *Goddesses, Whores, Wives and Slaves: Women in Classical Antiquity*. New York: Schocken.

Powell, A. and Welch, K. (ed.) 1998. *Julius Caesar as Artful Reporter: The War Commentaries as Political Instruments*. London: Duckworth.

Pribichevich, S. 1982. *Macedonia: Its People and History*. Pennsylvania: The Pennsylvania State University Press.

Rice, E. 1999. *Cleopatra*. Gloucestershire: Sutton Publishing.

Rossi, L. 1971. *Trajan's Column and the Dacian Wars*. London: Cornell University Press.

Sallust (trans. Handford, S. A.) 1963. *The Jugurthine War / The Conspiracy of Catiline*. London: Penguin Classics.

Salway, P. 2001. *A History of Roman Britain.* Oxford: Oxford University Press.

Speidel, M. 1970. The captor of Decebalus. In *Journal of Roman Studies 60*, pp. 142–53.

Stark, F. 1966. *Rome on the Euphrates: The Story of a Frontier.* London: John Murray.

Stoneman, R. 1992. *Palmyra and its Empire: Zenobia's Revolt Against Rome.* Ann Arbor: University of Michigan Press.

Syme, R. 1964. *Sallust.* Berkeley & Los Angeles: University of California Press.

Tacitus (trans. Mattingly, H.) 1971. *The Agricola and the Germania.* London: Penguin.

Todd, M. 1987. *The Northern Barbarians, 100 BC – AD 300.* Oxford: Basil Blackwell.

— 1992. *The Early Germans.* Oxford: Blackwell.

Trevino, R. and McBride, A. 1986. *Rome's Enemies: Spanish Armies 218–19 BC.* London: Osprey.

Trow, M. 2003. *Boudicca: The Warrior Queen.* Stroud: Sutton Publishing.

Vaughan, A. 1967. *Zenobia of Palmyra.* New York: Doubleday.

Volkmann, H. (trans. Cadoux, T.) 1958. *Cleopatra: A Study in Politics and Propaganda.* London: Elek Books.

Warmington, B. 1964. *Carthage.* London: Hale.

Watson, A. 1999. *Alaric, Aurelian and the Third Century.* London & New York: Routledge.

Webster, G. 1978. *Boudicca: The British Revolt Against Rome AD 60,* 2nd ed. London: Batsford.

Whittaker, C. 1994. *Frontiers of the Roman Empire.* Baltimore: The John Hopkins University Press.

Wiesehöfer, J. (ed.) (trans. Azodi, A.) 1996. *Ancient Persia: From 550 BC to AD 650.* London: I. B. Tauris.

Wilcox, P. 1982. *Rome's Enemies: Germans and Dacians.* London: Osprey.

Wilcox, P. and McBride, A. 1986. *Rome's Enemies: Parthians and Sassanians.* London: Osprey.

Wyke, M. 1997. *Projecting the Past: Ancient Rome, Cinema, and History.* New York & London: Routledge.

Yarshater E. (ed.) 1983. *Cambridge History of Iran: The Seleucid, Parthian and Sasanian Periods 4, part 1.* Cambridge: Cambridge University Press.

Zeev, S. 1994. *The Economy of Roman Palestine.* London: Routledge.

SOURCES OF ILLUSTRATIONS

Line drawings
Dominic Andrews 25; Cartographica Ltd. 3; Peter Inker 22; Martin Lubikowski main map, 1, 4, 5, 7, 9, 10, 11, 13, 15, 17, 23, 24, 27, 29, 30, 32; Ben Plumridge 12, 18, 19, 20, 26, 28, 31; Schelay Richardson 33, 34; Drazen Tomic 14; Claire Venables 2, 8, 16, 21.

Plate sections
Frontispiece Bryna/Universal (Courtesy Kobal). 1 Châteaux de Versailles et de Trianon, Versailles. 2 British Museum, London. 3 Museo Nazionale, Naples. 4 Delphi Museum. Photo Ecole Française d'Archéologie, Athens. 5 Photo Hirmer. 6 Delphi Museum. Photo Ecole Française d'Archéologie, Athens. 7 Prado, Madrid. Photo Scala. 8 Staatliche Antikensammlungen, Munich. 9 Cabinet des Medailles, Bibliothèque Nationale, Paris. 10 Ny Carlsberg Glyptotek, Copenhagen. 11 Louvre, Paris. 12 British Museum, London. 13 Museo Archeologico Nazionale, Chieti. Photo Giovanni Lattanzi. 14 Photo Ancient Art & Architecture Collection. 15 Photo Roger Wilson. 16 Photo Heidi Grassley, © Thames & Hudson Ltd., London. 17 British Museum, London. 18 Staatliche Museen, Berlin. 19 Musei Vaticani, Rome. Photo DAI, Rome. 20 Kingston Lacy, The Bankes Collection, Dorset. 21 Staatliche Kunsthalle, Karlsruhe. 22 Musei Capitolini, Rome. Photo akg-images, London. 23 Colchester and Essex Museum, Colchester Castle, Essex. 24 Thames Embankment, London. Photo National Monuments Record. 25 Photo Giovanni Lattanzi. 26 Musei Capitolini, Rome. Photo Alinari. 27 Photo Professor F. B. Florescu. 28 Photo DAI, Rome. 29 Photo A. F. Kersting. 30 Ny Carlsberg Glyptotek, Copenhagen. 31 British Museum, London. 32 Photo Roger Wood. 33 Aosta Cathedral. Photo Alinari. 34 Cathedral Treasury Monza. Photo Hirmer. 35 Kunsthistorisches Museum, Vienna. 36 Stanza di Eliodoro, Musei Vaticani, Rome.

SOURCES OF QUOTATIONS

All quotations are the author's own translations, apart from the following:

pp. 232, 235, 238 Extracts from Shapur, *Deeds of the God-Emperor Shapur*, inscribed at Naqs-i Rustam, taken from Fergus Millar, *The Roman Near East* (Harvard).
p. 278 Extract from Prosper of Aquitaine, *Gallic Chronicle* An.452, taken from the Fordham.edu website.

INDEX